Praise for *Leading with Vitality and Hope*

"*Leading with Vitality and Hope*'s emphasis on moving beyond *why* schools need to change to the *how* change is done is on point. The book is a welcome call to action from an eclectic group of author collaborators, each of whom adds an essential element of insight into the present and attainable variety of evidence supported best practices that schools can and *should* use to serve their students, staff, and communities in more meaningful ways today."

—Ken Wallace, PhD, superintendent, Maine Township High School District 207, Park Ridge, Illinois

"An invaluable resource for any leader working with today's youth! In the best of times, educators are challenged to meet all students where they are and provide instruction and curricula that enables them to thrive in the 21st-century workforce. The pandemic has disrupted our society in ways that have reverberated from across the globe to our communities, schools, and homes. Mason, Patschke, and Simpson have gathered the insights of educational visionaries who are leading the way to address systemic inequities and societal issues that impact cognition and student achievement. With practical strategies, optimism, and hope, these thought leaders provide a sound roadmap to revolutionize the educational experience with vitality, hope and healing."

—Melissa Hughes, PhD, author, *Happy Hour with Einstein* and *Happier Hour with Einstein: Another Round*

"*Leading with Vitality and Hope* is a strategy-filled resource that educators need right now as they lead our schools out of the pandemic. The stories of successful change include voices of those in the field and even students as they help lead us forward to engage and include all stakeholders. The best part of the book, though, is the insight from leaders and references to research that ground the work so that we can better understand the underlying issues of trauma and advocacy. Schools have the amazing power to heal and connect so don't miss this amazing tool to help you make this happen in your school community!"

—Dr. Andrew M. Jacks, principal, The Nokesville School, NAESP fellow, author, and podcast host of *Discipline Win*

"Educators will find much inspiration and support in this book, one that offers a heart-centered approach to healing. This compassionate work addresses the roots of the growing emotional health crisis in our schools. The solutions offered, based on a deep understanding of human development, provide a path toward change that is both profoundly human as well as practical.

A comprehensive resource for educators that wish to grow joyful, resilient learning communities."

—Hannah Beach, co-author, *Reclaiming Our Students: Why Children Are More Anxious, Aggressive, and Shut Down Than Ever—And What We Can Do about It*

"This is a momentous time in our history when challenges are profound and yet opportunities are limitless. It is through this paradox that Leading with Vitality and Hope: Embracing Equity, Alleviating Trauma, and Healing School Communities provides educational leaders with real stories, strategies, and provocations to vision and navigate transformational change. The book's vision–practice–change model equips and empowers leaders to deliberately, yet urgently, address today's challenges and opportunities for a better future."

—Dr. Johnna L. Weller, chief academic officer, Learning Care Group

"A must read for today's educators committed to being successful with all students during these challenging times. The authors give us concrete steps for developing relationships in times of trauma and stress and to ensure that hope, joy, and love are in the lives of all our students in our schools. This book will make a positive difference in the lives of students and educators."

—Dr. Kendall Zoller, Sierra Training Associates and global consultant in communicative intelligence

"In *Vitality and Hope*, Mason, Patschke, and Simpson use the power of vision to paint a compelling picture for compassionate and equitable school community cultures that provide hope and renewal for adults and students. This book is a modern-day leadership bible. Use it to reflect on your most urgent change needs, focus your change efforts, and engage everyone you lead toward successful and sustainable change."

—Tim Kanold, educator, author, consultant, and former superintendent, Adlai E. Stevenson School District 125, Illinois

"Vulnerability. Hope. Vision. Student voice. As school leaders how do you embrace these concepts in building systemic cultural shifts to maximize student learning? This dynamic team shares the research and application of these ideas—and more—o build that student-centered learning environment you've always wanted. You'll find this to be a powerful read that'll be on your favorite shelf to reference again and again."

—Dr. Adam Drummond, associate partner, International Center for Leadership in Education

"A thought-provoking collaboration and collection addressing diversity, equity, inclusion and justice in schools today. Out of crisis comes opportunity, and the authors share how they are turning their visions into reality, each of them making a difference in the lives of students, staff, and communities. This book is for educational leaders who desire change but may feel 'stuck.' It gives both hope and inspiration to those in education who are ready to lead transformational change and have a sustainable impact within our educational institutions. I highly recommend this book to school leaders and anyone else who has the courage and compassion to begin the work of repairing the systemic inequalities that exist in education."

—Ann Little, international consultant

"*Leading with Vitality and Hope* is a much-needed book of wisdom, frameworks, resources, recommendations, stories, and provocations for leaders who are seeking pathways for real transformation in education. It curates wisdom from diverse identities, experts, and elders who have rooted and centered their work on humanity, especially those who have been historically and systematically marginalized. It pulls together research and narratives that are historical, contextual, relational, and intersectional.

It offers us a radical shift in leadership centered on liberation, by challenging us to examine self and systems, as well as our collective historical truth, harm, and trauma. It offers us a different way of seeing, holding, and enacting power, a kind of power anchored on compassion that has leverage, intention, and impact on our collective liberation. It challenges us to re-evaluate our moral imperatives, responsibilities, and obligations as current caretakers of our world, to be fearless in asking hard questions, as well as to value and harness the powers, purposes, peoples, and practices of our communities. This book will inspire leaders to humanize and mobilize action; to be bold and agentic in designing for radical shifts in school and organizational cultures, as well as ground us on the fundamentals of our shared existence and humanity.

I cannot wait for the world to read this book!"

—Joel Jr Llaban, M Ed, director of diversity, equity, inclusion, and justice, International Schools Services

"Our world seems to be so disconnected, even though we have countless ways to connect, and what we know all too well is that we are polarized based on political beliefs. All of this leads to a feeling of hopelessness, and that is the very reason why this book is so important. Our schools are places where we need to be more human, and in *Leading with Vitality and Hope*, the authors help us do just that."

—Peter DeWitt, EdD, author, blogger, and leadership coach

"Dr. Christine Mason, Kevin Simpson, and Dr. Melissa Patschke have put together a robust collection of articles that provides a pathway to a more equitable, compassionate, and sophisticated future for our schools. The book is equally evidence-based and practical with strategies and solutions that educators can put into action right away. Highly recommend this book to anyone who works in schools who believes in and is committed to change."

—Ellen Mahoney, CEO, Sea Change Mentoring

Leading with Vitality and Hope

Leading with Vitality and Hope

Embracing Equity, Alleviating Trauma, and Healing School Communities

Christine Y. Mason
with
Melissa D. Patschke
Kevin Simpson

ROWMAN & LITTLEFIELD
Lanham • Boulder • New York • London

Published by Rowman & Littlefield
An imprint of The Rowman & Littlefield Publishing Group, Inc.
4501 Forbes Boulevard, Suite 200, Lanham, Maryland 20706
www.rowman.com

86-90 Paul Street, London EC2A 4NE, United Kingdom

Copyright © 2023 by Christine Y. Mason, Melissa D. Patschke, and Kevin Simpson

All rights reserved. No part of this book may be reproduced in any form or by any electronic or mechanical means, including information storage and retrieval systems, without written permission from the publisher, except by a reviewer who may quote passages in a review.

British Library Cataloguing in Publication Information Available

Library of Congress Cataloging-in-Publication Data

Names: Mason, Christine Y. (Christine Yvonne), 1949– author. | Patschke, Melissa D., author. | Simpson, Kevin, 1976– author.
Title: Leading with vitality and hope : embracing equity, alleviating trauma, and healing school communities / Christine Y. Mason ; with Melissa D. Patschke, Kevin Simpson.
Description: Lanham, Maryland : Rowman & Littlefield, 2023. | Includes bibliographical references and index. | Summary: "Leading with Vitality and Hope provides a practical resource for educators who want to move beyond the challenges schools are facing today"—Provided by publisher.
Identifiers: LCCN 2022039424 | ISBN 9781475869606 (cloth) | ISBN 9781475869613 (paperback) | ISBN 9781475869620 (epub)
Subjects: LCSH: Educational leadership--United States. | Educational change—United States.
Classification: LCC LB2805 .M2848 2023 | DDC 371.2/011—dc23/eng/20221007
LC record available at https://lccn.loc.gov/2022039424

Contents

Foreword ix

Preface xi

PART I: BRINGING HOPE AND VITALITY 1

Chapter 1: Turning toward Hope 3

Chapter 2: Visioning with Compassion, Equity, and Empowerment 15

Chapter 3: Vitality and Visioning 25

PART II: HEALING TRAUMA, RACISM, AND INJUSTICE 35

Chapter 4: MindWell Education: Rethinking Education and Focusing *on* What Really Matters 37
Kevin Hawkins

Chapter 5: Compassionate Mindful Practices for Healing Racism and Trauma 47
Orinthia Harris, Christine Mason, and Jillayne Flanders

Chapter 6: Reclaiming the Brilliance of Native Youth 55
Holly Echo-Hawk and Melanie Johnson

PART III: CRAFTING COMPASSIONATE SCHOOL CULTURES 71

Chapter 7: Heart Centered Learning: Developing Cultures of Compassion 73
Christine Mason, Michele Rivers Murphy, and Meghan Wenzel

Chapter 8: Being a Mindfulness School Coordinator 85
Jeffrey Donald

PART IV: CHANGING SYSTEMS' POLICIES AND PRACTICES — 91

Chapter 9: HOPE Is NEAR: Healthy Outcomes and Positive Experiences Is Neuroscience, Epigenetics, ACEs, and Resilience — 95
Jesse Kohler

Chapter 10: Visioning to Achieve Desired Results: A Social Media Case Study — 105
Jeff Ikler

Chapter 11: Visioning in Michigan: Recognizing the Evolving Role of Leadership — 113
Paul Liabenow and Michael Domagalski

PART V: BUILDING CAPACITY — 119

Chapter 12: The Coalition for the Future of Education — 121
Melissa D. Patschke

Chapter 13: Preparing New Educational Leaders for Vision-Forward Leadership and the Neuroscience of Purpose — 131
Renee Owen

Chapter 14: Youth Leadership — 141
Julia Murphy

Chapter 15: Visioning at Peace at Home Parenting Solutions — 147
Ruth E. Freeman

PART VI: SCALABILITY AND SUSTAINABILITY — 157

Chapter 16: Advocacy and Equity for International Educators — 163
Kevin Simpson

Chapter 17: The Collective Efficacy of Compassionate School Practices — 171
Christine Mason and Martha Staeheli

Chapter 18: When Visioning, Educational Equity, and Educator Emotions Matter — 181
Victoria E. Romero

Chapter 19: Scalability and Sustainability: Leadership and Paths to Enduring Change — 195

References	205
Acknowledgments	217
Index	219
About the Editors and Contributors	227

Foreword

FINDING OUR WAY, TOGETHER

If you know someone who has worked in education the past few years, here are a few things they may confess to you about their job:

- They are overwhelmed.
- They are struggling to help *all* their students.
- They want tools to support their most traumatized students.
- They are short on time.
- They are losing their inspiration.

Simply put, the pandemic has been rough on everyone, but teachers (and frontline workers in general) have endured an extra dose of stress and challenge. In addition, the problems of today's world—from racial inequity and climate change to communal violence and the mental health crisis—create a sense of sadness and hopelessness for many of our students and their families. So, what's the answer? Another book on leadership? Well, yes.

Leading with Vitality and Hope: Embracing Equity, Alleviating Trauma, and Healing School Communities by Christine Y. Mason, Melissa D. Patschke, and Kevin Simpson is the educational leadership book to meet this moment. This book provides both inspiration and practical support for school leaders who are searching for guidance for navigating these tumultuous and traumatizing times. Mason, Patschke, and Simpson profile 20 educational leaders who know how to focus on hope, healing, and building a collective vision for school transformation. The first three chapters provide a grounding framework for improving your educational leadership practice through collective visioning with colleagues, exercises to build your vitality and the vitality of your staff, and strategies for initiating the process of positive school change.

For 30-plus years, I have strived to center my teaching and leadership around a few key principles of cultivating kindness, fostering student voice and purpose, embracing community, struggling for justice, and developing the real-world skills of students. This book hit home for me because it provides tools and inspiration in all these areas. I recommend sharing and reading this book with your colleagues and new leaders and putting it on your nightstand so you can read a chapter in the evening or when you are getting your day started. Each chapter is a healthy, energizing meal that provides insight and inspiration along with practical tools you can implement right away.

If you make time for this book, you will be rewarded. We need educational leadership to meet the challenges of this moment, and *Leading with Vitality and Hope* will equip you with crucial tools for improving your leadership practice and guiding your team with hope and optimism.

Michael B. Matsuda
Superintendent, Anaheim Union High School District
Anaheim, California

Preface

Education is at a pivotal juncture. In the wake of the COVID-19 health crisis, after months of remote learning, transforming schools into family food delivery services, and worrying about the children they never saw, educators find themselves again in a new time and space. Across the country, faced with the uncertainty of what comes next, educators are adapting and doing their best to help students and families adjust to shifting expectations of instruction and learning. Even as most students are learning side by side with their peers in the same room as their teachers, teachers are facing extensive difficulties moving forward in the prescribed curricula. Try as they might, schools are not returning to the previous normal.

The pandemic has exacerbated the systemic inequalities and failures in the American education paradigm to an unparalleled degree. As attention is more centered around these inequalities and inequities, educators are examining curricula, discipline practices, and ways to provide scaffolded support to give students the boost they need. However, during the pandemic, students and families coped in a multitude of ways, with some having greater access to resources and enjoying more resiliency. The impact of these inequities continues.

Because of the disparities, it is taking a while for teachers to determine the best instructional level for each student. However, more difficult work lies ahead; once teachers understand what a student needs, they have the immense task of planning and organizing instruction that delivers relevant and appropriate content and instructional level for each student. Many students missed essential learning in 2020–2021, so now more than ever, teachers need to help students through a focus on personalized learning and increasing student engagement with greater use of project-based and hands-on learning, among other things, with attention on a student's preferences for learning (Domenech, 2016).

However, teachers are only human, and they, too, have experienced their own trauma, grief, and losses during COVID, even as they spent endless hours striving to reach and teach all their students. But all hope is not lost. Out of crisis comes opportunity—opportunity for recovery, renewal, and rejuvenation. As Peter DeWitt says, "crisis can be a teacher. It is through crisis that we can learn some of our greatest lessons" (2021, p. 47). There is something about weathering a storm that often brings increased insight and wisdom. Educators now find themselves in a unique situation where they can revolutionize schools with vitality, hope, equity, and healing, all of which support improved cognition and academic learning.

SEEKING CHANGE

The authors' quest in *Leading with Vitality and Hope* is to provide food for thought for educational leaders who desire significant change; for leaders who are leading by teaching and by joining with others; and leaders who, as visionaries, are leading the charge for renewal and are trying to respond authentically to the task at hand. In the pages that follow, readers will learn about the visions and evolution of dreams of 20 leaders, including the intersection of their personal visions with the missions and visions of their organizations; how their conceptualizations and their leadership changed over time; and what differences their innovations and their leadership are making in the lives of children, staff, and communities.

As Lee Bolman and Terrance Deal (2013) explain in *Reframing Organizations*, visioning is particularly important in times of crisis and uncertainty. "When people are in pain, when they are confused and uncertain, or when they feel despair and hopelessness, they desperately seek meaning and hope" (p. 355).

VISIONS TO TRANSFORM REALITIES

In *Leading with Vitality and Hope*, leaders articulate how their visions are being transformed into reality and how their leadership is propelling the hopes, dreams, and lives of others. This edited collection is intentionally designed to be inclusive of the perspectives of educational leaders, technical assistance providers, entrepreneurs, professors, principals, district-level administrators, authors, and youth. Even as the contributors continue to advance their causes in their own way, each is also addressing trauma, adverse childhood experiences, and individual and collective mental health and well-being.

Whatever your interest in leadership, any educator intent on leaving the current quagmire behind will find something of value in the stories these authors tell of their own transformational change effort. If you are seeking greater justice, healing, increased student engagement, or other significant changes, then this book will be a timely addition to your reservoir of resources.

THE NEED FOR *LEADING WITH VITALITY AND HOPE*

Thousands of books have been written on leadership. There are many classics that set the stage for furthering our insights into the most effective leadership styles, skills, and strategies. Consider the groundbreaking works of Peter Senge, who describes leadership and learning organizations; the inspirational writings of Margaret Wheatley on an organic approach to leading during times of chaos; and Peter Drucker's efforts to empower employees and decentralize leadership.

More recently, Brené Brown has taken the stage to help us understand the importance of vulnerability, Simon Sinek has urged us to start with the "why" to lead purpose-filled lives, and Angela Duckworth has brought grit and resilience into conversations on planning and implementing change. In the field of education, there are books on leadership written by such giants as Michael Fullan, James Kouzes, Barry Posner, and Todd Whitaker. The list goes on and on. So you might wonder, "Is another book really needed?"

How satisfied are you with education right now? Feeling the impact of societal trauma and drama, the hopelessness during the pandemic, and the uncertainty of being not yet back to normal, educators are finding a huge and urgent need for stronger, more resilient, and more impactful leadership. But it is not only about your satisfaction with education. There are also so many societal needs calling out for solutions. Here are a few facts:

- Childhood adversity, which encompasses experiences involving threat (e.g., abuse, domestic violence) and deprivation (e.g., neglect, parental separation) accounted for approximately 439,072 deaths annually in the United States in 2019 (and that was before the pandemic began; Grummitt et al., 2021).
- Deaths by suicide have increased 24% over the past 15 years across all people in the United States, with 1 in 5 teens contemplating suicide in 2019. Suicide is the second-leading cause of death for adolescents (LeFevre & U.S. Preventive Services Task Force, 2014; VanOrman & Jarosz, 2016).
- Beginning in April 2020, the proportion of children's mental-health-related visits among pediatric emergency room visits increased and remained elevated through October. Compared with 2019, the proportion of mental-health-related visits for children aged 5–11 and 12–17 increased approximately 24% and 31%, respectively (Leeb et al., 2020).

- LGBTQ+ youth are three times more likely than straight kids to attempt suicide at some point in their lives, with trans kids especially at risk (di Giacomo et al., 2018; Suicide Prevention Resource Center, 2021).
- Native American youth are most at risk for completed suicide, with African American/Black youth second-most at risk (National Indian Council on Aging, 2019).
- African American, Latino, Native American, and Asian American people who are lesbian, gay, or bisexual attempt suicide at especially high rates (Kalibatseva et al., 2022; O'Donnell, Meyer, & Schwartz, 2011).

WHY THIS BOOK?

First and foremost, the needs of children and educators are significant, and educators are hungry for change. They are looking for ways to reduce the stress. They are looking for hope, and they care: about the students they teach, about helping students get back on track, and about helping families feel more at ease. Yet schools seem uncertain about how to handle what has been unprecedented in our lifetime.

Second, the planet needs help. We continue to turn to fossil fuels, spread nano particles of plastic into our oceans, and kill off species. Although scientists explain the needed changes, we the people and the organizations we serve are unwilling to make serious changes. It is not only individuals; it is also businesses that continue to produce plastic, consume resources, and contaminate our earth, our skies, and our waters. Perhaps if our youth can experience transformational change in schools, then they will be more willing and able to undertake the substantial changes that are needed as we rediscover how to live in greater harmony with mother earth. If educational leaders can be just a bit bolder, then perhaps we can better lead schools down a path of significant change.

We invite you to consider the initiatives described in this book, including

- The Childhood-Trauma Learning Collaborative, whose mission was to provide technical assistance supports to educators in New England as part of a Mental Health Technology Transfer Center (see Chapter 17)
- The Coalition for the Future of Education (see Chapter 12)
- An offshoot of that project, the Collaborative to Alleviate Childhood Trauma (see Chapters 9 and 10)

Each of these initiatives shares this in common:

- Each has a leadership component, with recommendations for mindful, heart centered leadership that is inclusive, inspirational, and defined by its attention to self-care; conscious awareness; and the elevation of compassion, confidence, courage, and creation of a community of connectedness and belonging (Mason, Asby, et al., 2021).
- Many include strategies for listening to youth, increasing their engagement, and helping them find meaning and purpose.
- Each has recommendations and assessments for evaluating your individual paths and practices.
- Each shares a theme of "starting with self" and ensuring that each of us are learning and adopting/adapting practices before bringing them to others.

Grounding Our Work

The work described in this book is always grounded in the context of what schools do: the learning and academic achievement of students and the efficacy, well-being, and excellence of school staff and administrators. This work is also grounded in theory and research on executive functioning; the factors that mitigate student focus, learning, and academic achievement; and recent and long-standing research regarding the most effective teaching and leadership strategies as well as a deep understanding of metacognition, student leadership, and school culture.

Your Journey

- Where have you focused your efforts?
- Where have you made your greatest gains?
- Are there new areas that spark your interest?
- Do you have concerns for well-being and social-emotional learning?

So how does this current initiative for *Leading with Vitality and Hope* fit with other efforts, including other publications by the contributors of this book?

As portrayed in Figure 0.1, *Leading with Vitality and Hope* cuts through the other work of the Center for Educational Improvement. If you were putting a puzzle together, this might be considered the last piece of the puzzle. As we have shared our hopes, dreams, and progress with others over the past few years, we have found that many educators still need help to get unstuck (see Richert, Ikler, and Zacchei's [2020] book, *Shifting: How School Leaders Can Create a Culture of Change*). Christine Mason, Paul Liabenow, and Melissa Patschke guide others in implementing the visioning process in their

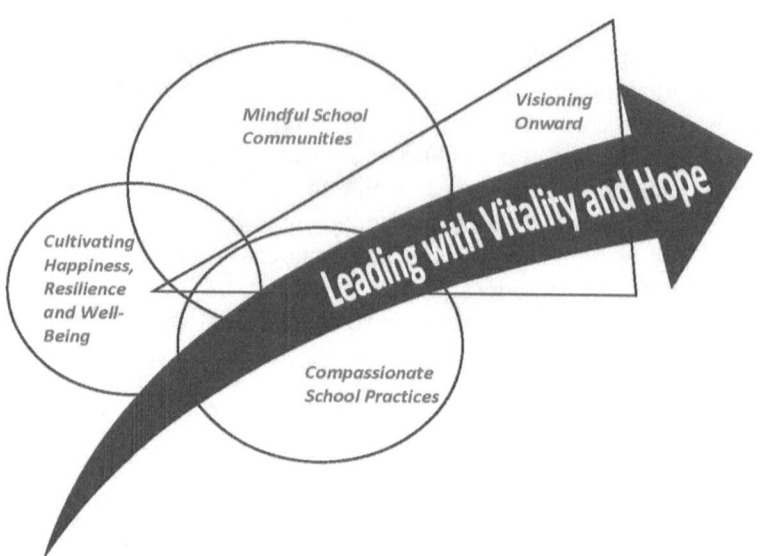

Figure 0.1. The Relationship of *Leading with Vitality and Hope* to Other Leadership Initiatives

book *Visioning Onward* (2020), but we realized that many educators needed additional examples of what can be achieved.

A Prescription for Action

In *Leading with Vitality and Hope,* you will learn from leaders about their visions—including the genesis for their visions—and how they have garnered support, fleshed out action plans, and moved forward on their journeys as they communicate, reflect, guide, and support their communities. Because of mutual interest in scalable, sustainable change, you will also learn about steps these leaders are taking to ensure their visions and actions will stand the test of time and survive challenges that arise, including changes in leadership and staffing.

To reach the goal of fundamental changes in education, educators must start to lead with passion and conviction as they address their most pressing needs, including the need for healing and helping students feel a sense of meaning and purpose. These are addressed in the visions laid out in this book. It begins with a vision for healing: healing from trauma, racism, and injustice and healing on personal, community, and global levels. However, these broad, philosophical shifts must be implemented in schools, and for them to stick, changes are needed in policies and practices. While this is happening, educators need to scale up for a full, all-out effort to make a difference. This will necessitate capacity building, which includes building leadership, preparing staff, and engaging in coordinated efforts for this to remain a priority. Schools are part of a broader ecosystem, so this is not an effort to be done in isolation.

Yet, as leaders and communities gain ground in advancing hope and healing in schools, three primary supports must also be advanced: advocacy, self-care, and collective efficacy. This blueprint is designed with sustainability in mind, and each chapter of this book contributes a key component to guide the necessary transformational changes.

Your Vision, Your Vitality, Your Hope

What do you know and what would you like to learn about each of these visions:

- Vision for healing?
- Vision for foundational shifts in school culture?
- Vision for policy and systems change?
- Vision for collective efficacy and capacity building?
- Vision for advocacy?
- Vision for self-care?

HOW TO APPROACH *LEADING WITH VITALITY AND HOPE*

One way to approach this book is by comparing and contrasting your current situation and mindset to the leadership stories the contributors lay out in their chapters. From podcasts to policy, you will learn how to implement bold, inspiring visions. You will also read about the importance of involving youth, building their leadership capacity, and giving them a seat at the table.

The first few chapters provide background information, including research support, for a process that you might consider using (see Figure 0.2).

This book is about leadership, and that leadership must start from a place of vitality, where educators are alert, centered, and grounded in collective visioning. Do you agree with this sentiment? Significant research substantiates the value of being less stressed. When staff feel more calm, more competent, and more valued, they are more likely to be effective.

The process for *Leading with Vitality and Hope* begins with exercises and activities to enhance your vitality and the vitality of your staff. When you are exhausted and overwhelmed, the visioning process is more difficult, and

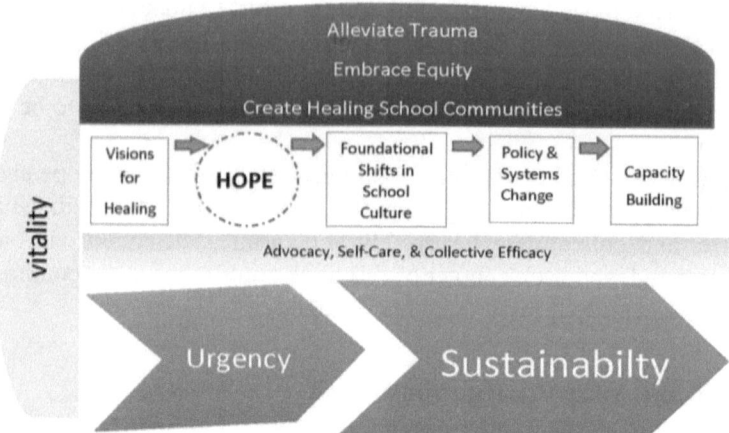

Figure 0.2. Leading with Vitality and Hope

oftentimes, the barriers may be overwhelming in these moments. Chapter 3 focuses on this process. However, even as leaders are putting out fires, there is a pronounced urgency for societal change.

Keeping It Real: Barriers

While Mason, Liabenow, and Patschke have received an overwhelmingly positive response to their visioning work, without care, staff could perceive visioning as "one more thing to do." There are barriers of time, space, resources, staffing, and community needs that may make this work difficult.

- What are your barriers?
- Do you have any ideas for how to address the barriers?

Chapters 1–3 provide some ideas for addressing barriers. See also *Visioning Onward*, and particularly the discussion in Chapter 7, which includes a guide for conducting a force-field analysis.

Questions to Guide Your Reading

Here are five key questions to keep in mind as you read each chapter:

1. Do you agree with the contributor's vision?
2. Would you want to adopt this vision? Or could it inform your vision?
3. What is inspirational about the contributor's story?

4. In what ways does the contributor address vitality, hope, equity, alleviating trauma, healing in schools, and a sense of urgency?
5. How does the contributor's message resonate with your own experiences or connect to your work?

Chapters 1–3 will ground readers in both some important leadership considerations and reflective exercises and materials related to leadership and the visioning process that Mason, Liabenow, and Patschke recommend in *Visioning Onward* (2020). If you are curious about visioning and considering whether it will be worth your time and the time of others in your school or district, or if you want to reflect on leadership, then read these chapters first. However, if you are most interested in policy or capacity building, for example, then head quickly to those parts of this book.

Features

Effective leadership involves a reflective process. To help guide your reflection, each chapter includes questions; ideas for "Keeping It Real"; and recommendations for practical implementation, advocacy, self-care, and collective efficacy. You will have opportunities to identify your strengths and areas for improvement, with suggestions for what you might do to strengthen your leadership. As you journey through this book, you will also find scenarios that bridge the underlying principles and recommendations to direct implementation in schools.

PART I

Bringing Hope and Vitality

The chapters in this section address foundational principles underlying the leadership narratives included in Chapters 4–19. If you have ever tried to influence a group, then many of the ideas in Part I may already be familiar. If you have sometimes been less than successful in getting others to buy in and support your ideas, then some of these basic principles may be essential to increasing your influence and impact. Whatever your perspective, these three chapters provide you with background knowledge so that you can gain the most from the subsequent narratives.

"CASCADING DOWN"

As you consider how to move forward, please consider what your students and their families may have experienced. Ta-Nehisi Coates in the novel *The Water Dancer* (2019) tells the story of a young man who was born into bondage, his experiences on the Underground Railroad, and his resolve to rescue his family, even as it took tremendous courage and meant untold hardships and risk for himself. When he was 19, "it all finally came cascading down upon me" (p. 37). So many of us have had experiences cascading down upon us, affecting us in so many ways. Consider the need to transform education right now. It really rests with educators to prepare youth for the future so they turn civilizations around, reduce trauma, and build a common concern for people in communities around the globe. In light of the recent pandemic, divisiveness, and complexities in our rapidly evolving world, the necessity of revisiting how to approach education is even more pressing. Paul Tough reminds us,

Helping children in adversity to transcend their difficult circumstances is hard and often painful work. It can be depressing, discouraging, and even infuriating. But what the research shows is that it can also make a tremendous difference, not only in the lives of individual children and their families, but in our communities and our nation as a whole. (2016, p. 114)

The work that lies before us will not be easy. At this point, there are no quick fixes. Uncertainty abounds regarding how many more years of masking lie ahead of us, how far astray people will continue wandering before the needed leadership emerges, and how to find the resolution and healing for wounds that have injured so many in so many different ways.

Yet substantial changes have occurred throughout history, and there are many options to learn from others as you move ahead. This requires paying attention to similarities and differences in circumstances; significant will; and caring, competent leadership.

Chapter 1

Turning toward Hope

Education is in a period of great turmoil and angst, with widespread public outrage and what some are referring to as the "Great Resignation." What will happen next? While America and countries around the world may not be quite post-COVID, most schools are operating in person, and masking right now is greatly reduced. However, nothing is what it once was. Unfortunately, many in the United States are blaming education for their own disappointments. Somewhere along the way, it appears that many have chosen to not understand how COVID affected schools. They ignore or forget how schools had to make the best of what they had available and rapidly set up remote learning, despite knowing it was a far from perfect solution.

People now wonder why students are struggling to readjust to being back in school. Parents are questioning school curricula, whether critical race theory is being taught, and even whether schools have a role in social-emotional learning. However, as Albert Bandura (1977) has said, all learning includes a social learning component. It is the way our brains are wired. The pressure on schools right now, the extent of trauma within America, the ugliness of racism and discrimination, and the absence of solutions all point to an urgent need to redesign school cultures and communities and to make transformational changes.

WHAT COULD LEADERS DO RIGHT NOW?

To accelerate the gains that educational leaders might make in the near future and to further a collective sense of hope and efficacy, let's first tune into what matters most. Educators have learned a lot since Dewey expounded on the value of education. Hopefully, educators have learned from failures as well as successes of various innovations.

Educators know how to provide developmentally appropriate education, to implement early interventions, to accommodate for students needing additional supports, to match student interest with instruction, to motivate and inspire students, to let teachers and families know they are valued, and to overcome barriers to learning. Despite these gains, many seem to be stuck with educational policies and practices from 20, 30, or even more than 100 years ago.

However, recent research on the neurobiology of trauma; how our brains work; and how supportive, nurturing environments can further student learning and well-being shows that teachers should shift their mindsets to understand students and reduce punitive discipline practices (Beach & Strijack, 2020; Hughes, 2018). Research on mindfulness and conscious awareness of self and others has shown us that caring practices can alleviate the impact of trauma, open minds to learning more efficiently, and foster more positive feelings about oneself (Mason, Donald, et al., 2021).

Strong, caring, and competent leaders who are sensitive to the needs of staff and students are essential (Smylie, Murphy, & Louis, 2020). And many educators are using several practices to keep students engaged. They are introducing hands-on, project-based learning and STEM to ignite students' interest and deepen their comprehension, critical thinking, and engagement. Yet, there are some things that educators still need to figure out. Many are transitioning from systems designed for the assembly-line production of the industrial age to systems that can prepare students to thrive in rapidly changing, highly competitive, and information-dense environments, and the change continues to be long, slow, and arduous.

How might you address the needed changes as you draw on these insights and incorporate them in your day-to-day practices as well as your long-term visions? To begin, let's acknowledge some common leadership strategies that are applicable across a wide array of circumstances. As you review the following five points, consider the implications for your current situation and whether you need to address any of these:

1. Begin with the end in mind (Covey, 2013).
2. Be mindful of the needs and concerns of your community.
3. Listen to students, learn from them, and be a magnet for their learning.
4. Have patience, realizing that timing is key and that the right initiative at the wrong time could lead to setbacks and disappointments.
5. Remember: What gets measured gets attention.

You can see additional strategies in the following section.

KEY CONSIDERATIONS FOR *LEADING WITH VITALITY AND HOPE*

For the past 24 months, several contributors have engaged in dialogues with others about visions for the future of education. What is required of leaders in education right now? Here are some key considerations:

1. Begin with a Sense of Urgency, Focusing on What Is Most Crucial.

Even as we acknowledge the need for patience and the importance of timing, without a sense of urgency, vital initiatives can take a back seat to change—so it is a balancing act: being patient but acting with a sense of urgency at the right moment.

Kirtman and Fullan, in their book *Leadership: Key Competencies for Whole-System Change* (2016), describe an urgency that is "not reactive and crisis oriented: rather it is strategic and purposeful to prepare students in their work and in their life" (p. 27). They go on to say that such urgency "means moving key initiatives forward quickly without too much process" (p. 27) and that decisive leaders will adjust strategies to reach desired results. Such a sense of urgency tells key stakeholders that this is a priority and that leaders are serious about taking action. However, being urgent does not mean being reactive to crises that arise. The needed leadership is planned and purposeful.

2. Acknowledge Stress and Trauma, and Build Self-Care and Vitality.

As much as you might want, it will not help to close your eyes and wish the stress and trauma away. It will also not help to ignore it and pretend it is not there. Educators must first consciously recognize the trauma around them. Only once it is acknowledged can they begin to manage and control it through individual and collective self-care.

Peter DeWitt (2021) explains how collective leadership efficacy, mental health, and well-being need to be a priority, emphasizing that "when we are stressed and our negative emotions get the best of us, it can negatively impact our creativity, which means we will not be as innovative as our potential allows" (p. 56).

3. Then, Do Something to Help Students, Families, and Staff Heal.

This isn't only an altruistic view of what schools can do. Significant research on trauma and the brain suggests that with healing can come greater self-esteem; caring for self and others; readiness for learning and academic achievement; and ability to cope, adapt, and make wise decisions. Mason, Donald, and colleagues (2021) point out that healing is also very individualistic: "While some people with high levels of resilience are able to process difficult emotions associated with a trauma quickly and move back into their normal emotions and activities, others can be left numb, hurt, or in crisis by these same events. In the same way, each person's healing journey from trauma is unique" (p. 113). In these days of uncertainty, healing involves not only examining what is happening with students and families but also attending to the individual and collective care of staff, including staff working conditions (DeWitt, 2021). DeWitt suggests examining five factors:

1. Job benefits (including salary)
2. Staff relationships with students
3. Workload (including setting personal boundaries and the school climate and culture)
4. Negativity and how the school handles student engagement and discipline
5. Proactive leadership practices and communication

As districts struggle to keep teachers and administrators, it would be wise to examine each of these factors more closely to see how to better support staff. Certainly, there is a need to reexamine working conditions and job satisfaction.

However, to lead, there must be movement from conversations to actions. Healing can be a community-wide effort, and it has ramifications for people around the world.

Rebuilding a Hopeful Culture: Permission to Be Human

At the Pennsylvania Educational Leadership Summit in August 2021, more than 80 school leaders participated in an EdCamp model organized by the Pennsylvania Principal's Association. The purpose was to demonstrate the structure of an EdCamp, with the hopes that leaders would take the PD model to the building level and implement it with school staff. For many of these principals and supervisors, this was the first face-to-face in-person learning experience outside their school districts since the initial COVID-19 shutdown in March 2020. What happened during these interactions was an authentic sharing about all that was happening in schools due to the pandemic. This led to a communal sense of understanding, similar emotional experiences, and a sharing of ideas across multiple educational platforms.

Once collective thoughts and experiences were shared, these school leaders knew instinctively that the 2021–2022 school year needed to value in-person relationships and encourage teams to mourn and heal through their struggles. The profession needed to heal, and it was a beginning for those who participated at this gathering. COVID was hard. Teaching and leading was hard. Educators needed permission to be human, grow, and move forward.

4. Remember and Embrace Equity and Justice.

Far too many have been traumatized over the past few centuries, and the inequities and injustice continue to persist. Whether genocide, slavery, or the trauma of immigration have affected your ancestors, you personally, your community, or others, much work needs to be done. This personal and societal trauma leaves scars that are not quick to heal, and each of us stands to benefit from the greater justice and compassion that will prevail with these efforts. Zaretta Hammond (2014) notes, "When we look at the stress some students experience in the classroom because they belong to marginalized communities because of race, class, language, or gender, we have to understand their safety threat detection system is already queued to be on the alert for social and psychological threats based on past experience" (p. 45).

One way to start addressing the needs of marginalized communities is to invest in equity consciousness. But what does this mean? Yvette Jackson and Veronica McDermott (2012) suggest beginning with a "conscious awareness of the innate potential of *all* students for engagement, high intellectual performances, and self-determination."

5. Increase Your Conscious Understanding of Yourself and Others.

There is a need to examine ourselves for implicit and explicit biases that further discrimination and injustice. Teachers can provide both the scaffolding and supports to elicit students' innate potential while also removing barriers that hinder progress. In *How to Be an Antiracist*, Ibram Kendi (2019) is clear: There is "no neutrality in the racism struggle" (p. 9). He talks about the "antiracist strategy" to fuse "desegregation with a form of integration and racial solidarity" (p. 180). He continues, "To be an antiracist is to champion resource equity by challenging the racist policies that produce racial inequity. . . . To be antiracist is to equate and nurture differences among racial groups"

(p. 180). Kendi also talks about antiracism as viewing "national and transnational ethnic groups as equal in all their differences" (p. 84).

In *Caste*, Isabel Wilkerson (2020), best-selling author and winner of the Pulitzer Prize and the National Humanities Medal, adds to our understanding of our need to change, saying, "When others suffer, the collective human body is set back from the progression of our species." Wilkerson compares social classes and disenfranchisement in America to caste systems of India:

> If each of us could truly see and connect with the humanity of the person in front of us, search for that key that opens the door to whatever we may have in common . . . it could begin to affect how we see the world and others in it, perhaps changing the way we hire or even vote. Each time a person reaches across caste and makes a connection, it helps to break the back of caste. . . . In a world without caste, being male or female, light or dark, immigrant or native-born, would have no bearing on what anyone was perceived as being capable of. (pp. 386, 388)

Wilkerson goes on to describe the need for radical empathy, or "putting in the work to educate oneself and to listen with a humble heart to understand another's experience from their perspective, not as we imagine we would feel." This includes a moral duty to act when you see someone being treated unfairly. For educators, this implies not only acting with a sense of moral authority and purpose when you see or hear racism but also helping our students develop a sense of radical empathy so they can be part of the solution.

6. Turn to Others: It Takes Teamwork.

Kirtman and Fullan (2016) assert, "Every leader needs a team of leaders who can be open and honest in their feedback on when to push and when to pull" (p. 16). Bill George in *True North* (2007) also talks about recognizing that success comes from empowering others and establishing a support team to help guide and support you along the way. He identifies six types of leaders, five of which rely heavily on teamwork:

1. Engaged leaders, who actively involve many, questioning them, listening to them, motivating them, and encouraging them
2. Coaching leaders, who take a long-term approach to building the capacity of those around them
3. Consensus leaders, who encourage everyone to participate in decision making
4. Affiliative leaders, who build bonds of trust and harmony with restrained and subtle leaderships

5. Authentic leaders, who are primarily involved in being engaged, coaching, developing consensus, and furthering affiliation
6. Expert leaders, who rely mainly on themselves and listen primarily to other experts

Your Leadership Style

Review the six styles identified by George:

1. Engaged leaders
2. Coaching leaders
3. Consensus leaders
4. Affiliative leaders
5. Authentic leaders
6. Expert leaders

Which styles best reflect your approach to leadership? Are there areas you might want to improve?

Shared leadership can lead to greater participation in intended shifts in operations and outcomes. In their book *Shifting: How School Leaders Can Create a Culture of Change*, Kirsten Richert, Jeff Ikler, and Margaret Zacchei (2020) describe the many benefits of collaborative leadership: "Shifting is about a move away from the top-down, command-and-control type of leadership to one where leaders seek to develop their own curiosity, vulnerability, and authenticity, all in the service of meaningful collaboration" (p. xxviii).

Teamwork

Great teamwork is also crucial to what Jenni Donohoo and Stefani Arzonetti Hite refer to as "collective efficacy" or a "shared belief in a team's ability to positively impact student outcomes" (Donohoo & Hite, 2021, p. 3). As Donohoo and Hite explain, collective efficacy can be a "key factor in motivating [their] productive and collaborative efforts" (p. 3).

When educators band together and dare to believe, they can foster transformational change. DeWitt (2021) explores how collective efficacy can be enhanced by working in productive and supportive groups. He explains that collective leadership efficacy is best built through understanding one another, truly collaborating, and understanding the impact that can be made.

As DeWitt reminds us, anxiety diminishes efficacy, and excitement increases it. Bringing curiosity and voice to instructional leadership teams can help create a positive affective spirit. Increasing the efficacy of teams takes modeling, planning, challenging each other's thinking, and having the ability to drop whatever status leaders may have based on their position to focus instead on raising the status of those sitting around the table (DeWitt, 2021, p. 2).

Effective groups include diverse voices and perspectives, and they focus on developing the leadership capacity of others. Additionally, leaders' self-care and well-being are essential to success. If leaders don't take care of themselves first, they are in no position to vigorously fight for others.

7. Share in the Visioning.

As you move forward, don't only share the teamwork; also share your dreams, and listen and learn from others and their dreams. DeWitt (2021) helps us understand the tragic flaw of visions driven only by those at the top: "school building leaders may have beliefs and a great deal of competence when it comes to certain situations, but those beliefs may not be exactly what the school community needs at that time" (p. 19).

In *Visioning Onward*, Mason, Liabenow, and Patschke (2020) urge leaders to establish a small steering committee to help guide visioning efforts, suggesting that you will want to include "people who are creative, progressive, and perhaps even those who know their field well. You want people you can trust, who will share openly with you, and who will also be influence wielders with their peers. . . . Considering the type and magnitude of change that a vision requires will lead you to who needs to be at the table" (p. 81).

8. Implement for Success and Sustainability.

In *The Global Fourth Way: The Quest for Educational Excellence*, Andrew Hargreaves and Dennis Shirley (2012) identify the essential role courage plays in making transformational changes:

> Leadership needs courage: the courage to head into unknown territory, to overcome resistance, to make a judgment call when the evidence isn't clear, and to take the first step forward when fear holds everyone else back. . . . It is what we do with our fears, how we face them, and whether we do the right thing anyway, despite the wounds that may be inflicted upon us, that defines whether we are courageous leaders or not. (p. 186)

As indicated in *Visioning Onward*, to make a significant difference, *usually substantial rather than incremental changes are needed*. That book presents the advantages of bold visions. To set bold visions often requires courage because it usually means going up against the status quo. This involves not only garnering support but also demonstrating the value of the proposal through providing evidence of its successful implementation, either in smaller projects in your school or district or elsewhere. As you initially consider your vision, look not only for evidence of its successful implementation but also for requirements for changes in policy, habits, or protocol within your school or district.

For lasting change, robust, long-term plans are needed. In *The Art of the Long View*, Peter Schwartz (1996) suggests ways to test how a vision might hold up against a variety of future scenarios, including a downturn in the economy, the disruptive influence of staffing shortages, or the emergence of new technologies or other innovations. In any case, you will need to make changes that go beyond your immediate domain and that may be helpful this week or this year—changes that will survive leadership transitions, our current crises, and unknown challenges to come. (Learn more about sustainability in Chapter 19.)

9. Lead with Heart and Hope; Your Vision and Your Plans Will Evolve Over Time.

Esteemed educational leader Michael Fullan (2021) describes "learned hopefulness," or the ability to focus on hope. He urges educators to turn toward hope, teach hope, and help people not only to cope but also to have hope.

Bill George (2007) in *True North* asks leaders, "Can you recall a time when you felt most intensely alive and you could say with confidence, 'This is the real me'? This can lead to authentic leadership" (p. xxiv).

What About You?

Review the nine key leadership considerations:

1. Begin with a sense of urgency, focusing on what is most crucial.
2. Acknowledge stress and trauma, and build self-care and vitality.
3. Then, do something to help students, families, and staff heal.
4. Remember and embrace equity and justice.
5. Increase your conscious understanding of yourself and others.
6. Turn to others: It takes teamwork.
7. Share in the visioning.
8. Implement for success and sustainability.
9. Lead with heart and hope; your vision and your plans will evolve over time.

Where do you excel? Where are your greatest needs? Are these related to areas where you might need mentoring? If not mentoring, then how else can you learn more to strengthen your leadership?

CARVING OUT TIME: URGENT PREPARATION FOR AN ARDUOUS JOURNEY

In *Leading with Vitality and Hope*, the contributors ask readers to set aside some of their mundane day-to-day tasks, to delegate some tasks to others, or to find other ways to build in time for reading and reflection. As other educational leaders have advised, leaders who are the most effective find ways to carve out time to contemplate change and how to advance the innovations that they deem to be most needed.

If you are striving to find a way out of the hardships, harsh realities, and setbacks education is experiencing today, then the narratives of our 20 contributors can be a resource as you head down what Michael Fullan (2020) calls an "extremely challenging path—one that calls for urgent, joint action that has leading in a culture of change as its continuous theme of salvation and flourishing" (p. 154).

Keeping It Real: Not Everyone Will Love This

Even with all the great leadership advice presented in this chapter, you can't count on being successful. Even the best initiatives sometimes fail. Here are a few things to consider:

- Watch out for staff overload and burn out.
- Make sure staff have a time and place to air their grievances, but ensure that an air of doom and negativity doesn't become the dominating vibe at your school or district. If you have less experience as an administrator, then you may want to seek advice from a mentor to help guide you through this process.
- Do your best to make sure that staff have release time for any extra responsibilities and that the visioning and planning you are proposing isn't just one more thing.
- Consider how to address the naysayers—perhaps by listening to them privately, building a relationship with them, and seeing if any compromises can be made to give them some sense of winning. However, sometimes it is best to simply not do too much with those who protest the most loudly.
- Find opportunities to involve families and students in the visioning process.
- Not everyone loves teamwork, and not everyone is a great team player. Know your teams, and consider how to ease in change with more buy-in and support from your most enthusiastic staff.

Aspirational Leadership: The Power of Mentoring!

An aspirational leader is someone who intentionally focuses on positively influencing the capacity of their people to flourish and to strive to perform their best for the world. Aspirational leader Jack Canfield (2015) notes in his book *The Success Principles* that successful people focus on their past successes. They never keep their focus on past failures. They never allow any distraction to distract their vision for moving forward. He explains,

> As a seasoned school principal, I reflect across my career and it's clear that the best leadership lessons, collegial projects, and general learning opportunities have come through interactions with fellow educators. Every educator knows something that I need to learn. Always take and provide opportunities to engage with those in like positions and those who do things differently. Dive into the reasons for their success. Find out the details of how, what, when, and why. Ultimately, these mentoring relationships result in experience compound interest. The more you learn, the more you grow, the better you become at problem solving, being empathetic, and looking beyond what is to see what can be.

Emmy Award–winning keynote speaker Clint Pulver helps organizations that want to retain, engage, and inspire their younger workforce. Clint has helped leadership teams diminish turnover, increase engagement, and create an organization that prioritizes people. Clint uses the video *Be a Mr. Jensen* as a message of motivation and gratitude for all the mentors of the past and those yet to be created (https://youtu.be/4p5286T_kn0).

How do you encourage other educators to be their best for the world?

Chapter 2

Visioning with Compassion, Equity, and Empowerment

A shared vision can make a crucial difference for schools. In *Visioning Onward*, Mason, Liabenow, and Patschke (2020) began their description of visioning by saying, "Our vision extends to the hearts and minds of our schools through the collective networks that share the same beliefs. Thus, many visions become streamlined into a powerful shared vision. This path ultimately illuminates with promise, hope, and passion" (p. 3). They go on to say that

- A vision establishes purpose.
- Creating a collective vision contributes to a culture of learning.
- Educators who challenge themselves start on a path to growth and improvement.
- A shared vision leads directly to collective efficacy (p. 9).

To help you find your way out of the deep distress our planet is facing, let's take a few moments to reflect on Gregory Cajete's (1994) writing about Indigenous visioning and learning. Cajete suggests that visioning focuses on the full spectrum of possibilities—the good, the bad, and the truly horrific. He realizes that visions occur in context, and to consider the full context, look to where you have been as well as where you want to go. Now, as the people around the planet are attempting global recovery, it may help to consider Cajete's advice. To recover, he suggests,

> It is important that we again give credence to the ways that primal people around the world have established their right relationship in their community and natural environments. Educators must again teach for "living the sky," "living the plain," "living the desert," "living the mountain." We must again "look to the mountain," climb it, and after that struggle and journey of understanding, complete the pilgrimage to our higher selves. We must look with new vision upon

where we have been, where we are, and where we wish to go in the evolution of education as a process within natural community. (pp. 113–114)

REFLECTING ON CAJETE'S SPECTRUM OF POSSIBILITIES

- What might you do to "live the sky" or "live the mountain"?
- What might your journey to your higher self entail?
- Where might the "evolution of education as a process within a natural community" take us?

EXAMPLES OF VISIONS IN *LEADING WITH VITALITY AND HOPE*

To examine visions more closely, review Tables 2.1 and 2.2, which include visions from 5 of the 20 contributors and include a school administrator, a state principal association leader, an international mindfulness leader, a leader combating racism and inequity, and a parent advocate. Each of these entrepreneurs developed a vision that was focused both on compassion and equity empowerment. Each vision also demonstrates a positive response to alleviating trauma. As you dive into this text, you will encounter examples of leaders who, like Paul, used visioning to catalyze an educational movement in their communities. Use the three questions from Tables 2.1 and 2.2 to test the vision statements of other leaders whose journeys we share with you in the coming chapters.

When crafting or revising your own vision statement, there are two additional considerations to keep in mind:

1. Be bold.
2. Include a call to action.

In the examples in Tables 2.1 and 2.2, the authors include such phrases as

- eliminate aggression
- remove barriers
- transform schools
- champion children's mental health
- help children learn how to best share this planet

Each of these vividly portrays action and suggests a radical impact.

Table 2.1. Framework for Common Components of Vision Statements in *Leading with Vitality and Hope*

Case study	Vision statement	Does the vision focus on compassion?	Does the vision focus on equity or increasing empowerment?	Does the vision focus on increasing a positive response to alleviating the impact of trauma?
Paul Liabenow and Michael Domagalski, Chapter 11	"MEMSPA is the vital knowledge network and voice for principals in Michigan, shaping effective solutions for everyday problems and emerging challenges. We are an engaged community of remarkable instructional leaders, furthering the practice of skillful leadership and connection with our peers."	MEMSPA's strategic plan focuses on diversity, equity, and inclusion (DEI) and uses the DEI lens as it conducts all activities in the future.	School administrators are empowered to help make change at a legislative level. Educators, staff, and students are taught mindfulness practices and are empowered with the knowledge of a new way of learning and life.	In some districts, ESSER funds are allocated to teacher self-care and increasing classroom use of mindfulness. In others, the funds have gone toward hiring mental health professionals and social workers to be available to high-risk students.

HEART CENTERED AND COMPASSIONATE LEADERSHIP

The Center for Educational Improvement's approach to visioning and leadership is heart centered and compassionate. These themes are reiterated in multiple ways throughout this book. You may be wondering if this is essential for visioning and for leadership. Could you be an effective leader without the focus on compassion and alleviating racism and trauma? Perhaps. But why would you want to do that?

Fullan (2020) addresses a related construct, "moral purpose": "Moral purpose is usually accompanied by a sense of urgency. . . . In our latest work

Table 2.2. Additional Examples of Common Components

Case study	Vision statement	Does the vision focus on compassion?	Does the vision focus on equity or increasing empowerment?	Does the vision focus on increasing a positive response to alleviating the impact of trauma?
Kevin Hawkins, Chapter 4	"To help our students, in the context of this community, learn how best to share this planet."	Developing school as a space where our children can learn to understand and care for themselves, for each other, and for this beautiful but fragile planet we call home.	Shifting our perspective of learning from teaching to doing; "The human mind is better equipped to gather information about the world by operating within it than by reading about it, hearing lectures on it, or studying abstract models of it."	Building foundational skills to grow equilibrium and resilience through social emotional learning; prepare students for life's many challenges.
Victoria E. Romero, Chapter 18	"When educators are conscious of barriers that impede the social-emotional and academic growth of their students, they can change their practice, policies, and procedures. When barriers for one group are removed, all students regardless of their gender, sexual identity, or ableism benefit. Hence, the curb-cut effect."	Removing barriers to help all students thrive.	Empowering one group by ending racism and other barriers empowers not only that group but also others who are marginalized. "Why do our mission statements continue to promote a vision of educational equity that schools in our nation rarely achieve?"	"Educators must be intentional about mitigating the impact of structural racism."

Visioning with Compassion, Equity, and Empowerment

| Ruth E. Freeman, Chapter 15 | "Eliminate aggression visited upon children in their homes through alternative techniques, mindfulness, and acknowledgment of generational trauma." | Connecting parents with inspiring experts and each other so they can gain the skills and support they need to build positive, peaceful, and joyful families. | Researching and evaluating the program to ensure that the alternative techniques being shared can actually be implemented with results. The "session you offered has given me actionable steps and a new frame of mind around how to best help them 'self-regulate' without squelching their will, independence, spirit, or personality." | Accepting parental trauma and being mindful that it is not passed down from parent to child. "Our bodies remember our losses and our fears. Our bodies remember the terror." |

on deep learning we find in students a greater sense of wanting to make a difference in society, immediately, and in the long run" (p. 15). Describing leadership effectiveness, he goes on to say that leadership effectiveness will be increased "[i]f they pursue moral purpose, understand the change process, foster deep knowledge building, and strive for coherence—with energy, courage, and relentless, and a share of doubt and anxiety" (p. 17).

As Fullan (2020) explains, from 1990 to 2010, education had the "wrong policy drivers," which negatively affected the efficacy of educational leadership during those years. He provides numerous examples of moral purpose and the dynamic process involved in pursuing moral actions, decrying developments that are "soul and planet destroying" (p. 39). He also sends a strong message about the need for educators to be deeply "concerned with the evolving state of moral purpose in their organizations and beyond" (p. 40).

Your Personal Vision

Use two to three sentences to describe your personal vision.

- Where are you on your journey toward fulfilling your personal vision?
- Are you centered on moral purpose or compassionate actions?
- Is that vision reflected in the work you do?

COLLECTIVE VISIONING: THE POWER OF YES

Paul S. Boynton is a best-selling author who advocates for his followers to overcome fears and discover their purpose by stepping into opportunities for growth and change. Paul believes that there is power in "yes" actions because they spark next steps. Thanks to a willingness to step forward, new choices and experiences will present themselves.

As a school leader, Melissa Patschke often begins her own visioning process with being aware of her vulnerability and *being vulnerable enough to let go of what is and say "yes" to something different.* She has found that taking ideas and individual energies from her team allows for a productive flow of trust. This momentum builds among the collegial network, and it also grows a passion within her core.

Melissa has learned that not everything works the way she planned, but with effort, there's a very good chance that your best will be enough to get you to the next step toward greatness. Teams take leaders who are willing to cultivate and nurture them. The synergy that's formed along this journey turns quickly from trust to belief. That's the power of *yes* in education. Always focus on all that's going right because it's quite possible that the collective vision being created will turn out far better then you could have imagined.

Examining Your Vision More Fully

Dan Heath (2020), in *Upstream: The Quest to Solve Problems Before They Happen*, not only explains the "upstream" metaphor but also describes the spirit of that metaphor: "With some forethought we can prevent problems before they happen, and even when we can't stop them entirely, we can often blunt their impact" (p. 231). To be effective, Heath offers three suggestions to leaders:

1. Be impatient for action but patient for outcomes.
2. Macro starts with micro: "You can't help a thousand people, or a million, until you understand how to help one" (p. 236).
3. Favor scoreboards over pills: that is, strive not for a medical model of double-blind testing but rather a "mindset focused on continued improvement" (p. 238).

A Comparison

Compare your personal vision to the upstream model that Dan Health suggests. Are there or could there be any upstream components to your vision?

Interviewing Team Members

Interview individuals on your team to learn what needs to change moving forward. Gather focus groups of team members that represent different roles, including some that are of like thinking.

- Ask them key questions to spark discussion about growing and improving in specific areas.
- Survey your team to find out what needs to be let go. What doesn't work any longer, and why?
- What do we need to do to get ahead of issues instead of constantly trying to fix problems?
- Put all this information together, and give it back to the team. What big ideas emerged? Were there undercurrents of messages? What felt like it should have been said but wasn't clear?
- Dive into these ideas deeper, and start to format a collective vision.

THE GENESIS OF VISIONS

In *Mindfulness Practices: Cultivating Heart Centered Communities Where Students Focus and Flourish*, Mason, Rivers Murphy, and Jackson (2019) describe the need to practice first before teaching mindfulness to our students. We, like many other mindfulness practitioners, realized that it just doesn't work to try to teach mindfulness to others if you haven't had your own internal experiences. Your experience with mindfulness will affect what and how you teach. As you continue to pursue visioning, dialoguing with others, and seeing the barriers to visioning, you may come to a similar conclusion. The small seeds that become a catalyst for visioning at work or school often have started with our own personal visions—our dreams—sometimes from childhood.

Vitality and Your Visions for Yourself

- Where are you with your own visions for yourself?
- Are you pursuing your lifelong dreams?
- Are you doing your best to live your dreams?
- Do you feel that you are on your path, or perhaps you have taken a detour?
- Where is your passion?
- Is there a disconnect between your dreams or vision and your life? If so, why? What's going on?

- If your life has been disrupted by the pandemic, racism, divisiveness, or concern for the future of our planet, then what thoughts do you have about needed changes?
- If you are not living your dreams, then what is feasible?

As you become more and more familiar with visioning and vision statements, you may start to notice that the birth of a vision could stem from a variety of places: perhaps a leader's childhood or their own lived experiences. Maybe inspiration was found during encounters with others or through the witness of dysfunction as an educator, paired with the desire to bring about change. After all, ideas can come from anywhere, and visioning is no exception.

Table 2.3 explores the commonalities and differences among the vision statements put forth by the leaders we've studied so far. When did a lightbulb go off for them? What steps did they take to unite people under their vision? Just by glancing through this table, it is easy to see that visioning is not a one-size-fits-all exercise. Rather, each leader must make unique decisions best suited for their students, their educators, and their community.

Keeping It Real: Is It Worth It?

As you consider visioning, it might be helpful to consider the questions asked by entrepreneur Kevin Simpson:

- Is it going to be worth it?
- Is it the right time?
- Are those taking the lead the right leaders?
- When your vision comes to fruition, how will it affect everything else? (Mason, Liabenow, & Patschke, 2020, p. 183)

Table 2.3. Genesis and Support for Visions

Case study	Vision statement	Personal vision from childhood?	Formal group activity at the school or community level?	Formal group activity at the district or state level?	Formal activity of a national or international group?
Paul Liabenow and Michael Domagalski, Chapter 11	"Transforming Michigan schools into champions of their children's mental health through mindfulness and social emotional learning. Looking at problems and solutions through the lens of diversity, equity, and inclusion. Advocating for this change to become more widespread through participation in the legislative process."			✓	
Kevin Hawkins, Chapter 4	"To help our students, in the context of this community, learn how best to share this planet."				✓
Victoria E. Romero, Chapter 18	"When educators are conscious of barriers that impede the social-emotional and academic growth of their students, they can change their practice, policies, and procedures. When barriers for one group are removed, all students regardless of their gender, sexual identity, or ableism benefit. Hence, the curb-cut effect."		✓	✓	✓
Ruth E. Freeman, Chapter 15	"Eliminate aggression visited upon children in their homes through alternative techniques, mindfulness, and acknowledgment of generational trauma."	✓	✓		

Chapter 3

Vitality and Visioning

What should you bring to your visioning process? Given the specific nature of grief, loss, and trauma we faced in 2020–2021, as you continue to address needs and collaborate, consider the wisdom of operating from the positive space of vitality. When we are stressed out, we are far more likely to make less-than-ideal decisions. This is where vitality comes in. Leaders, as they focus on the outward journey with others, also are traveling a road inward. With this inward journey, they learn about themselves and gain clarity and insights that come with experience and practices that reduce stress. With practice, they, too, will become more able to filter out the noise that sometimes keeps us from understanding what is needed at a deep level.

BEGINNING YOUR VISIONING JOURNEY

In Chapter 2, you considered your personal vision and reflected on its relationship with your life and your life journey. Now, imagine a time, as Bill George (2007) says in *True North*, when you were most fully alive, when you felt a sense of purpose. What images come to mind? Are you still on your path? Consider your life or your work. You may want to close your eyes and imagine what you want for the world or for your world. Think out 5–10 years from now.

As adults, we continue to go through developmental phases, and some of us may be envisioning the pinnacles of our careers, even as others of us edge toward retirement. Wherever you are on your journey, you can take steps to improve the quality of your life and your future. Consider how you want to spend your time, who you want to be with, and where. Consider your children, grandchildren, parents, other relatives, or friends. What do you wish for them?

ESTABLISHING A VISION BASELINE

As you vision, imagine your lifestyle, your hours, and how you feel.

- Are you rushed or relaxed?
- Are you hunkered down at home, at the beach, traveling, dining out, taking gourmet cooking lessons, sailing, hiking, or engaged in animated conversations?
- Are you enjoying your work?
- Do you feel the excitement of being with others, discovering new paths, or paving the way forward?
- How is your health?
- Are you finding time to smell the roses, to watch the grass grow, or to follow leaves as they float to the ground?

In your idyllic wonderland, are you feeling pressure or stress? Why or why not?

Preparation and Initial Steps

Gregory Cajete (1994) describes a period of initial preparation needed for visioning. This involves setting your intent, asking questions, and feeling psychologically empowered to take the time to indulge in your visioning. According to Cajete, this is followed by a time of exploration—considering the landscape through which one must pass and learning its story and physical nature. As Cajete reminds us, this landscape "may be internal as well as external." It involves self-knowledge and reflection on the stories, people, and events that are important to you and your journey.

In Cajete's view, this may also involve reclaiming one's history and cultural traditions; such a focus on history can be helpful in constructing a transformative vision. Think about it: You are influenced by your life events, including the stories of people in your life. These experiences and your memories of them will influence your vision. Cajete reminds us that there is wisdom not only in critiquing the past but also in appreciating those who have played a role in formal and informal ways, in big and small ways, in the past and in the present. You can frame the context for your vision by taking a few moments to reflect on your history and the history of your people, your country, and your culture.

VITALITY AND VISIONING: AN INWARD AND OUTWARD JOURNEY

Since *Visioning Onward*, we have dialogued about visioning many times with many people, and we have learned. The following are a few key considerations for you:

- As leaders, continue your inner journey, your reflections, and your dreams.
- As leaders, encourage others to pursue their inner journeys, reflections, and dreams.
- Consider not only your needs but also your strengths and the strengths of your school community. If your school excels in project-based learning, for example, how could you enhance that asset?
- Sometimes, when things get really tough, sit with it a bit. Often problem solvers feel a sense of urgency to solve a crisis. Allow yourselves to be fully conscious without judgment—to be mindful—of what is happening and what you are experiencing.
- Use your whole capacity—mind, body, and heart—to vision.
- As you vision with others, stay in touch with your inner journey.

DREAMING, SEEKING, REFLECTING WITH EMOTION AND CONVICTION

Cajete gives us a glimpse into what is needed for visioning, with some guidance for our inner journey. He talks about dreaming, seeking, reflecting, and bringing our emotions to our visions. Kevin Hawkins in Chapter 4 also discusses mindful awareness and emotional intelligence. Visioning is more than a cognitive, intellectual endeavor. It is the most authentic, the most powerful, when it is done with a sense of inner conviction and a sense of heart. You've heard the phrase, "I know in my heart it is true."

As "fully human" beings, you also learn from your bodies. Your bodily reactions (distress, discomfort, disease, excitement, vitality, well-being) can also guide your visioning. You may also know "it" in your body—perhaps it is a sense of fear or perhaps an inner joy—before you are fully aware of how you are reacting to what's happening around you.

Paul Gilbert (2017) refers to three steps to build a new sense of wholeness and well-being: (1) calming down neurological systems to become less reactive through breathwork, meditation, visualization, and self-compassion; (2) building social relational capacities and enjoyment, including "immersion in fun prosocial group activities"; and (3) "communal imagination," which he suggests can be built by "respecting natural processes; speaking up with concern for all entities as partners; [and finding] ways to embrace our common humanity."

So, bring your whole self to your visioning, and use your heart intelligence, your body intelligence, and your intellect. Stay in touch with your heart and your inner journey, as you vision and as you implement your visions.

THE THREE VS

During the past few months, Jeff Ikler, Jesse Kohler, and Christine Mason have led a series of podcasts to share stories of innovations that educators, school psychologists, social workers, and others are implementing to address the trauma from the COVID pandemic. At the same time, Chris has been pursuing an advanced yoga teaching certificate by taking a course on stress and vitality (Mason, 2021). These activities have led her to understand the power of visioning, vitality, and victory.

Consider the power of each:

- **Visioning:** A way to dream big as we plan for the future.
- **Vitality:** A way out of stress. Stress is exacerbated not only by external conditions but also by your inability to handle stress, to cope, and to adapt to your circumstances. Although stress can be reduced by redirecting one's thoughts and beliefs and through exercise, meditation, and mindfulness, it can also be reduced by adding energy or vitality to our lives.
- **Victory:** Rick Hanson (2013) is among those who point out that far too often, people dwell on the negative and merely glance at their successes. To build your resilience and your ability to move forward, we can strengthen neural pathways that help us "absorb the positive." Others have spoken of the power of celebration. When we aim for victory, we aim for celebration. Consider a time when you celebrated. How did it feel?

If, as you vision, you vision with a sense of celebration (victory), then you will bring another dimension to your activities. A spirit of celebration can help your community stay with its visioning even as the going gets tough, which can happen with strong differences of opinions and any number of factors that can derail visioning. It takes some grit to stay with visioning.

Visioning is a crucial step for achieving a more positive, hopeful future. Now pair it with vitality and victory, and you have a powerful trio. Visioning while feeling energy, positivity, and a sense of being alive: Power that up a notch with the thought of celebrating, being victorious, achieving your goal, and moving beyond your current circumstances to a better time and space.

Visioning with Vitality and Victory

As you read through the stories in *Leading with Vitality and Hope*, we urge you to look at not only the visions of the authors but also how they express vitality and victory. As you think of your own circumstances, we urge you to also consider where you are on a visioning–vitality–victory scale.

Visioning–Vitality–Victory Scale

See Figure 3.1. On each 5-point scale, where do you fall right now? Why did you respond as you did? What could you do to move forward? Throughout this book, you will have opportunities to not only reflect on the content, but to consider how to use the information as you collaborate with others.

Vital Versus Stressed Out

Imagine visioning from a vital versus a stressed-out state. When you are stressed out, you are more likely to be fearful and pessimistic. You may be exhausted and have difficulty bringing your whole self to visioning. Your vision of the future may not be quite as a bright. If you are stressed, then it might be wise to work on increasing your vitality before visioning.

Imagine the joy, enthusiasm, and excitement you or your community may feel if you achieve your vision. Imagine you are victorious. Imagining your

Visioning

1	2	3	4	5
Haven't begun		Mid-way		Implementing

Vitality

1	2	3	4	5
Stressed-Out		Okay		Energized, vibrant

Victory

1	2	3	4	5
Haven't Considered		Small Victories		Celebration!

Figure 3.1. Ratings for Your School District

team celebrating victory is one way to make a vision more real and to help everyone keep the end in mind.

Increasing Your Vitality

If you are feeling stressed out, your brain is likely to be stressed out, as well, and the quality of your activities and decisions you make will likely suffer. While you can sometimes push yourself to keep moving forward, to make tough decisions, and to advance your causes, it is usually more enjoyable (and often your results will be more insightful and impactful) if you can come from a place of vitality.

In *Cultivating Happiness, Resilience, and Well-Being through Meditation, Mindfulness, and Movement,* Mason, Donald, and their coauthors (2021) spend close to 300 pages describing how to increase your sense of vitality and well-being and how to introduce this to students in schools. Their research-based approach involves yoga, mindfulness, and meditation, with activities for children and youth from preschool through grade 12 and beyond.

The quality of your life is often influenced by the quality of your breath, and when you slow down your breath and focus your mind intentionally through meditation, you provide ways to set the stage for better intake of new information, as well as better, more efficient processing of input. All of this leads to better heart-mind-body connections, to greater coherence, and to a better sense of well-being.

Other ways to increase your vitality include the usual list of ways to improve your health and well-being: diet and nutrition, sleep, and exercise. Here are a few additional recommendations:

- Spend time doing things you love.
- Spend time with people you enjoy.
- Envision healing.
- Live a life of gratitude.
- Take a break.
- Give back.
- Get outside.
- Find time to really be involved with something you love—making it more than a brief experience. (Is it a weekend of cooking? Gardening? Hiking? Carpentry? Volunteering?)
- Amp up your listening. Put on headsets, and be with what's piped into your brain, or take a brush or charcoal in hand, and return to the peace and tranquility of being with yourself, an artist.

And on the other side of the equation, you can also increase your vitality by

- Removing negativity.
- Finding ways to do less of the things you don't enjoy.
- Finding ways to let go of worries, stress, and pressures to meet deadlines and expectations.
- Acknowledging your stress, your bodily reaction, your "pain points," simply observing without an expectation of change.
- Learning to live with a certain degree of stress and uncertainty—life will not be perfect.
- Changing your mindset—being more positive and optimistic.

Your Vitality and Your Staff's Vitality

What is your overall assessment? How stressed out are you? Your staff? Read through the previous list. Where might you begin? How could you support your staff so that they, too, are increasing their vitality? Recognize as you do this the power in just observing and just being. Sometimes it pays to just be with our emotions and stress, without trying to fix anything. We encourage you right now, before you go further, to just sit with your awareness of self. You might even coach your staff to do this—to begin by identifying their emotions and their levels of stress, including their bodily awareness of self.

Now as you read over the list, make sure you consider the children and youth you serve. What are you doing for them? How are you involving them in making daily decisions and in visioning? Looking to the future, educators need to make sure they are engaged with youth and asking them questions, listening, and using their input to help shape plans for the future.

Reflecting on Your Vision

Where are you with visioning right now personally? What about your school or district? How are you involving youth? What conclusions did you reach about vitality and the vitality of your staff? What about your students? If you vision from a stressed-out state, then your visioning may be constrained by your doubts, fears, and uncertainty.

Establishing a Collective Vision

What are you doing in your district to help leaders increase the collective self-efficacy that could be so healing for so many students and their families? Do you have a vision for the path forward in your community? Who can you partner with to implement your vision? How might you increase your collective impact?

As you move forward with a collective vision for your school, consider how to keep it ever present across all aspects of your school community. Consider posting the vision statement in your office and around the school—in the office, hallways, classrooms, and cafeteria. Add it to your website. Include it, perhaps in a separate box, on written materials and announcements.

VITALITY AND A PATH FORWARD

As you reflect on visioning as a path forward, consider walking on a path. When you are on a path, you are grounded. You are not hovering around, lost in space. On a path, you are actively headed some place, not standing still. As you envision some paths, you might even think of a favorite trail. Perhaps it was a trek in the Himalayas or a simple walk beside a nearby stream.

Wherever it may be, as you are on a path, you have opportunities to take deep breaths, observe the beauty around you, and sometimes to even challenge yourself, walking just a little further, balancing on boulders that suddenly appear before you or climbing over a fallen tree. You are mindful of the ground beneath your feet. You are mindful of the weather, of the temperature, and of the interdependence of various ecosystems.

What Path Are You On?

In this book, you will learn about the collective visions that our contributors are pursuing. The pursuit begins with the visions themselves. See Figure 3.2.

Life is moving on. However, at one moment, it may seem as if you are past the danger point, only to learn a few days later that there is a new COVID variant. You may be uncertain of many things, including whether the risks you are taking are acceptable. There is huge disagreement person to person and state to state. Psychologists are also uncertain of the long-term impact of all the recent stress, even as they tell us that trauma does not disappear overnight. So as you consider the ground beneath your feet, where are you headed? What's most urgent? What are you most excited about? Are you doing your best to help lighten the load as you journey with your staff and students? Is there more you might do?

ELEVATING YOUTH VOICE

Many school leaders feel the weight of decisions right now. Many are uneasy about what lies ahead. They may be concerned about student learning, health, and safety, including their mental health and well-being. However,

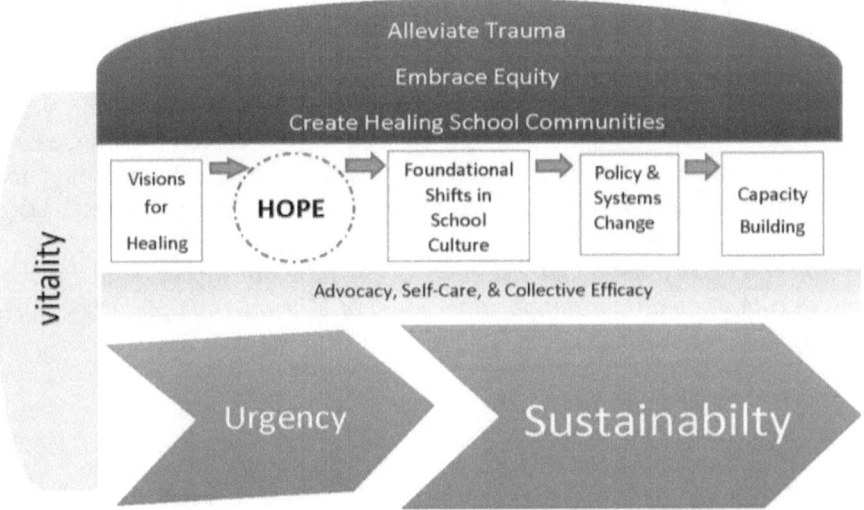

Figure 3.2. Leading with Vitality and Hope

visioning is future planning. When the voices of our youth are considered, their experiences will be enhanced by opportunities they have to voice their preferences and concerns. Educators need to listen to youth, learn from them, and welcome them to the table as partners to move things forward (Becker & Chen, 2021).

Based on the youth listening tours conducted by the Center for Educational Improvement (CEI) and the Coalition for the Future of Education, we know the following:

- Youth value being asked their opinions and would like to be more involved in planning for and designing their futures, including their courses of study, requirements, and instructional preferences.
- While many students struggle with online learning, some students thrive. Many students appreciated the flexible schedule afforded to them as they worked from home; some students also learned a lot about self-motivation.
- Some students don't want to sit in classrooms for six hours a day.
- Many students experienced a profound trauma during COVID-19 shutdowns, missing their social interactions with peers and teachers. Just as some thrived, others found it difficult to stay focused with virtual learning.
- When considering education in the future, youth want greater use of hands-on learning and more mindfulness to help alleviate their stress and anxiety and to create a greater sense of peace, calm, and well-being.

- Students realize the value of the current focus on equity and diversity and are looking forward to a future where more educators really look at them and can relate to them.

We also found out that students may need help to come up with creative ideas for what could be improved. They may need some help exploring and pondering options. They may need to learn about some of the innovative things others are doing.

You can learn more about visioning for the future of education and listening to youth at the Coalition for the Future of Education (https://www.edimprovement.org).

PART II

Healing Trauma, Racism, and Injustice

Unfortunately, American history is rife with trauma, racism, and injustice. To move forward, we must understand the past; acknowledge our shortcomings; and work to create a more equitable, inclusive, and compassionate future. Reflection, introspection, and visionary leadership are crucial tools in healing our wounds and fostering change.

To understand how we all can best live on this planet, in Chapter 4, Kevin Hawkins, an author and cofounder of MindWell Education, asks us to stop and reflect on what really matters. We must uncover and question our assumptions in order to try new things and drive change. He asks us, "What hidden assumptions might underlie our own beliefs about how children learn best?" After this internal examination, we can begin to build consensus and find common ground. As educators, we need to go beyond the classroom and align our efforts with the real world—current events and pressing problems. He suggests that we need to move beyond the ordinary and have a mindful awareness, and he urges us to strive for a more equitable and just society.

Kevin provides hope and a way to take us beyond time and space to a kinder, more insightful world. Kevin's passion is clear. He challenges us to determine how all of us can best live on this planet and implores, "This is not just an academic activity. It's an urgent call to action for all of us." As he suggests, authentic and connected leadership can foster a wiser and more compassionate, equitable, and sustainable future.

In a similar vein, Orinthia Harris, Chris Mason, and Jill Flanders in Chapter 5 ask us to "strengthen our hearts, our compassion, and our will to make a difference." Describing the need to dismantle racism, they urge us to consider not what is wrong with people but what is wrong with systems. They discuss how we might acknowledge racism, prejudice, and bias; begin to implement systemic changes through thoughtful policy; and slowly move forward as a nation. For their part, educators can continuously facilitate dialogue, avoid totalizing assumptions, and support students of color as they navigate the difficult terrains of systemic racism.

We end Part II with Chapter 6 by Holly Echo-Hawk and Melanie Johnson on the too-often-underestimated brilliance of Native American youth. Referencing cultural differences, Echo-Hawk and Johnson recount how the American educational system was not designed to embrace diverse cultures, life experiences, and accumulated knowledge. The authors both decry how the strengths of Native American youth have been overlooked and explain the urgent need to turn things around.

Chapter 4

MindWell Education

Rethinking Education and Focusing on What Really Matters

Kevin Hawkins

MindWell Education (https://www.mindwell-education.com) supports educational communities around the world in developing awareness and well-being through mindfulness and social-emotional learning (SEL). Since 2012, we have furthered individual and systemic mindfulness to help enhance the meaning and the validity of educational practices.

SHARING THE PLANET

A simple yet profound vision statement for any school on earth at this point in time is:

> *To help our students, in the context of this community, learn how best to share this planet.*

This is not just an academic activity. It's an urgent call to action for all of us. Key areas of learning—academic, technological, physical, and social—can be enhanced as we tackle this central issue. Within this context, we can develop foundational skills for building the inner equilibrium and resilience needed to navigate life in this moment in history and into the future.

At this increasingly pressurized point in time, we must now use everything we know about learning, both inside and outside the classroom, to create conditions that will truly make our schools *centers for human development*:

spaces where our children can learn to understand and care for themselves, for each other, and for this beautiful but fragile planet we call home.

My visioning of the bigger picture of education was radically revitalized through meeting John Abbott many years ago. He twice came out to work with our school community in Tanzania, and his profound thinking about the history, purpose, and potential of education influenced my own thinking and leadership on a deep level.

John often quoted Schank and Cleave (1995): "The method people naturally employ to acquire knowledge is largely unsupported by traditional classroom practice. The human mind is better equipped to gather information about the world by operating within it than by reading about it, hearing lectures on it, or studying abstract models of it." John questioned at a deep level our current outdated approaches to education. In *Overschooled but Undereducated*, Abbott and MacTaggart (2010) assert,

> The world crisis that is upon us is the unintended consequence of an education system designed in another time for another purpose, and now utterly inappropriate to human and planetary needs. . . . Learning is not dependent on schooling. We humans have been using our brains to learn for several million years. Maybe the very institution of school is now being side-lined by our deeper understanding of how humans learn.

Addressing the Full Range of Human Capacities

Even in 17th-century Europe, Czech educator, educational philosopher, and (for many) father of modern universal education John Amos Comenius was urging teachers to follow the example of nature, to keep learning "easy and pleasant," and to ensure that

- the pupil is not overburdened by too many subjects;
- the intellect be forced to nothing to which its natural bent does not incline it, in accordance with its age and with the right method;
- everything be taught through the medium of the senses; and
- the use of everything taught be continually kept in view (Comenius, 1638).

Comenius's approach, in line with many modern thinkers, demonstrates an awareness of the need to go beyond our traditional academic curricula and to *evolve more natural, more humanized systems of education.*

John Abbott was also a woodworker. In explaining the need for a revolution in schooling, he sometimes referred to learning that "goes with the grain of the brain." His work, like Comenius's, provides vivid examples of how educators can find ways to develop teaching and learning approaches that nurture the intrinsic strengths of our students in alignment with the "grains of their brains."

SHIFTING THE FOCUS

In a parallel attempt to simplify what really matters in education, Daniel Goleman and Peter Senge coauthored a book that urges educators to organize all learning around three key areas of focus:

1. Focus inwardly to increase our understanding of ourselves.
2. Tune into others to form connected relationships.
3. Focus outwardly to learn about and connect better with the world that lies beyond ourselves and our personal relationships while understanding better the systems in which we live and operate.

Their book *Triple Focus: A New Approach to Education* (2014) shows how we can combine mindful awareness, SEL, and systems thinking to shift the focus of education to areas that really matter—for ourselves and our planet.

What Do We Really Want?

We ask parents and teachers around the world, at the heart level, "What is it that we really want for our children?" Regardless of culture or economics, the answers are universally about deeper qualities of health, well-being, and happiness. Education is so busy, so overstuffed, and so fast moving that we seldom have time to pause and reflect on the deeper purposes of learning.

Yet unless we find ways to deepen this understanding, we will continue to turn out the same old approaches and content, even when it appears in shiny new packaging. In our experience of leading change in schools, we have found that unless we get down to this deeper level of reflection and communication, nothing really changes. We have to find ways to look together at *what really matters* and to rewrite our own narratives for the purpose of schooling.

"Culture Eats Strategy for Breakfast!"

As principal of the middle school at the Intentional School of Prague (ISP), I inherited a well-resourced team of educators. The school had a forward-looking administration, and we were able to make dynamic gains in overhauling the traditional curriculum. These gains occurred despite the generally conservative nature of the community. Yet within a few years, we began to question what else we might be doing. We wanted to learn how to make more fundamental changes to our approach to teaching and learning.

Seeing the System

Peter Senge's influential book *The Fifth Discipline: The Art and Practice of the Learning Organization* (1990) spoke to our needs. We used some of his ideas and techniques directly in our revisioning of the middle school. As we worked with school staff, we found an opportunity to implement two of Senge's principles:

1. We sought to develop a deeper dialogue in ways that would more fully engage teachers.
2. We found ways to question our own assumptions about our current situation and to understand more fully what we might achieve if we could learn to acknowledge and then let go of our preexisting notions of education, learning, and schooling.

We have all been to school, and so we all have our own notions (our mental models) of what constitutes a good education and what doesn't. But it's only when we surface and compare these assumptions that we can begin to move beyond them and see with greater clarity both what is and what is possible.

Applying Senge's Work at a Middle School

At ISP Middle School, we decided to use Senge and his coauthors' *Schools That Learn* (2000) to help us review our position in relation to the school's overall mission targets. A few of the teachers led us through a process of reviewing some common assumptions about learning from this book—and we found ourselves questioning the relevance of some of our underlying industrial-age thinking as we proceeded with this review. We focused on the following seven false assumptions that are implicit to most school systems:

1. Children are deficient, and schools fix them.
2. Learning takes place in the head, not in the body as a whole.
3. Everyone learns or should learn in the same way.
4. Learning takes place in the classroom, not in the world.
5. Knowledge is inherently fragmented.
6. Schools communicate the "truth."
7. Learning is primarily individualistic, and competition accelerates learning (Senge et al., 2000, pp. 35–48).

In the process, we learned a lot about ourselves, and we were able to visualize what we might be able to let go of to radically transform our approach to teaching and learning. Creating the space for this deeper dive into underlying obstacles to change had a profound effect. Rather than creating a detailed strategic plan, we evolved a set of shared intentions that over the next few years really did help bring us closer to achieving our ideals of what really matters in our middles school. (See my book *Mindful Teacher, Mindful School: Improving Wellbeing in Teaching and Learning* [Hawkins, 2017] for more details on how I applied Senge's ideas and *The Mindful Teacher's Toolkit: Teaching and Embedding Awareness-Based Wellbeing in Schools* [Hawkins & Burke, 2021] for further exploration of applying systems thinking to educational change.)

Evaluating Senge's Common Assumptions About Learning in Your School

After reading Senge's seven assumptions, review your vision, mission, values, and practices at your school, checking to see if any show up. If so, what modifications might you be able to make? (See Senge and colleagues [2000] for further details of this process.)

MINDFUL AWARENESS

Adding a mindfulness course for students into the curriculum can be a good way to get things started in a school. But if we really want to start to shift the focus of education, then we stand a much greater chance of stimulating sustainable change when we take our time to look holistically at connecting with existing initiatives and approaches and building a more coherent framework.

Situating mindful awareness training within the context of existing pastoral approaches and social and emotional programs can be an effective first step for schools. Positioning mindfulness and SEL within a broader school framework of well-being (we have come to call this *awareness-based well-being*) takes this a step further and provides an integrated view that can inform future curriculum planning.

Reflective Exploration

When looking at new initiatives in schools, we need to foster change in a broad-minded, thoughtful, and sensitive way. Rather than trying to force new ideas onto a school community, a healthier approach is to consider this as the beginning of a dialogue with faculty, administrators, support staff, students, and parents. If we are concerned with creating flourishing communities where the aim is improving well-being, then a good place to start is by involving interested parties in a reflective exploration of the issues.

Be Mindful, Teach Mindfully, Teach Mindfulness

It's important also to recognize that introducing mindfulness courses and increasing the emphasis on SEL can be a practical challenge for schools. It requires teachers to develop their own practice first and get trained up in methods of delivery. To become sustainable, this type of change needs a shift in the school culture and provision of ongoing professional-development opportunities.

The Messages We Give Students

Understanding the overall impact of the system within which we operate as educators is fundamental to helping to change that system, to help it become more humane. Despite our best intentions for our learners, schooling often ends up giving messages to students that may not be wholly beneficial.

A young person could be forgiven for thinking that education is all about getting the grade so that you can book your place in a university, so that you can get the job you most want and deserve, so that you can earn the money you need to buy the house for the family that you want, that you work hard so you can finally retire and relax, that life is a journey from A to B to C to D, so that at some point in the future we can end up someplace where we will be happy and successful. But learning is about life, not just preparation for college.

A Mindfulness Exercise

Find somewhere quiet to sit and focus for 5 to 10 minutes. You can sit or lie down for this mindful breathing exercise:

1. Place one hand on your waistband and the other on your chest bone. This hand will help you to notice how deep or shallow your breathing is.
2. Open your mouth and gently breathe out. Let your shoulders and upper body relax. Pause for a few seconds.
3. With your mouth closed, breathe in slowly through your nose, making your belly expand. Once you've inhaled as much as you comfortably can, pause again.
4. Breathe out through your mouth, and notice your belly drawing in. Pause again.

5. Repeat steps 3–4 for the rest of your available time. Take time to notice how you feel, how your body changes and reacts to each inhalation and exhalation (MindPanda, 2021).
6. After a few cycles of this, allow your breath to return to its natural flow, and see if you can continue to follow each exhalation and inhalation, anchoring your attention on the physical sensations of breath coming and going. Notice when the mind wanders off into thought, and then gently but firmly guide your attention back to the breath. If the breath is not readily accessible for you, try anchoring your attention on the physical sensations of the body: for example, the feet, seat, or hands.

BEYOND THE CLASSROOM

We urge educators to go beyond the walls of our classrooms to truly align our efforts with what is already happening elsewhere in education and in the wider world. For example, when we ask a question about what we really want, it can help us to rediscover the deeper purpose of education and the role it plays in society.

As countries around the world begin to show increased interest in the welfare and quality of life for people in their own countries and beyond, such governments as Bhutan, Finland, Iceland, and New Zealand have begun to revisit the question, Is there something beyond economic growth that is more important for our planet? In Bhutan, the government uses a measure of "Gross National Happiness," which provides a gauge for measuring progress through tracking various well-being components. The United Nations has now adopted this approach to global development targets.

As educators, when we ask ourselves, "What should come next?" we need to give our teams time and space for these deeper reflections on what could be. Perhaps a partial answer to the question lies in the realm of our value systems: What do we value most? Rather than valuing what we can easily measure, we need to develop skillful ways in schools to measure what we value.

Well-Being at Universities: A New Metric?

Many colleges and universities around the world are establishing mindful-awareness and well-being programs, partly out of an interest in the potential benefits of mindfulness training, but also out of a concern about increasingly disturbing levels of mental health of students. Here are some examples of recent developments in tertiary education:

- At the University of Montréal, Québec, it is now mandatory if you want to train to be a doctor that you take well-being courses that include learning some mindfulness strategies for yourself. Again, this is partly because they know that self-care in an extremely demanding profession is increasingly vital and because student stress and distress levels are quite high in medical training.
- The University of Rochester School of Medicine and Dentistry, New York, and Monash Medical School, Australia, have integrated mindfulness into their curricula. Many medical schools around the world now offer mindfulness training to students. Dobkin and Huchinson (2013) explain, "Studies show that students who follow these programmes experience decreased psychological distress and an improved quality of life."
- Many universities now offer undergraduate student courses in mindfulness. For example, at Duke University, North Carolina, Koru Mindfulness is an evidence-based curriculum that has been specifically designed for teaching mindfulness, meditation, and stress management to college students and other young adults.
- George Mason University, Virginia, works with faculty and students to focus on well-being, drawing on positive psychology and mindfulness. Gallup carried out research on the project, and Brandon Busteed, executive director of Gallup Education, believes,

> Just simply showing that someone has a diploma is not going to be the currency of the future. It's going to be, "Did that diploma significantly increase my likelihood of having a great job and a great life?" *That may be the new metric against which universities are measured in the future.* (quoted in Hawkins, 2017)

So far, few teacher training institutions have incorporated mindfulness training into their courses, but this is a much-needed development, both as basic introduction to educator self-care and as a foundation for bringing this work to future students. Two examples of universities that have made very good progress in this area are University of Vienna, Austria, and VIA University College, Aarhus, Denmark.

Developments in the United Kingdom

The United Kingdom is at the cutting edge of leadership in its approach to using mindfulness tools in government and business. Here are a few highlights from this journey:

- In 2012, Jon Kabat-Zin met with the British prime minister, and in 2013, Thich Nhat Hanh led a meditation in the House of Lords.
- Mark Williams, Chris Cullen, and Richard Burnett started a program to train members of Parliament on 8-week mindfulness courses (currently more than 240 politicians have been trained). Several politicians have described the impact of mindfulness on their lives. For example, Lord Andrew Stone explained how he used mindfulness during difficult government negotiations while on a trip to Egypt, and Conservative member Tracey Crouch has shared how she used the mindfulness training for relief from anxiety (Halliwell, 2014).
- In 2015, the Mindfulness All-Party Parliamentary Group released a report on the potential of mindfulness training in prisons, mental health, and education, and this work has continued to spread within the United Kingdom and to other governments internationally through individual efforts and the work of the Mindfulness Initiative (https://www.themindfulnessinitiative.org/).

AUTHENTIC AND CONNECTED

Mindfulness can help us stay connected—more connected to our authentic inner selves and more connected in relationship to others. In many ways, it is the antithesis of the busyness so many experience on a daily basis, helping us find meaningful ways to simply slow down, pause, and recharge while teaching and studying. Young people are growing up today in a world full of distraction and disruption. Many feel a sense of isolation and an anxiety about the state of the planet and about their own uncertain futures. Some are drawn to try to escape that sense of isolation and uncertainty through drugs, alcohol, and other addictive behaviors. Mindful-awareness training can be one crucial tool they can use to help them find a sense of calm in the storm, learning how to enhance their well-being and become more resilient in challenging situations.

Slow down, and step cautiously; just keep moving mindfully forward.

A Reflection

Missie Patschke reflects on how mindfulness was used in her district:

> In our school district, the concept of mindfulness practices was introduced in a slow, informational manner. We touched base at faculty meetings. The SEL committee shared many resources across the K–12 platforms that would match content areas and needs. Several staff modeled the ideas and joined colleagues'

classrooms to demonstrate lessons. Even with all of these efforts, not all staff have bought into the ideas.

Over the years, no matter where we introduce a practice or intervention—whether it is 2nd or 3rd grade, math or reading or PE—the new strategies are rippling into learning environments where they have never been before. It's really amazing. Teacher to teacher, leader to leader, what's being shared over time is what works. Mindfulness practices work for classroom management, self-regulation, peer collaboration, compassion, and empathetic supports. Go slow, but go forward. Continue to share what's working across settings, and the success will spread.

Keeping It Real

Not every leader, not every school, not every community is ready for the mindfulness that Kevin Hawkins recommends. Here are some considerations:

- Have you had any pushback in your community around SEL or mindfulness? If so, how might you proceed, realizing that you will experience some resistance?
- What competing initiatives must you consider? Is there a way to link to any of these?
- Is the timing right? How much support will you get for this work? What resources will you need?
- Do you have knowledge of how other schools or districts have addressed mindfulness and global change? If not, how might you find out about progress that others have made?
- If you have identified obstacles, what might you do?

Kevin's Leadership

Through MindWell Education, Kevin is pursuing a dream to bring about global societal change through mindfulness and improving conscious awareness of how education can help us address urgent planetary concerns. Over the course of his career, Kevin has journeyed with others to create mindful school communities, helping educators create authentic learning environments that empower students to find a sense of connection and purpose.

A guiding question for us all in this work is, "Can we, through understanding ourselves and each other better, learn how to cope, thrive, and flourish?"

Chapter 5

Compassionate Mindful Practices for Healing Racism and Trauma

Orinthia Harris, Christine Mason, and Jillayne Flanders

ANTIRACIST LITERACY VISION

Dismantling racism in America begins with embracing the fact that America is wrought with racism, prejudice, and bias, and we (all of us) have played a role in perpetuating these racist ideologies. The healing that is needed is a mind-body-soul experience. We must strengthen our hearts, our compassion, and our will to make a difference and to act with compassion from an informed base of knowledge. For this to happen, classrooms need to be transformed into compassionate centers of healing for all.

May 31, 2021, marked the 100th anniversary of the Tulsa race massacre. This past year, as we watched images of the prosperous Tulsa Black community being burned to the ground a century ago, we were also reminded of the historic cruelty that lingers to this day. Racism and bigotry run deep in the veins of America. What are we as educators called to do as these incidences of our inhumanity surface? Whether it is the ugly wound of slavery, the slaughter of Indigenous people, the caging of immigrant children at our borders, or the frequent microaggressions and implicit bias that are part of our culture and our history, healing is needed.

This healing does not come easily. Generations of tragedy cannot be easily erased from our DNA. Ignoring racism and whitewashing American history is not a solution.

DISMANTLING RACISM

Dismantling racism in America begins with embracing the fact that America is wrought with racism, prejudice, and bias, and we (*all of us*) have played a role in perpetuating these inhumane ideologies. Dr. Kendi (2019) states, "Denial is the heartbeat of racism, beating across ideologies, racists, and nations" (p. 9). We the People must come together and remove the filter that portrays America as a postracial society because the Civil Rights Act of 1964 was passed and a Black man was elected president. We cannot abolish what we refuse to acknowledge.

To become an antiracist, one must engage the world, seeing all racial groups as equals, and intentionally promote equity. Antiracists

- don't try to figure out what's wrong with people; they try to figure out what's wrong with policy.
- openly push back against misleading statistics and faulty premises that try to make a case that there's something wrong with a particular racial group that is genetically, culturally, or even behaviorally different from the dominant or accepted culture.
- understand that people are not broken; systems are.

When *We the People* stop judging differences by our own cultural standards, pursue dialogue filled with diverse perspectives, and remove ourselves from the echo chambers in which our biases thrive, we will be well on our way to dismantling racism and can truly experience "liberty and justice for all."

HEALING THE TRAUMA WITHIN

As much as education has focused on the six- to seven-hour school day, the children in our classes, no matter their culture, race, religion, or gender, have stored experiences from a world that is much larger. Bruce D. Perry and Oprah Winfrey (2021) describe the trauma of slavery and its aftermath in their recent book *What Happened to You* as "[h]undreds of years of internalizing the trauma of racism, segregation, brutality, fear, and dismantling of the nuclear family—all of it replicated and repeated over and over again at the micro level of the individual and eventually seen and felt at the macro level of society" (p. 129).

Trauma is embedded within each of us. Sadly, when anyone (adult or child) tries to suppress our own trauma or pretend it isn't there, further damage is done. When we try to flee our own trauma through diversion or to fight it with anger, it remains, and we have created response mechanisms that often sabotage our own best interests.

Neuroscience tells us that our brains are wired to respond to threats of danger—it is a matter of survival. Once traumatized or when in the midst of a traumatic experience, we are especially alert to danger. When this happens, instead of focusing on the teacher's words, five-star alarms may be ringing in our heads. In a class of 20, at any point in time, several students are likely to hear these alarms. However, trauma affects each of us differently, and what may be a minor stressor for one child could have a major impact on another.

What Can Be Done?

As much as we may wish it to be so, trauma cannot be erased by counting to 1, 2, 3, and on *3*, presto, it is gone. Human beings will not immediately become less cruel. Child abuse, domestic violence, bigotry, and injustice will not disappear overnight. Looking back over the past few decades, we can easily say that No Child Left Behind and the Common Core did not eradicate violence, racism, prejudice, or other trauma. The solution lies elsewhere, and education must play a role. Education as the social system established for the good of our children must wake up and do more:

- **Establish a foundation of healing.** The foundation we are calling for can be the undergirding for all that happens within a school. We want this foundation for healing to be solid so that what happens in individual compassionate classrooms across the span of grades will be maintained. Compassionate school cultures are an essential part of the solution.
- **Implement compassionate school practices.** Compassionate school cultures can be built with school leaders and staff who demonstrate significant caring and concern for students and families. In *Compassionate School Practices*, Mason, Asby, and colleagues (2021) recommend four overarching guidelines: (1) prevent the causes of stress and trauma, (2) support the child, (3) develop protective factors, and (4) build resiliency (see Figure 5.1).

Increase Awareness and Healing through Mindfulness

Mindfulness, the practice of being fully present in the moment without judgment (Kabat-Zinn, 2003), can be another key. *Cultivating Happiness, Resilience, and Well-Being through Meditation, Mindfulness, and Movement* (Mason, Donald, et al., 2021) describes how when "teaching a unit and using reframing or facilitating discussions to deepen understanding of racism, discrimination, equity, and justice," yoga, mindfulness, and meditations help by

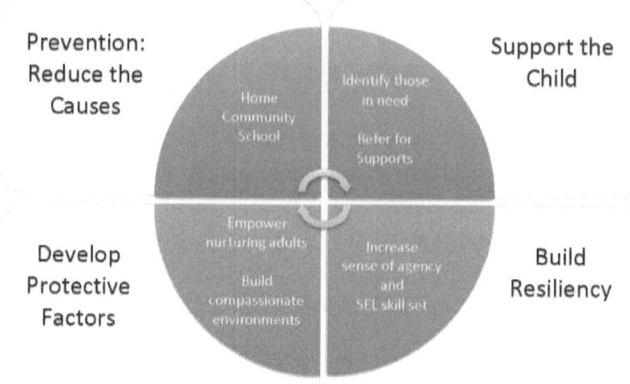

Figure 5.1. Four Overarching Guidelines for Compassionate Schools. *Courtesy of Mason, Asby, et al. (2021, p. xxvii). Used with permission.*

increasing mindful awareness and opening up our bodies, souls, and minds to remove blockages to healing, deepening understanding and caring (p. 142).

ANTIRACISM IN EARLY CHILDHOOD

When addressing racial equity in early childhood education, one has to consider early childhood mental health. The intersectionality of diversity, equity, and inclusion (DEI) and trauma-informed practices cannot be overstated. Early childhood professionals who are insufficiently or inappropriately trained on trauma leave students at high risk for racial retraumatization. Creating antiracist spaces in early childhood education requires a deeper understanding of how

- trauma gets passed down through generations, oftentimes involuntarily.
- traumatic memories get stored in the developing brain in a way that is distorted, which can change the brain's architecture.

To build capacity for understanding racial equity, we must go beyond physical representations of equity in our classrooms (i.e., books, toys, and images of representation in spaces and environments that young children spend time in). Adding these elements to your classroom does not fully address the deeper racial trauma and retraumatization experienced by young children daily.

Creating antiracist early childhood spaces requires recognizing that implicit bias exists in early childhood systems and must be mindfully dealt with by all stakeholders within the system. This mindful reflection requires those vested in changing the system through professional development and training to resist teaching and facilitate reflection.

The goal should not merely be the measurement of outcomes but the planting of seeds for mind shifts. Transmuting trauma into resilience through dismantling negative belief systems requires conscious deconstruction and reconstruction by each individual. Belief systems are constructed unconsciously but reconstructed consciously.

Reconstructing Equitable Educational Spaces

The conscious reconstruction of equitable early childhood spaces requires practitioners to engage in self-reflection and to gain new information, observation, exposure, and experiences. When this occurs collectively, we can consciously reconstruct equitable early childhood spaces at the belief level. Believing in the message of equity will ensure that collectively we can implement the practical aspects of creating equitable early childhood spaces with fidelity.

The Shift: A Personal Reflection

Orinthia Harris reflects on her own educational journey and development:

> Like most children cycled in the American public school system, we were trained to believe in this great nation, to believe in the promise of liberty and justice for all. We said the pledge and sang the songs with a real sense of pride. By 12th grade, many of us fully believed in the American dream and even dreamed of participating in this great democracy where justice surely always prevailed. Perhaps a run for Congress? Commitment to local politics? Either way, we were so blindly vested in the red, white, and blue that we couldn't see how systemic racism would consistently place barriers in my path toward actualizing the American dream.
>
> Sure, we knew there was slavery, but it was so well romanticized in every curriculum that even as young Black children, we fantasized about how it might be to live in the antebellum South. What it would be like to be Kizzy in the movie *Roots* or Mammy in *Gone With the Wind*? This period was my favorite to study and learn about. Even studying African American history in undergrad didn't fully expose racism in America for what it really was.
>
> And while my passion for the advocacy and advancement of Black people began to sprout in college, I still blindly placed my faith in the American public education system. A major shift came while studying for my PhD in educational leadership. EDU-772, "A Historical Perspective," was the catalyst for my great awakening to the true history America and how populations have

been negatively affected by racist policies and practices. The various systems that many people of color looked to help them actualize the American dream were the same ones that placed barriers in their way. What was brushed off as mere coincidences were actually racial microaggressions. We were victims of systemic institutionalized racism. This began a journey of self-reflection that led to acceptance that antiracist work in education is a process that requires self-reflection and collective activism.

Antiracism can't be "tokenized" as something handled by one professional-development session. My goal as an antiracist educator is to ensure that educators continuously facilitate dialogue, avoid totalizing assumptions, and support students of color as they navigate the difficult terrains of systemic racism.

Antiracism and Your Early Childhood Program

How has your early-years program moved to being antiracist? Review this Rosemarie Allen and her colleagues' (2021) article on the racial history and current status of racism in early childhood programs with your team. Then hold a discussion with your staff, addressing the following questions:

- What is the history of racism in your early childhood program and your school?
- How has racism been addressed?
- How are inequities being addressed?
- Consider staffing, mispronunciation or shortening of non-White names, statistics on suspensions, and other examples of racism. Is further work needed?
- Are you intentionally addressing antiracism?

Looking Ahead

Racism will not be easily extracted from the American culture. Generations-old biases and fears must be addressed. The healing that is needed is a mind-body-soul experience. We must strengthen our hearts, our compassion, and our will to make a difference and to act with compassion from an informed base of knowledge. For this to happen, classrooms need to be transformed to compassionate centers of healing for all.

Orinthia, Christine, and Jillayne's Leadership

To dismantle racism, healing is needed—for both the current and intergenerational trauma. Building on the work of Yale's Childhood Trauma Learning Collaborative and a model for compassionate school practices, Orinthia,

Chris, and Jill are following Ibram Kendi's recommendations to focus on antiracism as schools also acknowledge racism in its historical and current contexts. They also urge a complementary focus on prevention, supporting the needs of each child, and developing protective factors and resiliency through compassionate school leadership.

Chapter 6

Reclaiming the Brilliance of Native Youth

Holly Echo-Hawk and Melanie Johnson

American Indian and Alaska Native youth are frequently misunderstood, despite our responsibility to nurture their future and see them for what they are: innately intelligent and vital community assets.

Our vision is that public educators understand the strengths, resilience, and innate intelligence of Native people. We envision a world in which all educators understand that their training is based in a western world view that supports western superiority and lacks understanding of Native contributions to history and contemporary society. We envision a future where educators are aware of the ancestral strengths of Native youth and that the innate intelligence Native youth is assumed and nurtured.

Many non-Native educators in America underestimate the intellectual capacity of Indigenous students. This is due, in part, to a historical American educational system that was not designed to embrace the knowledge found in diversity of culture and life experiences.

Thousands of Native American school-age children and youth are dependent on underfunded public school systems, and when combined with an educator who lacks knowledge about Indigenous life or who possesses a romanticized view of Native American culture, the intellectual capacity of Indigenous students can be frequently underestimated. This can lead to the systemic writing-off of thousands of youth, ignoring or dampening their potential to contribute to society.

IMAGINE THE BRILLIANCE

Take a moment and imagine that you are a young Native person who has been a lifelong witness to the psychological intelligence, cultural strengths, and resilience of your family. But you keep this knowledge to yourself because you believe that only a blood relative or another tribal person would understand. You hold this awareness as your private gift, like a secret stone of power that you alone possess and control. You remain quiet about this inherited gift, as you were taught not through words but through observation that being reserved, respectful, and silent are warrior strengths. This ancestral power source of being watchful and silent, nourishes your natural brilliance. United South and Eastern Tribes (2022) explains, "Native brilliance refers to the innate intelligence, balance, resources, and resilience by acknowledging the strengths of Native people."

In a February 2022 presentation, Holly Echo-Hawk and Jeff King described the brilliance of Native Americans with numerous examples of how Native tribes have influenced how we approach disease prevention, sustainable food practices, fire prevention and containment practices, and even informed much of modern Western psychology. Interactions with Native people led to such fundamental psychological concepts as Jung's conception of the unconscious and psyche, Maslow's hierarchy of needs and self-actualization, and Erickson's stages of psychosocial development. Additionally, Echo-Hawk and King noted how the West mainly relies on hierarchical and linear ways of knowing, while Indigenous people rely more on shared and holistic ways of knowing. Fixico (2003) elaborated, "The linear mind looks for cause and effect, and the Indian mind seeks to comprehend relationships."

Native Youth Demonstrate Untapped Brilliance

The innate strategic thought capacity of Native young people is not something born in a classroom. It is more accurately viewed as an inherited gift from their ancestors. In other words, the innate brilliance that lives within each Native young person is grounded in their ancestral and cultural DNA. This untapped brilliance of Native youth demands safe nurturing to ensure their right to expand their brilliance and to explore ways they can be a positive force within their tribal and broader societies.

The Art of Joy, Resilience, and Movement

Madeline Gupta is a student at Yale University and an Ojibwe woman who recognizes the resilience of her ancestors and carries on their legacy through her work. She explains that for many Indigenous people, dancing is an art of joy, resilience, spirituality, and emotion:

> I believe that dance is for everyone, no matter age, background or ability. The passion and freedom I find in moving my body is something that everyone deserves to feel. These values are drawn from and align closely with one of my biggest Indigenous role models—Maria Tallchief. Tallchief, who was one of the first Native American dancers to pursue ballet, spent her career representing people who did not previously have access to this art. She devoted her life to ensuring all life—no matter community, gender, or access—could appreciate a love of movement and music. . . .
>
> For me, ballet is a place beyond time and space where I feel most at home with my body and the world around me. My ancestor's strength and wisdom propel my grand allegro, guides my turns, and keeps a watchful eye over my epaulement. Although I am in control of my body, I am not alone on stage. With me are all of the Indigenous dancers who came before. (Gupta, 2020)

As educators and role models, we should assume Native brilliance and double our efforts to nurture and support the unique intellectual and cultural gifts of Indigenous youth.

Don't Squash the Brilliance of Native Youth

Unfortunately, that same young Native person who is watchful and silent is likely to be in a mainstream classroom, where words are rewarded and silence is misinterpreted as "less intelligent." It is likely that most of their classmates are not Native and the classroom topics (e.g., science, government, etc.) are taught in a linear fashion with no Native inclusion or Native interpretation. There is no mention that

- Native people were early astronomers.
- The US government was modeled after the Iroquois Confederacy's Great Binding Law.
- The Penobscot Nation is the oldest continuously operating government in the world.

When there is no mention of the positive influence of Native brilliance or there is no mention of Native people in history, it can send a message to students that Native people are not important.

Add to this scenario the same young Native person who faces daily prejudice or racism because they look Native or they have brown or dark skin in a White neighborhood or they are quiet or they communicate in a way that others don't understand or any number of attributes that are interpreted as being "different." Too many young Native people face the emotional pounding of bigotry, but they can also absorb the most dangerous interpretation of the message that Native people are not important. When interpreted personally, the message is "you" are not important.

What Do You Know About the Brilliance of Native American Youth?

Reflect on any experience you have had teaching Indigenous youth.

1. What was your experience?
2. Were youth quiet?
3. Did you see brilliance?
4. What might you have missed?

The Voice of Youth

The National Indian Education Association annual convention in October 2021 featured Native youth. As part of the Healing Indigenous Lives Initiative, the United National Indian Tribal Youth (UNITY) and the Office of Juvenile Justice and Delinquency Prevention (2022) hosted a series of youth town hall meetings. Their report found that when asked about Native brilliance, the Native youth shared insights reflecting five general themes:

1. Mainstream society embraces misinformation and stereotypes about Native people that are not true.
2. Native youth should not be fearful to show who they really are.
3. Native youth should not be afraid to fail, and they should not be afraid to succeed.
4. History cannot change, but Native youth can influence the future.
5. Indigenous voices matter.

FOSTERING BRILLIANCE: CULTURE MATTERS

Identity development, including self-concept and self-esteem, is a crucial developmental process that occurs during adolescence and young adulthood (Kroger, 2007). For most Native people, cultural identity and cultural connectedness are the touchstones of their life as Native people and tribal members.

David O'Connor, the American Indian Studies Consultant with the Wisconsin Department of Public Instruction, is one of many influential leaders and advocates in the area for tribal education. His multilens passion as an

Anishinaabe member, an educator, and a storyteller has shaped his perspective on teaching Native studies: "When I think about teaching culturally, that's where an educator is becoming a guide with their students. . . . [T]hey are learning along the way with them. . . . I always tell teachers, don't look at it from the lens of telling someone else's story—tell your story. Tell the story of why you're interested in this content" (quoted in PBS Wisconsin Education, 2020).

Cultural Connectedness

Cultural connectedness refers to the degree to which an American Indian or Alaska Native is integrated within his or her Native/Indigenous culture. For many Indigenous people, culture, language, traditions, beliefs, and ceremonies are a living part of their heritage and an important part of their balance in life. Regardless of race or culture, young people across the world are increasingly involved in heritage protection and promotion, recognizing that heritage does not only belong to the past but is also part of their identity (United Nations Youth, n.d.).

Measuring How Culture Matters

Dr. Angela Snowshoe and her colleagues (2015) developed the Cultural Connectedness Scale (CCS) for First Nations/Indigenous youth in Canada to measure the degree of cultural connectedness and the link of cultural connectiveness to mental health and well-being outcomes. The CCS was later modified and adapted for use with California tribal and urban Indian populations.

As part of the California-based Culture Is Prevention project, a series of phased studies reviewed the adaptation the CCS-California (CCS-CA) and later investigated the relationship between culture (measured by the CCS-CA) and mental health and well-being [measured by the modified Herth Hope Index (mHHI)]. The goal was to evaluate if culture is a social determinant of mental health and well-being for a California population of Indigenous/Native peoples, with a sample of 344 Indigenous adults in the San Francisco Bay Area (Masotti et al., 2020). The study concluded that, in fact, culture is an important determinant of health for Indigenous peoples (King et al., 2019). Indigenous peoples around the world are promoting cultural revitalization and connectivity to reclaim and nurture what remains, bettering their health and well-being outcomes.

How do Native young people have their cultural identity and self-worth reinforced within the school environment, which accounts for much of their waking hours? How can their cultural identity and innate knowledge be supported in school settings if there is no mention or no accurate mention of their ancestral role in the history of the United States?

BACKGROUND

The 2020 US Census Bureau data reported a significant increase (86.5%) in the American Indian and Alaska Native population (alone and in combination) from 5.2 million in 2010 to 9.7 million in 2020 (Indian Country Today, 2022). This 10-year upsurge in the American Indian and Alaska Native population means that Native people now represent nearly 3% of the entire 2020 US population. The census also reported that more than 2.1 million American Indian and Alaska Native youth under the age of 24 live in the United States (Youth.gov, n.d.). There are more than 574 recognized tribes in the United States, 225 of which are in Alaska; 103 in California; and 68 in the Southwest (Colorado, Nevada, New Mexico, and Utah). A map showing the location of the tribes can be found at the Bureau of Indian Affair's Tribal Directory (https://www.bia.gov/bia/ois/tribal-leaders-directory/).

Despite this growth in population, the US mainstream population still holds many misperceptions about Native people (IllumiNative, n.d.a). One misperception is that Native American people live on reservations, yet the 2010 census reports that approximately 70% of Native people live within an urban setting (Norris, Vines, & Hoeffel, 2012). This means that most school-age Native youth are dependent on public schools for their academic education (Indian Health Service, 2018).

According to the National Indian Education Association (n.d.b), 90% of Native school-age youth attend public schools. They also report,

- The high school graduation rates for Native students who attend public schools is 72%, compared to the national average high school graduation rates for non-Native students of 85%.
- The remaining 10% of Native school-age youth attend reservation-based Bureau of Indian Affairs schools, and their high school graduation rates fall even further behind at 53%.

Unfortunately, suspensions and expulsions contribute to the low graduation rate. Native youth are more likely to be suspended than any other racial group, except African American students, and twice as likely than their White counterparts to face disciplinary actions (Pinto, 2020).

We Can't Ignore High Suspension and Low Graduation Rates

Disproportional rates of school suspension and low graduation rates of an entire group of culturally distinct youth cannot be ignored. We must examine the following:

- How do public schools identify and support Native youth?
- Do public schools accurately depict Native history and Native contemporary contributions?
- Is there a correlation between misperceptions or absence of Native peoples in public school curriculum and Native student perception of self-worth and their vision of success?

Remaining Resilient

The education of Native youth and the ongoing discrimination they face follows on the heels of long-standing catastrophic events. Nyché Tyme Andrew (2020) wrote about this in a short article "What Is Resilience?" posted on the website for the Center for Native American Youth:

> Indigenous people who suffer from the fatal policies and actions of a colonizing government use the strength from their ancestors and family, the love for their land, and people to rebuild their community, bountiful in life just as before. We as a people are part of the force of nature, following the pattern of a resilient ecosystem. It is in our nature to be resilient. Our catastrophic event(s) have already happened with the ashes of blood from the ancestors who braved the forest fire as best they could. We, the following generations, and the generations yet-to-be, grow our moss over the land ceased, sprout our trees by taking care of one another, and return to our ancestral lands to thrive on what it provides. We are resilient for surviving.

Andrew acknowledges how Native peoples have faced generations of systemic hardship, trauma, and discrimination, yet they've remained resilient.

HISTORICAL ADVOCACY OF NATIVE EDUCATIONAL RIGHTS

National and regional American Indian and Alaska Native organizations have long served as advocates for the educational rights and future well-being of tribal and urban Indian school-age youth. This includes Native advocacy for the 1969 Special Senate Subcommittee on Indian Education, led by Senator

Robert Kennedy (and, following Senator Kennedy's assassination, led by Senator Edward Kennedy), which was tasked with assessing the state of Indian education. The result was a report titled "Indian Education: A National Tragedy—A National Challenge," also known as the Kennedy Report (Faircloth, 2020–2021).

The Kennedy Report was influential in building momentum for Native educational change that ultimately gave rise to the American Indian education movement and the founding of the National Indian Education Association (NIEA) in 1969. The NIEA was founded by Native educators anxious to find solutions to improve the education system for Native children. For more than 50 years, the NIEA has continued to advocate for culturally meaningful education for American Indian, Alaska Native, and Native Hawaiian children. The NIEA mission is to promote comprehensive, culture-based educational opportunities for Native youth in three areas: (1) educational sovereignty for Native people, (2) continued use of traditional knowledge and language for Native education, and (3) improved educational opportunities to advance Native communities (National Indian Education Association, n.d.c). The NIEA also supports an annual convention established to serve as a national forum for sharing and developing ideas for Native education and to promote federal education policy on behalf of Native youth and families.

Two pieces of subsequent legislation contributed to the forward movement of Native educational sovereignty. These included the Indian Education Act of 1972 (US National Library of Medicine, n.d.), which created the Office of Indian Education and authorized a formula grant program for American Indian and Alaska Native students, and the Indian Self-Determination and Education Assistance Act of 1975, which delegated authority to Indian tribes to provide their own services created by the federal trust responsibility. The education component of the Indian Self-Determination and Education Assistance Act

- gave tribes control over the Bureau of Indian Affairs (BIA)–operated schools and
- created amendments to the Johnson-O'Malley Act, including a key amendment to mandate advisory boards made up of parents of Indian children for schools that receive federal funds through Johnson-O'Malley (University of Alaska, Fairbanks, n.d.).

Key to these successes were long-standing Native organizations like the National Congress of American Indians (NCAI) and the NIEA, respected throughout Indian country for their commitment to protect the cultural, political, economic, and educational sovereignty of American Indian and Alaska Native people.

Key Events

- **1969:** Special Senate Subcommittee on Indian Education, led by Senator Robert Kennedy, published the "Indian Education: A National Tragedy—A National Challenge" report.
- **1969:** The NIEA was founded by Native educators anxious to find solutions to improve the education system for Native children.
- **1972:** The Indian Education Act created the Office of Indian Education and authorized a formula grant program for American Indian and Alaska Native students.
- **1975:** The Indian Self-Determination and Education Assistance Act delegated authority to Indian tribes to provide their own services created by the federal trust responsibility.

The Annual State of Indian Nations Speech

Each year, the president of NCAI presents the State of Indian Nations address to members of Congress, government officials, tribal leaders and citizens, and the American public. Delivered the same week that the president of the United States delivers the State of the Union, the State of Indian Nations speech shares the positive and future-oriented vision of tribal nations (National Congress of American Indians, 2022). This annual speech outlines tribal leader goals, opportunities for success and advancement of Native peoples, and priorities to advance the tribal nation-to-nation relationship with the United States. The 2021 State of Indian Nations called for the

> federal government, state and local governments, school boards, and other key stakeholders to create, fund, and implement a comprehensive curriculum about tribal nations, tribal sovereignty, and the rich histories and contemporary lives of Native people. This curriculum should be designed by local tribal educational experts and provided to K–12 schools across this country. (Sharp, 2021)

Impact of COVID on Native Populations

Native peoples demanded executive action for recovery and resources during the COVID pandemic. Coronavirus transmission levels were recorded to be 3.5 times higher in American Indian and American Native populations than in non-Hispanic White populations, with a four times greater chance of hospitalization (Hatcher et al., 2020). These impacts spurred action from the Biden-Harris administration, centered around nation-to-nation engagement and healing, including the following:

- The American Rescue Plan (ARP) Act allotted $32 billion in funding for tribal community and Native economies.
- President Biden called for change within the education system. Included in the ARP was $19 million in supplemental grant funding toward preserving education in Native languages and amending curriculums of cultural histories (White House, 2021).
- The Bureau of Indian Education (BIE) funds Native language development and provides classes to increase Native language proficiency during the school day as well as professional development for teachers to incorporate Native language use in their curricula and integrate language and culture into their instruction (US Department of the Interior, Office of Congressional and Legislative Affairs, 2021).

The federal Every Student Succeeds Act (ESSA), signed by President Obama in December 2015, included provisions that deepened Native students' ability to succeed by requiring states and school districts to consult with local tribes and tribal organizations in the development of state and local educational plans. ESSA also acknowledged the importance of Indigenous languages and community in the lives of Native students by establishing a grant program to support the use of Native languages as the primary language of instruction.

To assist state education departments and local school districts with the implementation of tribal education requirements in ESSA, the National Indian Education Association developed a series of guides to ensure Native inclusion. The three guides focus on

- effective tribal consultation practices with Indian tribes and tribal organizations, which are required by districts that receive more than $40,000 for Title VI or have more than 50% American Indian student enrollment;
- an introduction to tribal consultation requirements for local education agencies (LEAs); and
- a brief introduction on how to evaluate state and local plans under ESSA.

These resources provide guidance to support tribes and local communities as they collaborate with state governments and local districts. Most importantly, the partnerships formed between local tribal communities and states are foundational relationships that can create and alter established education systems to better support and address the holistic needs of Native students.

NIEA continues to monitor Native education issues; to engage states with high Native populations; and to provide resources, technical assistance, and training to Native education advocates (National Indian Education Association, n.d.a). NIEA has now partnered with a Communities in Schools regional affiliate and developed a Tribal Communities in Schools project in Oklahoma to provide academic, cultural, and other supports to ensure Native student readiness for college, career, and lifelong success. In keeping with the Communities in Schools vision, the Tribal Communities in Schools project works directly inside schools, building relationships that equip students for success both inside and outside the classroom.

Tribal Colleges

The development of the tribal college system can be traced back to 1650. The Charter of 1650, the founding charter of Harvard University that continues to be Harvard's governing document, pledges the university to support the "education of English and Indian youth" (Harvard University Native American Program, 2022). Caleb Cheeshahteaumuck of the Wampanoag Tribe was the first Native American to graduate from Harvard (class of 1665). Unfortunately, despite Harvard's founding charter to actively facilitate the education of Native youth, it was not until 1970 that a Harvard program was established to support Native American issues and Native American students.

The American Education Higher Education Consortium

Important in this Native education history brief is the development of the American Indian Higher Education Consortium (AIHEC). The AIHEC was established in 1973 initially to provide a network of support for seven tribally controlled colleges. Today, AIHEC has grown to 37 tribal colleges and universities (TCUs) across Indian country. Each of these Native educational institutions was created and chartered by its own tribal government or the federal government for a specific purpose: to provide higher education opportunities to American Indians through programs that are locally and culturally based, holistic, and supportive. The AIHEC works to ensure that the principle of tribal sovereignty is acknowledged and respected and that the TCUs are equitably included in the US higher education system.

Actions to Counteract the Damage of Myths and Misinformation

The NCAI and the NIEA recently partnered with tribal researchers and emerging Native organizations, and between 2016 and 2018, they conducted a nationwide survey of Native content in K–12 public education classrooms. The Reclaiming Native Truth survey focused on the 35 states where federally recognized tribal nations reside. The survey revealed

- 72% of Americans rarely encounter or receive information about Native Americans;
- education is one of the most powerful opinion-shaping systems in the United States, yet the K–12 education system is a key driver of invisibility and false narratives about Native peoples;
- 87% of state history standards did not mention Native American history after 1900 (Shear et al., 2015); and
- 27% of states made no mention of a single Native American in their K–12 curriculum (IllumiNative, n.d.b).

IllumiNative

IllumiNative, a Native-led racial and social justice organization, was founded in 2018 with a mandate to translate the Reclaiming Native Truth project's research into action within society's key opinion-shaping sectors: K–12 education, pop culture, and the media. Led by tech-savvy and younger-generation Native leaders, IllumiNative uses research, narrative, and culture-changing strategies to increase the visibility and amplify the voices of Native peoples. IllumiNative partnerships are part of a growing movement to amplify contemporary Native voices and stories and change the narrative to set the record straight about Native peoples (IllumiNative, n.d.a).

Becoming Visible

"Becoming Visible: A Landscape Analysis of State Efforts to Provide Native American Education for All" (2018), a survey conducted by NCAI and NIEA, found that while Native American curriculum is included in content standards (primarily in social studies), for a majority of the 35 states surveyed, less than half reported that Native American education curriculum is required to be taught at some or all grade levels in the K–12 public school system. Given that efforts to adopt and implement Native American curricula in schools are not currently widespread, the report team chose to focus on the 35 states where federally recognized tribal nations reside.

However, the "Becoming Visible" report and call to action contributed to the momentum to transform K–12 education to accurately represent Native cultures, histories, diversity, contributions, and contemporary places in modern society. Success stories include the following:

- In 2019, an Oregon law required education to provide historically accurate, culturally embedded, place-based, contemporary, and developmentally appropriate American Indian and Alaska Native curriculum in five subject areas.

- Connecticut now requires schools to teach Native American studies, with an emphasis on local tribes, advocated by the Mashantucket Pequot Tribal Nation and other Connecticut tribes.
- A 2021 North Dakota law requires all elementary and secondary schools, public and private, to include Native American tribal history in their curriculum, with an emphasis on tribes within the state.

CHANGING PUBLIC EDUCATION TO SUPPORT NATIVE YOUTH

Native brilliance requires support and nurturing, but the American education system has a dismal track record of including Native history in state education content standards, ensuring accuracy in how Native history is taught, and conveying the Native perspective in history. It also lacks partnerships with local tribes and Native organizations to develop collaborations for curriculum development and support for Native students.

Key to systemic change is the concept of "essential understandings," which are understandings agreed on by tribal nations in each state to help educational content decision makers and educators understand and frame Native American education topics. The "Becoming Visible" report provides guidance for state education decision makers on how to understand and frame Native American education topics. In addition, the report describes best practice strategies for partnering with local tribes and tribal communities for formal tribal consultation.

Indigen(i)ous

Indigen(i)ous: An individual, collective, and/or movement who, through natural ability, inspires others in innovation and creation, by expressing one's traditional and cultural knowledge to advance community

Indigen(i)ous Education was founded in 2016 to administer the Cobell Scholarship Program and supports Native scholars representing a variety of tribes to Indigenize higher education in their respective academic fields. Their scholarship program supports high-achieving student researchers who might not otherwise have access to funds for research and related activities during summer months (Indigenous Education, 2021). During the fellowship period, scholars receive guidance from their faculty research advisor and support from the director of research and student success at Indigenous Education. Summer research fellows also enjoy networking opportunities with other fellows across the world and engage in future fellowship activities as new cohorts are added.

The American Indian Science and Engineering Society (AISES)

AISES is a national nonprofit organization focused on substantially increasing the representation of Indigenous peoples of North America and the Pacific Islands in science, technology, engineering, and math (STEM) studies and careers. AISES provides academic scholarships, internships, professional-development and career resources, national and regional conferences, leadership-development summits, and other STEM-focused programming to help the next generation of Native people be successful, influential, and respected (American Indian Science and Engineering Society, 2018).

Integrating Indigenous Knowledge

Western science has largely dismissed Indigenous knowledge of the lands, waters, and sky as anecdote, mythology, or superstition. But thanks to the hard work of Indigenous scientists and educators, this perspective is beginning to change. More Indigenous knowledge is being integrated into Western science, benefiting everyone.

An excellent example of cultural intersections in health care is Dr. Lori Alviso Alvord, the first female Navajo surgeon. Dr. Alvord quickly realized that simply healing bodies wasn't enough: "Navajo teachings and ceremonies emphasize seeing ourselves in connection to the environment. Tribal beliefs incorporate spirituality and metaphysics connected with everything around us. It's important to care for all of these." She explained that tribal ways of living, focusing on preserving the purity of the earth, the air, and the water, helps people live longer and happier lives.

Dr. Alvord has spent her career promoting the shift toward integrative medicine. She served as a faculty member and dean at several medical schools, where she advocated for whole-person care and raised awareness of how combining Native ways of healing with Western medicine results in better outcomes than medical intervention alone (Krol, 2018).

Changing Damaging Narratives

The US educational system is rooted in a Western worldview, which can systemically ignore and undervalue the intellectual capacity of Native students. Most adult Americans have attended a school where information about Native people is either completely absent from the classroom or relegated to brief mentions, negative information, or inaccurate stereotypes. This results in enduring and damaging narratives about Native peoples that, in particular, can negatively squash the brilliance of Native youth. Tribal and urban Indian people demand that public education portray an authentic and accurate portrayal of the history and influence of Indigenous peoples in the United States.

Today, 90% of Native young people attend public schools, with significant implications for urban and suburban public school educators. Public education teachers need to be informed, learn the truth about the past, and appreciate Native intellectual strengths and resilience. If you have a Native student in your class, then assume brilliance. While there is much more that is needed, this is a very good place to start. This vision will help guide us as we work to change racism and discrimination and work toward a better future for Native youth.

Holly and Melanie's Leadership

To begin to right the wrongs and end the long-standing discrimination and inequities faced by Indigenous people, Holly and Melanie are advocating for a bold shift in how teachers view the silence of Native American youth. Just as Yvette Jackson in Aim High, Achieve More (Jackson & McDermott, 2012) describes a need for high expectations for urban youth, Holly and Melanie say we must begin by "assuming brilliance" and from that perspective incorporate culture-based instructional strategies and opportunities to advance academic achievement, promote self-esteem, and set the groundwork for a greater sense of well-being.

PART III

Crafting Compassionate School Cultures

Compassion does not come easily for everyone. As Paul Gilbert reminds us, if an individual has been raised in an environment that is void of compassion, then the person is more likely to view it as a weakness and avoid being compassionate (Gilbert, 2017; Mason et al., 2022). Self-compassion for many is also difficult to obtain. We often blame ourselves, feel guilty, or feel shame. Some people believe being kind to yourself can lead to laziness, while others think practicing self-care can feel indulgent (Purbasari Horton, 2020).

Yet self-compassion is foundational to healing. Kristin Neff, a leading expert on self-compassion, explains, "Most people find that when they're absorbed in self-judgment, they actually have little bandwidth left over to think about anything other than their inadequate, worthless selves. When we can be kind and nurturing to ourselves, however, many of our emotional needs are met, leaving us in a better position to focus on others" (quoted in Purbasari Horton, 2020).

With all the divisiveness in the United States and the world today (Lauter, 2021), compassion toward strangers and even "enemies" is needed. Humans are social beings who thrive in communities, and compassion is a powerful tool that helps us relate to others, build trust, and forge strong connections. Compassion helps us approach situations with kindness and curiosity and solve problems, and it can even improve our health and well-being (Guild, 2020).

In Chapter 7, Mason and colleagues reference the need for consciousness to become aware of our own and others' thoughts and emotions, compassion as the basis for fruitful and enduring relationships, confidence for people to feel worthy and resilient, courage to be bold and do what's right, and community to support and empower us.

The vision that Chris Mason and Michele Rivers Murphy had for Heart Centered Learning (HCL) began with input from national educational leaders over several years. Through focus groups, interviews, and annual meetings, they distilled key ideas and components for the HCL framework. From there, they developed an assessment tool and piloted it in various schools and with fellows to collect feedback and refine as needed. They continue to evolve and adapt the framework based on ongoing discussions, implementations, and feedback. However, to grow this vision, they have continued to be responsive to the needs that emerge in schools and communities. Involving a broad range of stakeholders, building and empowering leaders, and acknowledging and embracing change can only strengthen their vision.

Again, with a focus on transforming school cultures to ones of kindness and caring, in Chapter 8, Jeff Donald shares lessons he has learned over the years about how best to grow an initiative within a school district. Imagining your ideal outcomes in vivid detail can help guide your visioning process. Bringing in diverse stakeholders and people you admire can drive the visioning forward. From there, training, implementation, and reflection are key to adapting and evolving the vision as needed. All these steps are transformative to Jeff as he helped schools move from punitive discipline to restorative justice and build a culture of conscious awareness of how to support oneself and collective care within schools.

Chapter 7

Heart Centered Learning
Developing Cultures of *Compassion*

Christine Mason, Michele Rivers Murphy, and Meghan Wenzel

Our vision is that Five Cs (consciousness, compassion, confidence, courage, and community) will be the cornerstone for school culture, climate, and learning for every classroom and school in the United States and internationally; that school policy and practices will reflect the belief and inherent norms of the five components; that teachers will model these Five Cs; and that the Five Cs will be naturally woven into academic curricula throughout the school day for each grade level, pre-K–12.

With this heart centered learning approach, students and staff will listen to their hearts and be consciously aware of their emotions and the emotions of others, and schools will be filled with joy as we transcend past practices to focus on a sense of purpose, empowerment, caring, and resilience.

UNDERSTANDING THE URGENT NEED FOR HEALING COMMUNITIES

As educators, we may hear about a challenging home situation or a recent loved one's death, or we may notice that Sam stopped participating in class or Keisha has become more distant from her peers. Traumatic experiences don't magically disappear when students enter the building. They carry them with them, and these experiences risk changes to their brain architecture, learning, behavior, and emotional regulation. Mason, Rivers Murphy, and Jackson (2019) explain, "These early, formative years serve as the foundation for all of life's later endeavors. If, as a society, we fail to meet the needs of our young children, it is not just the children who suffer. We as a society suffer as well. Their success is our success" (p. 16).

Heart centered learning (HCL) promises benefits for even the hardest-to-reach students and tools to achieve greater happiness, justice, and equity. Mason, Rivers Murphy, and Jackson (2019) elaborate, "At a societal level, our need is to deepen an understanding of and commitment to compassion at all levels, in all districts, with students from all different walks of life" (p. 32). Crafting more conscious and compassionate school communities can increase students' protective factors and well-being. Building strong and caring relationships; helping school community members better understand their thoughts, feelings, and reactions; and building a more responsive and supportive environment can help students manage and overcome their traumas.

THE DEVELOPMENT OF HEART CENTERED LEARNING

Heart centered learning is the hallmark of the books we have written on mindful practices (Mason, Rivers Murphy, & Jackson, 2019, 2020). Our approach has gradually evolved over the past decade, with decisive input from educational leaders through focus groups, interviews, and annual meetings of interested colleagues as well as implementation in schools and feedback from staff at these schools. Our initial concepts were grounded in heart centered compassionate practices that included yogic and meditative practices, like mindfulness, and connected (married) mindfulness to the social-emotional learning (SEL) competencies that allow school staff and students alike to work on both the inside and outside job of health and wellness.

To help others implement HCL practices, we developed the School Compassionate Culture Analytical Tool for Educators (S-CCATE; Mason, Rivers Murphy, et al., 2018) and used it as a measure to assess school culture and help educators determine interventions to further compassion and caring in classrooms and schools.

In developing S-CCATE and refining HCL, we conducted pilot projects in four schools in Pennsylvania, Massachusetts, and West Virginia and a social validation study with more than 800 responses to arrive at a simple self-rating assessment that teachers and other educators could use to rate the degree of implementation of various indicators of school compassion.

To further HCL and our Five-C approach to mindful practices, we also introduced the process to more than 24 fellows who were part of a childhood-trauma learning Collaborative in six New England states. To support their practices and encourage the adoption of the Five Cs, we conducted numerous webinars and developed and disseminated articles on such topics as the neurobiology of childhood trauma, alleviating childhood trauma, and how schools can further individual and collective self-care.

At the same time we were developing and disseminating information on the Five-C approach, we also studied such related educational initiatives as trauma-informed learning and the research and recommendations from the Collaborative for Academic and Social Emotional Learning (CASEL, 2021). We did not choose to design and implement HCL in a vacuum but rather to develop it with full awareness of the success and possible limitations of related practices.

We are continuing to promote HCL through such initiatives as the Coalition for the Future of Education; the *HeartMind Community eNews*; and a series of podcasts designed to cultivate resilience, an initiative of the Collaborative on Alleviating Childhood Trauma led by Christine Mason, Jesse Kohler (executive director of the Campaign for Trauma-Informed Policy and Practices), and Jeff Ikler (coauthor of *Shifting: How School Leaders Can Create a Culture of Change* and cohost of the podcast *Getting Unstuck: Educators Leading Change*). Additional information on each of these initiatives is available on the Center for Educational Improvement's website (https://www.edimprovement.org) and through dissemination to more than 11,000 subscribers.

WHAT'S UNIQUE ABOUT OUR WORK?

While we have been engaged in HCL since 2009, many similar practices continue to emerge. Certainly, there have been related efforts to promote SEL, to implement trauma-informed practices in schools, and to enhance school climate. However, the work toward positive school climate begins with school culture because it is a school's (students, staff, and leadership) foundational belief system (strength based), practices (heart centered/Five Cs), and actions (decision making and what is most important) that determine the characteristics of a positive school climate (how it feels and is experienced by stakeholders).

Here are five characteristics that we believe are unique to the Five Cs' heart centered approach we recommend. When combined the total is greater than the sum of the separate parts:

1. **The Five Cs:** The focus on consciousness, compassion, confidence, courage, and community provide the foundational practice for five well-defined components to further compassionate practices.
2. **A Way of Being:** The Five-Cs approach is not a separate curriculum; rather it represents a way of being and educating, with many opportunities for each of the Five Cs to be seamlessly woven into any of a number of social-emotional programs or curricula.
3. **A Coherent Approach:** We urge practitioners to implement the Five Cs in classrooms spanning from preschool to 12th grade. As such, it provides a coherent approach with a focus on the same five characteristics across academic grade levels while providing an underlying foundation of heart and compassion.
4. **Self First:** With the Five Cs, educators focus on self-care and understanding and using practices themselves prior to introducing them to students.
5. **Accompanying Measurement:** We have a validated tool that can be used to measure progress. Along with the S-CCATE instrument, we have S-CCATE action guides for educators to implement evidence-based practices to further compassionate school practices.

A Deeper Dive Into the Uniqueness of the Five Cs

In this section, we review and compare Michael Fullan and Geoff Scott, William Daggett, and CASEL's frameworks alongside the five characteristics of the HCL approach.

Comparing and Contrasting Frameworks

Others, including Fullan and Scott, Daggett, and CASEL, have developed related frameworks around fostering capable, responsible, and caring students and citizens:

- Fullan and Scott (2014) have developed a framework focused on six Cs: character, citizenship, collaboration, communication, creativity, and critical thinking.
- Daggett, with the International Center for Leadership in Education, established the three Rs: rigor, relationships, and relevance (DeWitt, 2012).
- CASEL (2021) identified five essential components to academic and social and emotional learning: self-awareness, self-management, social awareness, relationship skills, and responsible decision making.

Each of these frameworks provides a viable platform around which educators might organize and structure learning. There is some overlap among these systems, including an overlap with the Five Cs we recommend.

Let's take a moment to explore and compare these three frameworks in more depth. We do this by asking, "So what?" and inviting readers to envision what happens to our individual and collective well-beings if each of these is implemented with fidelity, from pre-K to grade 12 schools.

Fullan and Scott's Approach: Character, Citizenship, Collaboration, Communication, Creativity, and Critical Thinking

Imagine students across grade levels who are engaged in critical thinking, given many experiences to collaborate and communicate, encouraged to develop their creativity, learning about the importance of citizenship and culture, and participating in character education programs to enhance their connectivity. Imagine students graduating from high school with competencies in these areas. What are the values and benefits of these activities?

The world certainly needs better problem solvers and race relationships. Equity and justice might well be furthered, and many of the soft skills leading to better workforce productivity might be enhanced. Additionally, these six skills could reduce feelings of alienation and increase understanding of how to form and maintain healthy relationships with others.

The International Center for Leadership in Education (William Daggett): Rigor, Relevance, and Relationships

Envision classrooms where teachers focus on rigor, relevance, and relationships across academic subjects in grades pre-K to 12. Envision high expectations for students and academic learning, guidance on building and maintaining relationships, a focus on understanding the connections between academic learning and lessons for life, and implementation procedures to measure progress so that the focus is not on teaching the curricula but rather on helping students master content (Daggett, 2016). What would be the benefits?

It seems that we might see more individualized instruction and scaffolding to help students master content; teaching that furthers collaboration and connections to real-life scenarios; and more systematic use of formative assessment to ascertain individual students' skills, knowledge gains, and knowledge gaps that require further instruction. Students might well graduate with more competencies and be better prepared to enter the workforce.

CASEL's Five Competencies: Self-Awareness,
Self-Management, Social Awareness, Relationship Skills, and
Responsible Decision Making

In comparison to Fullan and Scott's and Daggett's approach, the CASEL criteria focus more specifically on SEL (CASEL, 2022). For just a moment, envision young children who develop a greater understanding of their own feelings and emotions and use that understanding to increase their self-monitoring and self-regulation. Over time, as these children and youth deepen their understanding of self, they will also develop a social awareness or consciousness about the needs of others. Couple this with relationship skills that students practice in a variety of contexts, and they will also learn about how to take responsibility for their decisions. Youth graduating from high school with these skills might have a greater understanding of themselves and others, leading to more thoughtful decision making and a deeper understanding of the implications of their actions.

So far, what can we conclude from analyzing these three frameworks (see Table 7.1)?

Trauma-Informed Learning

Before we compare these frameworks to HCL, let's take a moment to examine a related initiative gaining in popularity: trauma-informed practices. Trauma-informed teaching is designed to ensure that educators understand how trauma affects learning and behavior. West-Ed (2019) in a recent report

Table 7.1. Comparison of Frameworks

Similarities	Differences
• The components within each framework are synergistic: they complement and build on each other. • The qualities are both learnable and assessable. • All three frameworks focus on learning and developing skills in context, through relevant and collaborative learning, not simply learning information in isolation. • Educators are proactive learning partners, rather than all-knowing experts or passive guides.	• Fullan and Scott focus on helping students develop values and skills to succeed in the world. They envision students partnering with teachers to develop personal values, attitudes, and skills that will benefit them inside and outside the classroom. • Daggett places emphasis on academic proficiency. He imagines transformation leadership to drive change and foster "future-ready students." • CASEL focuses on social-emotional learning. It promotes building trusting and authentic school-family-community partnerships to create productive learning environments.

on trauma stated, "Trauma can negatively affect student learning at school by decreasing students' ability to pay attention, to regulate emotion and behavior, or to develop positive relationships with adults and peers."

Related to trauma-informed instruction is a movement for trauma-skilled schools, which focus on knowledge of trauma; building resilience; skill acquisition (for prevention, intervention, referral, and recovery); assessment and implementation; and maintenance and validation (Gailor, Addis, & Dunlap, 2018). By combining heart centered learning and trauma-informed learning, we invite students to bring their whole selves to school and set them up for success.

Heart Centered Learning: Consciousness, Compassion, Confidence, Courage, and Community

We suggest elsewhere (Mason, Rivers Murphy, & Jackson, 2019, 2020) that these five components have a hierarchical relationship; that *consciousness* (or mindfulness) is the necessary foundation for the other four components; and that consciousness needs to include a conscious awareness of self (our thoughts, feelings, and experience), as well as others. If that consciousness includes a heart component, then we go beyond mindfulness to a better holistic understanding of self. It is important to stay with our consciousness for a while, to sit with conscious awareness of self without any attempt to change

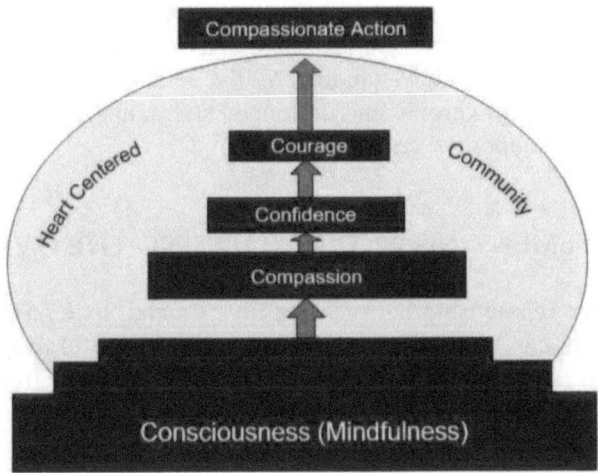

Figure 7.1. Heart Centered Learning. *Used with permission from* Mindful School Communities: The Five Cs of Nurturing Heart Centered Learning *by Christine Mason, Michele M. Rivers Murphy, and Yvette Jackson. Copyright 2020 by Solution Tree Press, 555 North Morton Street, Bloomington, IN 47404. 800-733-6786. SolutionTree.com. All rights reserved.*

anything. There is no need to rush in and make things better. Sometimes conscious awareness is all that is needed. Such awareness can lead to self-acceptance and compassion for self and others.

However, at times you may feel a need to shift—to slow down your breath; to let go of expectations; or to support your body, your mind, or your spirit with the intent of some level of improvement. That, too, is okay; however, we urge you to try "just being" as a first step.

After consciousness comes *compassion*, the undergirding to enhanced relationships and to our personal and collective action. So once again focus—this time on compassion. Check to see where you are, accepting who you are and your compassion gauge. Then, when you are ready, which could be months later, move on to *confidence*. For acts of compassion to increase, students need confidence, including a growth mindset and feeling of success.

However, to fully implement the changes we believe are needed to advance our civilizations and our humanity, we need to help students develop *courage*. Courage will evolve as confidence evolves. Although courage is individualistic, with it comes the attitude, the resilience, and the boldness to do what is necessary, even under difficult circumstances. Further, all this needs to be taught in the context of a heart centered, compassionate *community*, and as this happens, we will also find our sense of community evolving.

Imagine students graduating from high school with these Five Cs. How might they be able to apply these Five Cs in the context of work and personal relationships? The Five Cs' HCL approach has much in common with a trauma-informed approach, although it specifically and intentionally addresses each of the Five Cs. In school environments, both approaches include a fundamental understanding of the relationship of neuroscience and neuroplasticity to chronic and prolonged stress, and both emphasize the importance of a supportive community.

IMPLEMENTING AND EVALUATING THE FIVE CS

Because of the relationship between the Five Cs and S-CCATE (the unique assessment that can be used with HCL), it could be useful to imagine what might happen as the Five Cs are implemented with guidance from S-CCATE and the S-CCATE action guides. To do this, let's look for a moment at the five domains that S-CCATE measures (see Figure 7.2).

We recommend weaving the Five Cs into the curriculum so that students gain multiple experiences with them over time. S-CCATE reinforces key components, including assessing leadership, policies, and practices that influence the community; understanding neuroscience and mindfulness; focusing

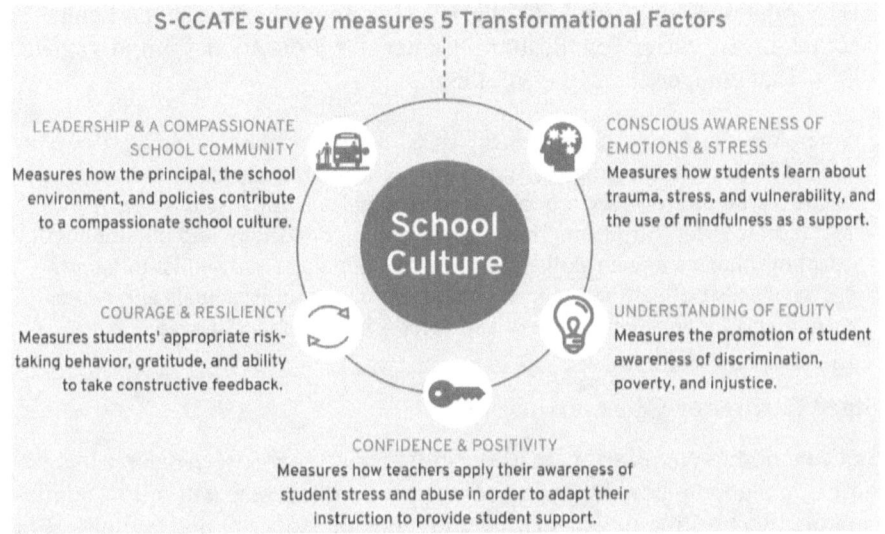

Figure 7.2. S-CCATE. *Used with permission from the Center for Educational Improvement.*

on equity; alleviating injustice and discrimination; and building individual and collective courage and resiliency.

What Conclusions Can We Draw?

What can we conclude when comparing the Five Cs of HCL to the other frameworks?

- The Five Cs include an important component that is not essential to some of the other frameworks: consciousness or mindfulness.
- The Five Cs also acknowledge the importance of rigor by focusing on building confidence and resilience.
- Connections and relationship building are a part of our focus on compassion and community.
- Communication is a key component of compassion, and character education and SEL are furthered in practical ways that are embedded in the academic content. [This is explained in detail in our book *Mindful School Communities* (Mason, Rivers Murphy, & Jackson, 2020).]
- By design, we encourage responsible decision making based on conscious understanding and compassion.
- Our platform is the only one that explicitly addresses leadership and community building.

The relationship of HCL to the CASEL competencies in particular is detailed in an earlier publication (Center for Educational Improvement, 2021). That comparison ends with this:

> When schools decide to implement HCL, and particularly with the use of S-CCATE to monitor progress, schools have a framework for addressing the CASEL criteria. However, schools implementing HCL will also have guidelines and resources for introducing information on neuroplasticity and mindfulness, enabling students to gain skills, and understanding that are essential to increasing knowledge of self and others, guidelines for school principals and recommendations for achieving mastery and success in use of the 5 Cs. (p. 20)

Stacy Bachelder-Giles, Principal

Stacy embodies compassionate leadership in many ways. She ensures that her staff is in a good place—showing compassion for teachers and fellow administrators by checking in and sharing strategies for self-care and wellness. For the students, Stacy greets each child with genuine excitement as they show up to school each day and helps them through difficult moments. Stacy believes that compassionate leadership comes from within. She models compassionate leadership in her day-to-day interactions with others. This practice inspires Stacy's team to be compassionate leaders to help implement her vision of becoming a compassionate school, district, and community.

Keeping It Real: Shifting to Heart Centered

Your school or district may already be going down a path. You might already be following another framework. Sometimes it takes tremendous will and ingenuity to modify a course or shift directions. Here are a few things to reflect on:

- Are you implementing any mindfulness or self-care provisions for staff and students?
- Are you weaving SEL—whatever brand you are using—throughout the school day?
- Are you building a sense of confidence, courage, and resilience?
- Are you building community and increasing connectiveness and a sense of belonging?
- How are you approaching the self-management skills that CASEL recommends, including self-regulation, which may include impulse control, stress management, self-discipline, self-motivation, goal setting, and organizational skills?

- Are you teaching these self-management skills and helping students self-monitor?

To reduce stress, it may make more sense to ease into some of these; that is, do not to teach directly, but rather set the stage and let neuroplasticity take over. This can be done with mindfulness and HCL where the focus is on the breath, calming the brain, and setting the physiology so that students automatically improve in many of these areas.

HEART CENTERED LEADERSHIP

Effective school leaders understand the importance of creating a compassionate school environment and helping students develop into their best selves. They need to take care of themselves and others while building trust and inspiring and encouraging change.

A leader's attitudes and actions will influence teachers' understanding of and interactions with students. Great leaders lead by example and exhibit strong emotional intelligence, gratitude, humility, and kindness; recognize others; and create a community of connectedness and belonging. Mason, Asby, and colleagues (2021) explain,

> Caring, competent leaders who are most attuned to the needs of vulnerable students are also attuned to the strengths of these students. They lead with a mindset of inclusion, inspiring others, and are always aware of self-care and the wisdom of establishing a sense of trust and elevating compassion, courage, and confidence in their school communities. (p. 125)

A Few Closing Thoughts about Heart Centered Learning

Our vision for HCL was not of a program but rather a way of being. It was designed as an overarching approach to be used with a variety of SEL curricula. Rather than being tied to textbook or a manual, the HCL Five Cs are a coherent approach that guides teachers as they make instructional, disciplinary, and SEL decisions across grade levels and curricula. (See Chapter 19 for more on visioning for HCL.)

Implementation Tips

To implement HCL, we recommend that teachers and others first try these techniques themselves. Whether it is implementation of mindfulness, breath work, yoga, or meditation, teachers need to practice and see and feel the results themselves before attempting to instruct others using heart centered techniques. As teachers begin practicing, they will increase their own self-care and learn more about how to help others with self and community self-care. Remember: HCL can be used with other approaches. It is designed to be used with a variety of SEL curricula. Because HCL has an accompanying assessment, teachers and others within schools will have opportunities to systematically assess needs and progress and to design and implement interventions that are a part of the S-CCATE action guides.

Christine, Michele, and Meghan's Leadership

Based on their long-standing advocacy for transforming school cultures to further compassion, Chris, Michele, and Meghan have engaged in multiple efforts to scale up compassionate school leadership and promote instructional practices that further a sense of community, confidence, and well-being. However, this must begin with a conscious awareness of self and others and include mindfulness practices that can increase vitality, alleviate trauma, build neuroplasticity, and further self-care.

Chapter 8

Being a Mindfulness School Coordinator

Jeffrey Donald

> *My vision is to provide systemwide foundational tools for students, staff, and communities to cultivate mindfulness and student self-care and mental health. These tools would be accompanied by professional development and training and curricular and instructional support so that they could be implemented with fidelity, reducing the use of punitive discipline and increasing resilience and positive educational and social-emotional outcomes for all students.*

We have been implementing mindfulness and restorative practices in Maryland for more than 10 years. I direct mindfulness interventions for the entire district with a staff of four who support outreach, training, and the use of the strategies we recommend. We rely on resources provided by Y.O.G.A. for Youth (Kaur, 2013) and Mason, Rivers Murphy, and Jackson's two books on mindfulness practices (2019, 2020) to help guide implementation.

Over the past few years, we have also developed a curriculum and a library of more than 100 videos to help staff with implementation, and the tools and techniques we recommend are being used in more than 168 schools in our district.

IMPLEMENTING MINDFULNESS WITH EQUITY AND JUSTICE

The application of mindfulness in our district includes an emphasis on individual and collective self-care. At each of our most engaged schools, there is a coordinator who serves as a point of contact, and we offer a weekly session for any staff who want to connect, problem solve, and share resources.

The mindfulness practices include three tiers of support:

1. Tier 1 includes mindfulness instruction to be used by all teachers in all classrooms, giving teachers and students tools to enhance understanding of self and others.
2. Tier 2 involves a deeper dive into mindfulness, restorative practices, and strategies to assist youth needing greater supports.
3. Tier 3 extends the capacity of schools and districts to develop the skills and leadership capacity of youth who are most at risk and most in need of strategies to overcome the impact of significant trauma and adversity.

To be fully implemented, the system I envision is one of growing capacity, with adequate leadership, supervision, and technical assistance supports available for implementation, problem solving, and ongoing refinements and improvements. Over time, the use of these foundational tools will expand to all schools, all districts, all staff, and all students in the United States and around the world, becoming a significant resource in enhancing school culture and staff and student well-being.

With the use of mindfulness practices—which includes breath work, yoga and movement activities, and games to increase students' social-emotional competence—we have seen a significant decrease in suspensions and expulsions and an increase in positive problem solving and relationship building.

During this past year, with the increased awareness of the need to address equity concerns, our mindfulness staff have combined forces with our district's department focused on equity and justice. We are using the Groundwater Approach developed by the Racial Equity Institute (Love & Hayes-Green, 2018). That approach advises us to look beyond the individual to systems to determine causes and solutions to racial disparities.

While we have made significant progress since this program began a few years ago, our resources are stretched to capacity. Like many districts around the nation, in the fall of 2021, we saw a substantial increase in the demand for restorative practices supports, and we are maxed out in documenting needs and providing triage to help schools.

RESTORATIVE PRACTICES

In addition to mindfulness, a key component of our work in Maryland is restorative practices. With restorative practices, teachers hold circle meetings to check in with students. When an unacceptable behavior occurs, the teachers rely on conflict resolution, dialoguing with the offenders and the offended students, who share how the offense made them feel. Over time, students develop a greater understanding of their own feelings and the feelings of others, and rather than implementing a punitive system of discipline, teachers help students problem solve about how to resolve the harm caused by any wrongdoing.

While we are thrilled to be able to support schools during this time of need and excited to see the expansion in the use of restorative practices, this has meant that we have had to scale back on planned professional development and training, at least for the near future.

THE SEEDS OF CHANGE: HOW MY VISION EVOLVED

I had been teaching in Montgomery County Public Schools for about two years when I hit a personal bottom. My life was an emotional roller coaster, and something needed to change. Seeking relief, I found it in a personal yoga practice, and within a year I was introducing it to students with the most serious emotional and behavior problems in an alternative high school setting. These practices provided a much-needed strategy to calm down their hypervigilant brains and introduce a sense of well-being and positivity.

Surprisingly, students at our school were enthusiastic, and practices quickly evolved in our district. As students implemented these practices and staff were trained to provide additional supports and guidance to students, we saw a decrease in office referrals and incident reports and an associated increase in interest in academics and academic achievement.

With the success we experienced, the mindfulness program in our district rapidly expanded. As it grew, we were able to obtain some foundation funds to research the impact of these practices. To date, we have trained more than 1,400 teachers in mindfulness practices, and 168 schools (more than 80%) are implementing at least some components of our programs. We have mindfulness intervention rooms in 51 schools and are also training student leaders to help colead mindfulness sessions. Recently we received a greenlight to start training "wellness coaches" for middle and high schools. It has been a busy year, as students have struggled returning to school, and we have seen an increased need for mindfulness and restorative justice interventions. However, we are in the middle of conducting that research and anticipate some preliminary results within the next year.

You Don't Need to Start with Perfect

Over time, I have learned that not everyone starts at the same place. One reason my program is so successful is that although excellence is an end goal, I have helped staff to understand the "wisdom of imperfection." With mindfulness, I often helps staff to find their comfort zones, urging them to implement mindfulness by beginning with what they can do and gradually improving their practice with disciplined and dedicated commitment, a mindful acceptance of themselves. As indicated in *Cultivating Happiness, Resilience, and Well-Being through Meditation, Mindfulness, and Movement*, "The ability to self-reflect and ask, 'How am I doing?' helps us as teachers and as students recognize and understand through self-reflection, assessment, and correction *how* we can plan to best get there" (Mason, Donald, et al., 2021, p. 24).

Mindfulness, yoga, breath work, and meditation include so many practices that can be used successfully in classrooms and schools. As mentioned in Mason, Donald, and colleagues (2021), educators and families can use the recommended tools "to maintain a healthy balance in the midst of current chaos, uncertainty and anxiety" (p. xv).

Key times to implement the practices are early morning, during transition times, before lunch, before afternoon academics, and before transitioning home at the end of the school day. These practices help with self-care and self-regulation (which includes self-monitoring, self-evaluation, and self-reinforcement). I have found that student metacognition, focus, learning, and healing are positively affected by these practices. Also importantly, through these practices, schools have been able to develop a sense of belonging to a community of caring.

Advice for Visioning for Mindfulness and Restorative Practices

The following are strategies learned from my years in the restaurant industry from an amazing leader, Daniel Harf. Even though these visioning techniques were applied toward food, service, ambiance, and so on, these principles have been universally effective in every part of life. Start from the end. Have a perfect vision of what you are creating, down to the smallest of details. What does it look like? The end goal is the beginning of the creation process, which is divided into:

- **Vision:** What do you want to achieve?
- **Planning:** How do you get there? What do you need?
- **Assembling:** What pieces or talent is required?
- **Training:** Are all stakeholders prepared to work at their highest level?

- **Implementation:** How will you execute the plan?
- **Reflection:** Does the product meet the vision you began with? What is not working as it should? What adjustments are required? Does the vision itself require tweaking? Are you meeting the need?
- **Manage/Feedback:** Provide continuous communication and professional development.

Keeping It Real: Don't Think You Have All the Answers

- Always bring in minds you admire for consultation and added ideas.
- Allow the vision to evolve and improve.
- As you proceed, life happens. Students, families, staff, and all around us are influenced by COVID, racial tension, immigration, the influx of people from other countries, national and international leadership, and more. Not every school leader will understand the importance of continuing with mindfulness.
- It may take problem solving, connecting with others outside your school or district, and continual innovation to move forward with implementation.

A Great Opportunity

Using these principles, being alert to the need for self-care, and being a catalyst for self-care for staff, together we can positively revamp education and enhance the lives of our students. While the fall of 2021 has been a time of great stress and an extremely heavy workload, it provided an opportunity to continue to spread the positive practices to reach additional classrooms in our districts. These are life-altering practices.

Our district is not relying on a few hours a week of social-emotional programming; rather we are building a life raft for each school, for each classroom, for each teacher, and for each student. This is a collaborative effort, and we are encouraged by the deep learning that is occurring, the spread of compassionate school practices, and the enhanced emotional well-being for all—teachers and students alike.

Jeff's Leadership

Over the past 10 years, Jeff has built capacity within one school district to incorporate mindfulness and restorative practices with students from pre-K to grade 12. Jeff now has a team supporting these efforts, even as he works on developing the leadership of youth and the self-care of teachers and students.

He is furthering his reach and his vision through curriculum developed for his district, staff development and technical assistance, and policy changes to reduce the use of punitive discipline. Also, in light of racism and equity concerns, Jeff's team has joined forces with others within his district to further positive systemic changes.

PART IV

Changing Systems' Policies and Practices

In their book *Shifting: How School Leaders Can Create a Culture of Change*, Richert, Ikler, and Zacchei (2020) examine why educational changes fail. Instead of focusing on human readiness and those actually responsible for implementing the changes, leaders often overemphasize such top-down factors as schedules, resources, and processes. To set leaders up for success, Richert, Ikler, and Zacchei developed a series of mental shifts that educators can use to focus on necessary processes *and* people to enact change. They suggest moving from an environment of command and control to one of leaders developing and supporting other leaders and reframing change as an essential shift in school culture rather than a series of episodic events.

Change may take a village to achieve shared goals. The following chapters walk you through how it all starts from a simple vision, pivots through obstacles, adapts with perspectives and resources, and spurs progress. This vision-practice-change model can be used to guide your reflection on these chapters.

Trauma can permeate day-to-day functioning, especially in young students whose developing minds are vulnerable to surrounding circumstances. In Chapter 9, Jesse Kohler, the executive director of the Campaign for Trauma-Informed Policy and Practice (CTIPP), explores how common childhood adversity truly is and urges educators to learn about its potential impacts on young brains and bodies.

Kohler paints a clear example of CTIPP's perseverance and passion in implementing their vision of increasing trauma-informed practices. CTIPP realized how little Congress members knew about trauma, neuroscience, epigenetics, adverse childhood experiences (ACEs), and resilience and recognized it as an opportunity to revamp their advocacy strategies. CTIPP worked with congresspersons on opioid legislation, partnered with neighboring organizations to form a coalition on trauma-informed care, and inspired school staff to bolster protective roles and resilience.

Implementing and executing change often calls on individuals who share similar drive and motivation, see the impact that it could bring to their colleagues and loved ones, and come together to make things happen. This is what Jeff Ikler calls "purposeful change" in Chapter 10. An educator, coach, and cohost of the *Getting Unstuck: Educators Leading Change* podcast, Ikler reveals how to masterfully weave ideas, talents, and resources in a saloon-style correspondence and elevate a *culture of change*. By thinking in new ways, generating more exciting ideas, and putting them into practice, Ikler aims to catalyze innovation. Exploring everything from neuroscience to leadership to mindfulness to communication to authenticity, Ikler hopes to help build inspiring leaders. He asks us, "How might we reimagine schools to better support kids for the world today?"

Paul Liabenow and Michael Domagalski in Chapter 11 explore how having a clear vision helps guide us to bring about desired change. While Ikler speaks about a *culture of change* in Chapter 9, in Chapter 10, Liabenow and Domagalski discuss a *community of practice* when spotlighting the work at St. Clair Middle School and the Michigan Elementary and Middle School Principals Association (MEMSPA). Cultures of change and communities of practice share a fundamental principle: Change happens in communities with shared leadership and a common purpose.

MEMPSA recognized the evolving nature of the principal's role and brought their leadership team and board of directors together to vision how they could best support principals committed to this important work. MEMPSA wanted to implement transformational change by advocating for funding resources for principal and staff care, retention, and recruitment; increasing professional-learning opportunities to build leader capacity and resilience; and ensuring diversity, equity, and inclusion by better supporting and empowering underrepresented populations. They are committed to fostering discussion, learning, and trust in order to surface, share, and enact new ideas.

Similarly, St. Clair Middle School piloted the three-tier TRAILS curriculum and resources to support students. The program promotes social-emotional learning (SEL) opportunities, designs prevention and intervention strategies, and provides access to care and risk management. MEMPSA sees this as a way to support educators, particularly by discussing how to address evidence of trauma in the classroom. St. Clair Middle School provides an example of how MEMSPA's framework could bear fruits in building relationships among students, families, and educators.

From these contributors' perspectives, sustainable change does take a village—a passionate and compassionate collection of individuals, educators, community leaders, families, and students. This allows for the vision-practice-change model to be filled with diverse mind-sets and talents to work toward shared goals. A culture of change and a community of practice drive progress.

Chapter 9

HOPE Is NEAR

Healthy Outcomes and Positive Experiences Is Neuroscience, Epigenetics, ACEs, and Resilience

Jesse Kohler

The Campaign for Trauma-Informed Policy and Practice's (CTIPP) mission is to create a healthy, just, resilient, and trauma-informed society where all individuals, families, and communities have the social, political, cultural, economic, and spiritual opportunities and support necessary to thrive.

CTIPP works to create trauma-informed and healing-centered systems, alleviate unnecessary suffering, and improve outcomes throughout society. We know that things can be different from the status quo, and we work to realize a better normal. We envision a world in which a continuum of care provides support for all people, so that everyone may reach their fullest potential. We achieve this vision by building sustainable investments in community coalitions to drive forward trauma-informed, resilience-focused, healing-centered, and grassroots-led initiatives.

In 2016, when CTIPP was created, one rarely heard the term *trauma* used by either congresspersons or their staff. Although the original adverse childhood experiences (ACEs) study (Felitti et al., 1998) had been published 18 years earlier and subsequent neuroscientific discoveries showed that ACEs and childhood trauma were major underlying causes of many of the toughest health-related problems Congress was trying to solve, this research had virtually no impact on congressional policy discussions, much less on legislation.

TRAUMA IS UNFORTUNATELY EXCEPTIONALLY COMMON

Two-thirds of all people in our country experience at least one ACE, and one in six experience four or more (Merrick et al., 2018). Childhood adversity is common, and professionals working with children need to be aware of its potential impacts on young brains and bodies. Higher ACE scores are not predictive on an individual basis—many with high ACE scores do not have correlated behavioral or health problems, while many with low ACE scores do—but across the population, higher ACE prevalence correlates with higher incidences of several negative behavioral and health outcomes, including with many of the top killers of Americans today. Two-thirds of all people who attempt suicide or suffer from alcoholism experienced at least one ACE, as have 69% of individuals with a mental illness, 78% of intravenous drug users, and 61% of incarcerated adults (Anda, 2013).

How has your school considered and tracked how ACEs could relate to your students' health, learning, and social-emotional outcomes? While the evidence of the significant impact of ACEs is clear, the legislation that Congress passed in response to youth suicide, substance abuse, obesity, diabetes, and heart disease addresses symptoms, not underlying causes. Congress missed an opportunity to obtain more substantial results.

What C-TIPP Has Done

To awaken the consciousness of Congress, CTIPP began its policy role by visiting congressional offices to determine existing awareness of trauma science and to provide relevant education to fill gaps in knowledge for staff and congresspeople. Existing trauma knowledge on the Hill was mixed, but the majority of staff had little or no exposure to the science of trauma and ACEs. However, when we presented the powerful science to them, the importance of these findings was largely understood. As a result, the terms *trauma* and *ACEs* have become more common staples of policy discussions.

Due to the rising opioid epidemic in our first full year in 2017, the first advocacy issue CTIPP focused on was the crucial role childhood trauma plays in increasing rates of substance dependence and opioid use disorder. After years of taking little action on the issue, Congress approved $6 billion to address the opioid crisis in 2018, but unfortunately, the legislation focused solely on treatment instead of prevention. CTIPP's first policy paper was "Trauma-Informed Approaches Need to Be Part of a Comprehensive Strategy for Addressing the Opioid Epidemic" (Campaign for Trauma-Informed Policy and Practice, 2017). It cites the growing body of research showing the link between adverse childhood experiences and opioid use disorder and examines effective prevention and treatment programs.

CTIPP then began working with the staff of Senator Durbin of Illinois and Senator Heitkamp of North Dakota to advocate for trauma-informed provisions in the opioid legislation. Thanks largely to the work of those staffers, five trauma-informed provisions were included in the SUPPORT Act (H.R. 6, 2018). While only a fraction of the $6 billion authorized by the bill went to trauma-informed programs, it was an exciting start that CTIPP continues to build on. With time and education, additional senators on both sides of the aisle have become advocates for incorporating trauma-informed provisions into federal legislation.

Today, CTIPP is mobilizing to leverage COVID stimulus funds and opioid settlement moneys for trauma-informed, resilience-focused, and healing-centered supports. CTIPP is also leveraging the power of the National Trauma Campaign to advocate for the passage of the RISE from Trauma Act, STRONG Support for Children Act, the ACERT Program, and other pieces of legislation recently introduced in Congress to build trauma-informed work around the country. CTIPP continues to look for new opportunities to create a country where all communities, families, and individuals have the support and opportunities they need to thrive. As our capacity grows, we are excited to work on local and state policy, as well.

Trauma: My Personal Story

Trauma can affect any of us at any time. As a young child, despite access to numerous advantages (quality childcare, exposure to books and intellectual conversations) and encouragement to dream big, trauma turned my life around.

Academic excellence ended for me in seventh grade, when I choked on a piece of food. Though my mom successfully gave me the Heimlich, my understanding of my own mortality shifted dramatically. Trauma is not an event itself but rather our perception of said event. Shaken to the very core by this experience, I could not eat solid food for four months and lived off the nutrition drink Ensure. Vicious anxiety attacks took over any time food was near my mouth. At the worst moments, I struggled to swallow my own saliva, and school, once a focal point, became irrelevant.

Neurologically this constant terror caused me to operate in a primitive brain state for extended periods, prioritizing survival instead of higher cognition. I struggled at different times, phasing between hypervigilance and dissociation, rarely finding the ability to be centered and regulated. Without access to my cortex, long-term thinking was nearly impossible, so why should homework or the lessons from school matter at all? Instead, day-to-day survival became the utmost importance. Many teachers quickly grew impatient with my acting out and zoning out.

Fortunately, with the support and love from family and friends, I was able to relearn how to eat and got back to acting and feeling like myself again. A huge player in my healing was my best friend, Doug, who had gone through a near-death experience of his own when he first found out that he was deathly allergic to seafood. Doug regularly told me that he knew I was afraid, but I would be okay.

About two years after the choking incident, Doug and his dad passed away in a plane crash. I was devastated. I had a nightly recurring nightmare of being in a plane but never figuring out how to stop the plane from crashing. Right before the moment of impact, I would jolt awake, unable to fall back asleep. Most nights for nearly a year, I got less than an hour of sleep. Just as difficult, I was forced to spend my days in the place that reminded me most of Doug: school. I was exhausted and depressed, unable to focus on school, and the frustration of most of my teachers grew over the months.

Though baseball was usually my passion and provided a refuge from my daily struggles, it was the wrestling team at school that saved me. One of the coaches, aware of my struggles, invited me to work out with them before school on Mondays, Wednesdays, and Fridays. Not able to sleep anyway, I decided to join them. A few remarkable things happened over the next several years.

Not surprisingly, I got much stronger. I felt better and loved experiencing the growth and change in my body. There were some other benefits that were less expected. Being physically exhausted by the end of the day, I started sleeping through the night and became more attentive during the school day and able to participate more in class. As I did more exercise repetitions, I was literally creating new neural pathways, further promoting healing. My grades improved dramatically, as did my social life, and I didn't feel as stuck anymore.

I share my story here for a few reasons. First, note that my trouble with school was caused by things that happened outside school, and the solution to these problems was not more school or to do even more classwork. The tracking system that plagued my educational experience by moments of extreme adversity was traumatizing all by itself. My potential was greater than my grades. It still is.

Another major point is that healing does not take place in isolation. We all need people who care deeply and are there for us, even under the worst circumstances Dr. Bruce Perry's research tells us that just one caring adult can help a child heal from traumatic experiences and that more caring relationships create more protective factors: "Relationships are the agents of change, and the most powerful therapy is human love" (Perry & Szalavitz, 2007, p. 258).

The Impact of a Trauma-Informed Approach

Trauma-informed, resilience-focused, and healing-centered school environments are a major step in improving school cultures for staff and students alike. When all staff at a school (custodians, bus drivers, teachers, administrators—everyone) understand basic principles of neuroscience and how stress and adversity affect the mind, they see behavior differently (including their own).

Children who act out are punished less frequently because adults see the behavior for what it really is: a cry for help. Staff have the skills and tools to help students regulate so they can be in their cortex more, unlocking one's ability to learn. This approach improves connectedness, meaning, and overall school outcomes.

Trauma-Informed Healing in Texas

In an elementary school in Fort Worth, Texas, shortly after implementing trauma-informed training and healing-centered practices at the school, suspensions dropped from 890 to 19 (a 98% reduction in two years). While student behavior changed over time, the necessary shift was in the staff's perception of said behavior and new approaches to support students. Though their work ultimately improved student behavior, the initial step to get there was staff changing the way they saw behavior and their jobs. The result (beyond discipline) was the transformation of a school culture into one where students felt cared for and wanted to come to school and learn, and it ultimately improved outcomes across the school, student body, and staff.

How has your school worked with students and staff to build and elevate a compassionate campus-wide culture? The impact in Texas is not an isolated example. Other schools have realized similar outcomes from similar approaches. Lincoln High School in Washington State saw an 84% reduction in suspensions and a 40% reduction in expulsions in a single year (McInerney & McKlindon, 2015).

Trauma-Informed Healing in Hawaii

Nanakuli-Waianae Schools in Hawaii saw reductions in suspensions and chronic absenteeism as well as increases in graduation rates, college enrollment, and dual-credit enrollment since rolling out their initiatives. In addition to improved student outcomes, many staff outcomes improved, including retention. The short-term benefits of trauma-informed and healing-centered practices continue to improve outcomes, and over generations, we can expect the long-term benefits to be even more impressive.

Multiple Traumas

We must also appreciate the adverse community environments (illustrated beautifully in Dr. Wendy Ellis's "When a Picture Tells the Story: The Pair of ACEs Tree [2017]) that children are raised in and the impact they have. Some of the students I worked with were abused and neglected and lost multiple people to gun violence and substance use in a single year. In addition to this increased potential for trauma, these students had fewer supports in their lives. Is it any surprise some of them struggled to concentrate in school?

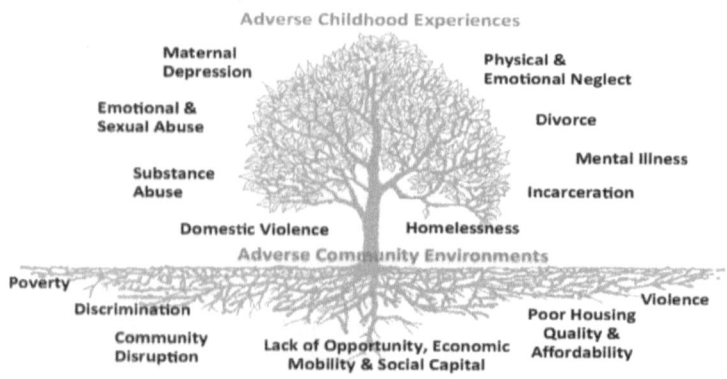

Figure 9.1. Pair of ACEs Tree. *Courtesy of Ellis (2017)* https://www.movinghealthcareupstream.org/when-a-picture-tells-the-story-the-pair-of-aces-tree

Implementing Trauma-Informed Practices in Walla Walla, Washington

In Lincoln High School (Walla Walla, Washington) just one year after implementing trauma-informed professional developments and programming, there was an 84% reduction in the number of suspensions and a 40% reduction in the number of expulsions schoolwide. The culture of the school changed because teachers and other staff better understood the impact of trauma, which led to a different way of analyzing student behavior and ultimately improving school practices. With this less punitive and more supportive environment, relationships and the educational experience overall (for both students and staff) improved.

Implementation in Philadelphia, Pennsylvania

Similar action was taken by Mastery Charter Schools (Philadelphia, Pennsylvania) with similar results. Across its network of 17 schools, a trauma-informed plan was embedded in a larger strategy to transform school culture to increase soft-skill development in students. The charter school network now requires staff members to partake in multiple trauma-informed-content trainings throughout the year, and instructional standards have been changed to reflect greater emphasis on creating community and nurturing positive relationships. This initiative has helped to improve school culture and therefore student outcomes (McInerney & McKlindon, 2015).

WHAT EDUCATORS CAN DO

We can put in place protective factors that prevent ACEs from occurring and build resilience that help mitigate the impact of ACEs when they do occur. We should work toward universal practices and precautions that create safe environments for all members of a school community.

There is a common mantra: We need to meet kids where they are. To do that, we need to understand neuroscience, epigenetics, ACEs, and resilience (NEAR) sciences. Meeting kids where they are means within their own brains most of all—understanding how to coregulate and help them tap into their cortex so they are as prepared for the learning process as possible.

Additionally, we cannot ignore the legacy that oppression has played in our education system. Communities of color were either given no formal education or forced to attend segregated schools for most of American history. The legacy of racism plays a major role in our education system today, and the historical trauma of the past needs to be addressed to promote healing. Though laws have changed, many communities of color live in underfunded school districts and are under the constant stress of systemic racism.

What does a trauma-informed, resilience-focused, and healing-centered classroom and school look like? There is no one way. The answer to this question depends on the school population, community context, and available resources. There are some commonalities across such environments, however. It is never about taking it easy or lowering expectations. In fact, as Cheryl Jorgensen (2005) spells out in "The Least Dangerous Assumption," it is better to have high expectations than it is to limit a child's potential.

However, there is safety (psychological, physical, emotional, social, and spiritual) intentionally built into the school environment and practices.

Keeping It Real: Lead with Compassion, Not Judgment

- What has happened to you? What needs do you have that are not being met?
- How do your lived experiences shape your own actions and feelings in the school?
- How do others' lived experiences affect their own actions and feelings in the school?
- How does creating connection and understanding support everyone in feeling safe and welcome in a classroom environment?
- What is the ultimate goal of education?
- How can we get the most out of our staff and students?
- In light of COVID-19, what should our educational priorities be?

Trauma Increased with COVID

While the coronavirus pandemic upended education and other systems, it also provided us with an opportunity to reanalyze the education system's priorities. All of us, especially children, experienced increased adversity and stress. Whether loss of a loved one, a routine, or a sense of safety, we all could use a little tender love and care. For many people who already had trauma histories, losses associated with the pandemic compounded these experiences even more. Our systems and the people who work and operate within them need to understand the emerging NEAR sciences to better support people and improve outcomes moving forward.

HOPE FOR THE FUTURE

There are so many reasons to have tremendous hope for the future of our education system and our world. Many places provide excellent tools, resources, and quality training, and if we invest time and money in these, then we will benefit tremendously. If our schools focus on quickly making up for the learning loss that many students have experienced from the pandemic, then we will cause harm to many who are in need of greater support. If, however, we collectively change our priorities and refocus our systems to support long-term growth and fulfillment, then we will benefit for generations to come. If we do that, then our education system should never look back.

My vision: Healthy outcomes and positive experiences (HOPE) is neuroscience, epigenetics, ACEs, and resilience (NEAR).

Jesse's Leadership

To address the neural, behavioral, and emotional impact of widespread trauma and ACEs, Kohler and the Campaign for Trauma-Informed Policy and Practice are working to create trauma-informed, resilience-focused, and healing-centered school environments. Kohler understands the urgency of this initiative, how important it is to embrace equity and justice, and the power of partnering with legislators to enact sustainable change.

Chapter 10

Visioning to Achieve Desired Results

A Social Media Case Study

Jeff Ikler

> *My vision for our district office is for us to take care of the building leaders so that the building leaders can take care of their teachers so that teachers can take care of their kids—so that we can all help these kids believe in themselves and help them believe that they have a future. It's not difficult to understand. It's not rocket science.*
>
> —Assistant Superintendent Dr. Debra Gustafson, Geary County Schools, Junction City, Kansas (Ickler & Richert, 2021)

ACT 1: BEGINNING

"Hey, how would you like to start a podcast?" Kirsten asked on the other end of the phone.

"Pratt has a one-hour opening in its radio station, and I think we should apply for it."

Pratt is the Pratt Institute, a private university in Brooklyn, New York, where Kirsten Richert, a colleague and friend from our years working at an educational publishing company, was teaching a couple of courses at the time.

"Sure," semiretired me replied, believing we had value to contribute. And with that, *Getting Unstuck*, our foray into the burgeoning world of podcasts, was born.

It's interesting to look back at our almost four-year old application: "This is a one-hour live, interactive talk radio program which shows you how to break through what's holding you back, generate more exciting ideas, and put those ideas into action to make progress towards your personal and professional goals." We never mentioned the phrase *purposeful change*, but that's what we were about in our respective hearts and minds—*purposeful* meaning designed to help you get where you wanted to be. We refined those words into a vision statement that we read on air at the start of our first broadcast in February 2018: "Welcome to *Getting Unstuck*. We intend to introduce you to different ways of thinking and tools designed to help you and/or your organization effect purposeful change and achieve your desired impact." Changing not for the sake of changing but to get desired results.

At the time—and still today—Kirsten was teaching at the college level and directing Richert Innovation Consulting, who describes its function, "We are innovation catalysts. We activate the value of your entire organization by combining fire with focus so you can transform your results. Together, we unleash the *possibilities*." Changing not for the sake of changing but to get desired results.

I was running Quetico (KWEH-teh-co) Leadership and Career Coaching—and still am—working with private individuals and organizational leaders to help them remove the inner constraints that are holding them back from the performance they desire. My mission states, "My coaching will help you gain insight into yourself, but then most importantly, it will help you choose meaningful actions—actions that develop you in ways that are aligned to your values and goals." Changing not for the sake of changing but to get desired results.

Our first 60 or so episodes concentrate on the general idea of changing to get desired results. Our format integrates brief instruction from one or both of us, thought-leader interviews, and wrap-up reflections. Our episodes cover the gamut of topics that could affect purposeful change, including neuroscience, leadership, mindfulness, project management, emotional intelligence, marketing, problem solving, communication, giving feedback, and authenticity.

And then we shifted.

ACT 2: TRANSITIONING

"Hey, how would you like to write a book on change?" Kirsten asked on the other end of the phone. "We've got experience and a load of good material we could leverage."

"Sure," semiretired me hesitatingly replied. The idea was very intriguing. Who doesn't want to see their name on a book cover? But the question we soon grappled with was "For what audience?" The business sector was overflowing with books on change. While our corporate and innovation experience could bolster our voice, we would figuratively be standing in a commodity pit with a plethora of authors all shouting, "Look at me! Look at me!"

But the education sector was a different matter. Both Kirsten and I had extensive teaching experience, and we knew the space through our work for the educational publishing company. And while there were lots of great books on *why* education needed to change and on *what* should be changed, the offerings were slim on *how* to change.

Shifting: How School Leaders Can Create a Culture of Change was born. One of the points we make in the book is why educational changes fail. One reason is that change agents tend to plan top-down on the mechanics of change: schedules, resources, one-size-fits-all training, and processes. The psychological underpinnings of those leading and implementing the change—*human readiness*—are not usually a consideration. We set out to correct that by outlining a series of shifts that most educators would need to make to lead successful change, shifts that focused on the processes *and* people needed to bring about desired results.

But as we planned *Shifting*, we had to grapple with the obvious question, "Does our *Getting Unstuck* podcast stay as a general forum on change, or do we focus more specifically on *educational* change?" We ultimately decide to rebrand the podcast as *Getting Unstuck: Educators Leading Change*. But doing that involved much more than changing a name and updating our websites. As we explain in our first education-focused episode,

> With the publication of our book *Shifting: How School Leaders Can Create a Culture of Change*, we now focus on change in education: who is leading it; what they're trying to accomplish and why; and what obstacles they're encountering and overcoming. Central to that focus is contributing an answer to the question "How might we reimagine schools to better support kids for the world today?"

What's Worked for You?

What has and has not worked when your school has implemented changes to curricular planning and activities, teacher training, campus guidelines, and the like? Why do you think that is?

What Worked for Us

Our vision for *Getting Unstuck: Educators Leading Change* was to help improve teaching and learning to better prepare kids for today's world. We do that in three ways:

1. A Focus on Visionary Leadership

We believe that students need to be capable of collaborating effectively with others and applying their knowledge and skills in new and unrehearsed situations. Thus, our vision is one of supporting that shift by raising the voices of

- key thought leaders who bring proven research-based practices to schools for consideration and
- practitioners who are already leading their teams differently or working with students differently.

None of the voices we showcase are promoting or implementing change reflective of the latest fad or trend. Instead, they're engaging in practices that have the potential to lead to something better—to increase the likelihood of achieving desired results on behalf of students.

Over time, we conducted more than 120 education-focused interviews. That said, when we look at our guests in aggregate, many share three qualities:

1. **Mission-focused.** An innovators' mind-set within a clear, disciplined understanding of what the institution is trying to achieve
2. **Student-focused.** An unrelenting focus on helping kids develop as emotionally intelligent problem solvers
3. **Team-focused.** A desire to move away from top-down everything and instead unleash the spirit of leadership in others

2. Telling the Bigger Story through a Series

Hosting a long-running weekly podcast involves turning the educational soil for interesting and instructional stories that support our mission and considering requests from prospective guests to appear on the show. Sometimes we break the single-issue format by building a series of interviews around a key topic to bring greater cohesion to our audience. We've done this now three times:

1. **Schools: Leading in a Time of Crisis.** When COVID first hit, we conducted brief 15- to 20-minute interviews with educators across the country. What we found universally was that beyond the sheer

mechanics of switching to a virtual or hybrid model, there was an overarching concern for students' and colleagues' emotional health.
2. **Tomorrow: How Might We Reimagine Our Schools?** Schools are often the brunt of criticism that they're changing too slowly. We wanted to bring current research, scholarship, and direction to our listeners, so we developed a 17-part series that outlines a variety of considerations for listeners to weigh. Those considerations include everything from making sure that schools are inclusive to helping educators access open resources to understanding how the brain enables or shuts down students' engagement.
3. **"Unstuck": Educators Leading Change.** One of our guests in the previous series, an experienced field consultant who works with schools across the country, made the following observation:

> We have to stop talking about "why" education needs to change; that train left the station a decade ago. And we have to stop focusing on "what" those changes look like; there is broad agreement that education must become more student-centered, inquiry-based, and differentiated to the needs of the individual learner. The challenge for us is "how" we will make these changes, quickly and sustainably, in a world that changes more rapidly than at any time in human history.

So, we took that observation to heart and developed an ongoing series that reviews the efforts of organizations and educators in the United Kingdom, Canada, and across the United States who are already knee-deep in the "hows." And while we can't share all their stories, we discovered that there are literally hundreds of organizations and schools that are rewriting *how* schooling should be done to achieve desired results for kids.

3. Supporting the Vision beyond the Microphone

It's not uncommon in the podcast world for hosts to provide the bare minimum of support beyond the interview itself: the guest's bio and contact info and maybe a summary of the conversation. We always felt, though, that providing robust show notes that listeners could access before or after listening was vital to supporting our vision. So in addition to providing the recording and the standard guest bio information, we provide "Listen for" points or "Think about" prelistening questions to consider during the interview. We also provide context for the episode with "Why this conversation matters" and brief, targeted professional-development support with "How you can use this episode." We are under no illusion that all listeners will engage with these extended notes, but if a few listeners make more out of an episode than "That was nice," well, that's why we're in this.

Two other practices we engage in are worth noting:

1. **"Hello!" meetings.** We routinely ask prospective guests to meet with us for 20–30 minutes well in advance of a taping just to get to know one another a bit and flesh out a potential episode. The last thing we want is to presume that we possess all the wisdom about what's important to discuss and share with our audience.
2. **The "brief."** After each "Hello!" meeting, we generate a "brief" that provides the guest with some framing questions in advance of the taping. It's not that we're going to be religious about covering each question—our discussions are often organic as we respond to something the guest says—but we want to help the guest know our thinking and prepare for the actual taping.

ACT 3: GOING DEEPER

Today, the listening public can choose from well more than 3 million podcasts, and we know that at least 50 of those are high-quality K–12 education-focused podcasts! Clearly, if we want to be listened to on a regular basis, and we do, then we have to continuously provide quality content and support, and we have to stay fresh. To that last point, we created an extension podcast called *Worth a Listen, Look, or Read*, where in about five minutes, we go deeper on the main idea *Getting Unstuck* delivered that week. We do that by offering a new way of thinking, unique content, or crucial skills to help leaders at any level get unstuck and work toward achieving their desired results.

Vision: Bringing That Point on the Horizon into Focus

Years ago, a very stuck client had trouble envisioning a more desirable future for herself, so I posed the following: "Imagine two boats that symbolize your journey. One is a rowboat, and one is a canoe. Now, imagine that you're in the rowboat, rowing across a lake. Which way would you physically be facing as you row?"

After a long period of contemplation, she hesitatingly replied, "If I'm in a rowboat, I'd have to be facing the back of the boat. I'd be looking where I came from."

"Now, imagine that you're in a canoe heading across the same lake," I continued. "Which way would you physically be facing?"

"OK," she sighed. "I'd be looking forward."

"If your desirable future is that point on the horizon in front of you, then which boat do you want to be in?"

Getting Unstuck has been our canoe for almost four years now. As paddlers, we've always tried to visualize a point on the horizon where we help administrators, building leaders, and teachers help their students be the best they can be in today's world. Periodically we check in on our vision compass to see if we're tracking appropriately. As guest Dr. Debra Gustafson said of her vision, "it's not rocket science." It just makes sense.

How Have You Used Visioning?

How and in which specific ways has your school used visioning to support and motivate teachers and other staff members in their professional journeys as well as daily classroom-related functions?

Keeping It Real

- What is the vision you and or your organization has for what it's attempting to do and serve? How did you develop it? Have you needed to shift how you work toward your vision over time as we did with our *Getting Unstuck* podcast?
- Organizations are bombarded by well-intentioned thought leaders inside and outside their organizations suggesting new initiatives. As we describe in our book *Shifting: How School Leaders Can Create a Culture of Change*, adopting a new initiative because it's the sexy topic du jour can lead organizations astray of what they're ultimately trying to accomplish. Derailment is one of the reasons long-term change efforts fail and visions are left unfulfilled. How are you or can you use your vision as a filter to deliberately weigh new opportunities?
- Vision and mission statements are often relegated to flashy posters in hallways, and conference and break rooms, where they can eventually blend in with the painted wall. How are you or your organization verbally keeping your vision front and center? If a visitor were to say to you or one of your colleagues "Tell me about your vision," could you respond quickly in just a sentence or two?

Jeff's Leadership

To help educators reimagine schools to better meet students' needs, Jeff uses his writing, podcasts, and coaching to introduce educators to new tools and different ways of thinking to help them create purposeful change. He urges educators to share in the visioning to determine what matters most and foster collective efficacy with their peers and school communities in order to effect beneficial and lasting change.

Chapter 11

Visioning in Michigan

Recognizing the Evolving Role of Leadership

Paul Liabenow and Michael Domagalski

> *MEMSPA is the vital knowledge network and voice for principals in Michigan, shaping effective solutions for everyday problems and emerging challenges. We are an engaged community of remarkable instructional leaders, furthering the practice of skillful leadership and connection with our peers.*

The Michigan Elementary and Middle School Principals Association (MEMSPA) is a community of principals dedicated to advocating, leading, and learning. We recognize the evolving nature of the principal's role and support those committed to this important work. As difficult as developing a vision may seem, execution of the plan to move it forward is far more difficult. Agreement on shared values after establishing the "why" of your organizational vision is imperative.

STRATEGIC PLANNING AT MEMSPA

The MEMSPA leadership team and board of directors dedicated several months to identifying the desired outcomes of our visioning process. Most of our leaders used *Visioning Onward* as a guide. Coleaders representing each of four goals that evolved from the visioning and strategic planning process then used crowdsourcing for gathering ideas and questions from school principals across the state of Michigan.

Strategic plan goals include:

- Legislative advocacy focused on support for principals and the schools they lead. Advocacy for funding resources for principal and staff self-care, recruitment, and retention are paramount.
- Increased professional-learning offerings to build principal leader capacity and resilience.
- Strengthening MEMSPA by growing membership and the value the association brings to members.
- Resources for social-emotional learning (SEL), suicide prevention/intervention.
- Ensuring diversity, equity, and inclusion (DEI)—broadly speaking, viewing all association activities through a DEI lens in order to better support underrepresented populations.

MEMSPA dedicates significant time and energy to move beyond the conversation toward actions, helping to students heal wounds and deal with day-to-day challenges in their lives. To implement their vision, Paul and MEMSPA are gaining support from Michigan legislators and business leaders who see the importance of SEL for now and the future. To implement MEMSPA's vision, MEMSPA leadership teams each developed one to three action steps, time lines, and success metrics. These were reviewed by the MEMSPA board of directors.

When it comes to the DEI lens, we were particularly interested in how we could increase the number of teachers and leaders of color (particularly males) in the classroom and in leadership positions. Additional human resources and dollars were then dedicated to the efforts of each team.

A Focus on Social-Emotional Supports

As we implement our goals, we are acutely aware of the need for social emotional supports. Just dealing with the last 18 months of the issues related to COVID-19, we also lost connection with 62,000 students in Michigan, who were facing different levels of trauma. One of the ways we are doing this is by helping industries across the state access the TRAILS curriculum and resources. The TRAILS program, developed at the University of Michigan, focuses in the first year on SEL. The second focuses on suicide prevention, and the third provides access to psychiatric and psychological care for kids in desperate need.

Furthering Innovations

MEMSPA also is collaborating with 19 schools funded by special grants to form a community of practice. These funds support human resources, helping to build exemplary programs in their school districts. They are collecting data; administering pre- and post-tests; and using instruments (e.g., the Center for Educational Improvement's S-CCATE tool, see Chapter 7) to determine current and future needs for teacher professional development and student learning.

Turning to Crowdsourcing, Mindfulness, and Well-Being

MEMSPA is working systematically to bring information from peers about what they seek for the future through crowdsourcing and also through implementing a TIPS program: a guide of practice for classroom teachers to understand how and what to address in class when there is evidence of trauma. This guide, which has been tested over the course of the last several months in schools (particularly in Michigan), will help better equip teachers to assess when a student has been exposed to trauma using the ACES tool and other assessments and how to best deal with the trauma.

During the past few years, MEMSPA has

- increased efforts to influence advocacy and legislation regarding children's mental health, mindfulness, and SEL;
- brought staff together to complete exercises in mindfulness practices (Mason, Rivers Murphy, & Jackson, 2020);
- involved 295 schools in a Building Health Communities initiative, which focuses on students' mental and physical well-being;
- influenced the voice of school administrators in the legislative process (in some cases, legislators are now calling educators to get their advice as they design legislation); and
- implemented extensive programs to increase mindfulness in 147 schools, with an eye not only on student well-being but also on teacher and collective self-care.

Addressing Equity

MEMSPA recently completed its own strategic plan, with a decision to focus heavily on DEI and to use the DEI lens as it conducts all its activities during the coming year.

VISIONING AT ST. CLAIR MIDDLE SCHOOL

St. Clair's vision is to create empowered students who can advocate for what they need and can accomplish.

St. Clair Middle School is focusing on mental health and SEL and is revamping its mind-set to focus on mental health first and then academics. It is a public, magnet school located in Saint Clair, Michigan, with 745 students in grades 5–8, a student-teacher ratio of 20 to 1, and a center for students with cognitive impairments. To implement St. Clair's vision, teachers and students are having conversations (adult-adult, student-student, and adult-student) about trauma and stress, how they are doing, and what else can be done to provide additional supports. St. Clair is also providing parents with resources on how to parent and how to improve the social-emotional well-being of their families.

Actions and Progress

Over the course of the past few years, St. Clair has transformed its seminar time, which is 25–30 minutes a day, from focusing on academics (reading, working on homework, etc.) to an SEL block, where students have conversations about positive relationships, active relaxation, awareness of thoughts and emotions, mindfulness, self-care, dealing with conflict and adversity, equity, anxiety, and depression (through the Positivity Project and the TRAILS program).

The Positivity Project (https://posproject.org) has had a major impact on St. Clair. Its mission is "[t]o empower America's youth to build positive relationships and become their best selves." There is a focus on 24-character strengths. See Figure 11.1.

Options for elective classes help focus on the needs of students rooted in SEL. Since focusing on mindful conversations and SEL, St. Clair has seen a decrease in discipline referrals and fewer absences and tardiness.

Other Things St. Clair Is Doing

- When students have a hard time, they can come to someone they trust who has already had the conversation with them. Then they can work together to solve the problem.
- Instead of asking "What's wrong with you?" or "What's the problem with you?" students are invited in and asked, "What happened?" to open the conversation to cope with problems with a team around them.

Figure 11.1. The Positivity Project

- We ask students to think about where they are now, where they want to be, and how they want to get there.
- We look at our vision constantly, seeing where we are and what needs to change, and then we develop the mission and goals, monitoring progress every few months.
- Recently, St. Clair has implemented a P2 Prize Patrol where staff will pop into classrooms and acknowledge positive actions or interactions. This contributes to a sense of positive school spirit and well-being.

EXPANDING VISIONING IN MICHIGAN

Mike is working with other principals to form a consulting team to support other schools as they vision. They are beginning to partner with districts, schools, and businesses, providing customized supports based on *Visioning Onward* for improving school culture, leadership, and instruction. They are also facilitating conversations with other districts about SEL and trauma-informed practices so they can be the best they can be.

Paul and Michael's Leadership

To help principals be effective, inspiring leaders and keep up with their evolving roles, Paul and Michael have created an engaged community of leaders to support and learn from each other, determine their collective vision, and move their organizations forward. They understand the power of inviting community members to share in the visioning; ensuring diversity, equity, and inclusion; acknowledging stress and trauma; building self-care and vitality; and advocating at the legislative level to ensure sustainable change.

PART V

Building Capacity

Change is challenging, and driving transformational change can seem downright daunting. But visioning is an incredibly powerful tool to help you imagine what's possible, inspire others to get involved, and foster resilience when things get tough. Inviting others to help you develop and shape your collective vision creates a more inclusive foundation and increases commitment to taking action. You can't change the world on your own, but you can lead, inspire, motivate, and encourage others to join in and exponentially increase your impact and chances of success.

In Chapter 12, Melissa Patschke dives into the importance of visioning for the future of education. After schools, businesses, and society at large had to completely refactor daily life to adapt to COVID-19, we realized that change, while challenging, is possible. As COVID-19 exacerbated inequalities, trauma, and mental health challenges, it made us more committed than ever to driving positive change within schools. We need to better meet the needs of all youth, ensure equity and justice, increase the participation of youth in educational decision making, help youth develop a lifelong love of learning, and prepare young people for their futures. To achieve this lofty vision, the Coalition for the Future of Education is focused on disseminating neuroscience findings, advancing the use of technology, revising how learning is assessed, pushing an antiracist curriculum, distributing resources more equitably, and amplifying youth voices.

With more than 20 years of educational leadership experience, Renee Owen (Chapter 13) understands the power of visioning in sharing leadership and growing support for transformational change. After two successful school turnarounds, she realized that having a school community come together and create a shared vision can drive tremendous change. A shared vision provides guidance for challenging decisions, resilience during trying times, and motivation to inspire change.

VISIONING WITHOUT LIMIT

Too often we limit our imaginations and visions, hoping to stave off disappointment. But we need to be bold and dare to dream bigger. Doing so can actually benefit our brain and overall well-being! By defining, embracing, and pursuing an inspiring vision, we focus on purpose and positivity instead of simply getting by. Our brain releases dopamine and serotonin, making us feel good, whenever we make progress toward our goal.

Julia Murphy, a legislative aide at the Massachusetts House of Representatives, explores the power and potential of elevating youth voices and leaders in Chapter 14. Instead of dismissing youth as too lazy, inexperienced, and disengaged, we should be building their agency, inviting their perspectives, and making space for their leadership. By viewing young people as resources instead of problems, we invite them to engage, participate, and feel valued.

In schools, what if we taught students about various leadership styles and skills? What if we nurtured their innate potential and passions and developed an energetic generation driving change? As we face complex challenges across the globe from climate change to increasing inequality to strained social relations, we'd be wise to invest in building a new generation of strong, confident, and capable leaders.

Finally, in Chapter 15, Ruth E. Freeman, founder and president of Peace at Home Parenting Solutions, explores the power of personal experiences and passion to drive meaningful change. Her mission suddenly popped into her head at a workshop, and it has guided her career ever since. Her story illustrates how fearlessly pursuing a lofty vision and welcoming guidance and support from a variety of sources along the way can result in powerful change.

Chapter 12

The Coalition for the Future of Education

Melissa D. Patschke

This coalition envisions a world that leans in with heart and compassion for self, others, and our environment, where people and institutions are dedicated to expanding conscious acts of caring; building resiliency; and advancing learning, equity, and justice.

We envision safe and equitable schools with an education that serves as the foundation for our humanity; it is flexible and empowering. There is room for adventure, students drive their learning, learning and self-understanding are celebrated, and communities support their individual and collective self-care and well-being.

Established in January 2021, the Coalition for the Future of Education (CFE) is an outgrowth of the Center for Educational Improvement's (CEI) visioning. I recount the initial months of the coalition, steps taken to influence policy and practice, and plans for the next year.

OPTIMISM

CFE was created through an optimistic and time-driven need to provide the newly forming Biden administration research-based best practices to guide the foundation of their work. Dr. Christine Mason, executive director of CEI, was formative in the creation of the platform and keen in her political awareness that the time for the messaging was immediate. We began working with the youth leadership initiatives through listening tours and engaged with youth advocates around the topics that now embody the vision and mission of the coalition.

Once the work began, we were guided by a coordinating committee of professionals with diverse backgrounds, experiences, and expertise. This coming together of passionate minds allowed the momentum of the work to take hold and press forward. Along the way, we learned from each other, exchanged ideas and documents, and embarked on the visioning process of what was needed to elevate the future of education in a manner that would serve our society best as well as accentuate student achievement.

CFE: THE WHO

CFE represents a diverse group of individuals and organizations dedicated to supporting and positively influencing the future of education in the United States and globally. To shift to a culture where each student is guided on an individual path that honors oneself and others will require intensive efforts. Members of this coalition have spent decades growing our understanding of what can happen. We support research, policy decision making, and revamped teacher preparation and other training to focus on an empowering process with students at the heart of our efforts. Substantial evidence confirms the viability of what we recommend. However, the size and scale of our proposed changes will require intensified efforts, an expanding consciousness, and a change of mind-sets and practices for many.

CFE: Passions Shared

Dr. Liza Caraballo-Suarez, Coordinating Committee Member

I have spent my career working tirelessly to advocate for equity in education, I have seen firsthand how detrimental the inequities can be. I serve as the school principal in the very same neighborhood I grew up in. I experienced these inequities as a child, as a teacher, as a school leader, and as a community member.

Martin Luther King Jr. said, "The ultimate measure of a man is not where he stands in moments of comfort and convenience but where he stands at times of challenge and controversy." As a school leader active at the local, state, and national levels, I have stood alongside colleagues to demand for educational equity for all our children—no exceptions. I have had the opportunity to tell the story, their story, my story. I believe this is the path to the success, regardless of a child's ethnicity, race, color, or religion.

My first and only language as a little girl was Spanish. I lived in an economically challenged neighborhood. I was the target of biased comments. I couldn't speak English, and my family couldn't afford to buy me new clothes or shoes. I suffered many acts of bullying and discrimination due to poverty, language, cultural barriers. I experienced firsthand the hardships many of our students experience. Yet these memories have made me the transformational educational leader that stands before you today.

I advocate for equity. I am driven to make a difference. I am passionate to ensure that every child feels welcomed, respected, loved, and safe when they come to school—not just PS 120 but every school. Receiving an equitable education is a basic human right in this country for *all* children. I know our differences bring us strength. This is true in our profession, in our communities, and in our classrooms.

As we reimagine education, our students deserve equitable resources to achieve academic success. They need to believe in their own purpose, faith, ability to succeed despite the obstacles they may face. It's up to us to provide them an equitable and respectful educational experience.

CFE: THE WHY

Our pandemic-driven educational experiences have proven that change is possible and must continue to evolve to better meet the needs of all youth, ensure equity and justice, increase the participation of youth in educational decision making, and prepare young people for their futures. CFE is concerned about the trauma and injustice that accompanied the COVID pandemic in 2020–2022 and beyond. More supports are needed to address student and family mental health, well-being, and healing (Barron & Kinney, 2021; Zacarian, Calderon, & Gottlieb, 2021).

The coalition believes that students must be more involved in planning and determining their education. Their autonomy needs to be valued, and their voices deserve to be heard (Dueck, 2021; Kaur, 2018). We also know that visioning for the future of our K–12 system is crucial (Mason, Liabenow, & Patschke, 2020). We need to examine what works, reimagine what could be, and ultimately figure out how to head in that direction.

CFE: THE ASK

The education of the future needs to be focused on understanding neuroscience, heart-mind connections, and the adverse effects of childhood trauma; the importance of effective remote learning; and the essential nature of solidarity in affirming dignity, equity, and justice. The future must demand compassionate school practices bolstered by research on the significance of student engagement and student leadership (Mason, Asby, et al., 2021; Murray, 2019; Sanfelippo & Sinanis, 2016).

It is important to understand neuroscience, heart-mind connections, and the adverse effects of childhood trauma. Teacher education programs must update curricula to include the expanding body of research on neuroplasticity, executive functioning, heart intelligence, and building student resilience. Teachers must understand how supportive adults strategically employ strategies that build neuropathways to support cognition, well-being, and healing from trauma (Mason, Rivers Murphy, & Jackson, 2020; Zacarian, Calderon, & Gottlieb, 2021).

As technology continues to evolve, schools and districts must be able to give students substantial experiences with up-to-date technology. Schools need funding to ensure that all students have uninterrupted access to the technology they need to learn, collaborate, connect, explore, and receive virtual mental health supports (Dintersmith, 2018; Gustafson, 2017; Sheninger & Murray, 2017).

Schools need to help students find meaning while maintaining high academic standards. Learning can be enhanced by recognizing and responding to student interests; elevating their voices; and helping them find meaning, value, and purpose in their education. Students need experiential activities and community-based opportunities for problem-solving and entrepreneurial initiatives (Brown, 2012; Murray, 2019; Zacarian, Calderon, & Gottlieb, 2021).

Schools must revamp how learning is assessed and how assessment data guide instructional decisions. We recognize that the psycho-social-emotional needs of children and youth have been inadequately addressed with an over-reliance on standardized expectations and assessments. We envision a future of education that is driven not by lists of standards and high-stakes assessments but by individualized measures of growth over time (Dueck, 2021; Gustafson, 2017; Payne, 2018).

Schools need to encourage equity through antiracist curricula. We must review instructional curricula to ensure that our understanding of history is not dominated by one voice but rather that all voices are heard. For the future of our democracy, we must revisit history for accuracy and relevance—seeking truth, inclusiveness, and justice. We must also ensure that students have a better understanding of civics, citizenship, and their participation in democracy (Fergus, 2017; Kafele, 2021).

Schools need to increase equitable access to resources. Justice and equity for all children require equitable access to education, technology, and other resources supporting education (Brown, 2018; Payne, 2018; Wagner & Dintersmith, 2015).

We need to value the voices of youth; we must listen to them and help advance their leadership. We can shape the future by focusing on the needs of youth; urging mentoring and scaffolding for young people; and building on individual self-awareness, metacognition, and self-monitoring. By applying principles from neuroscience, educators can enhance executive functioning (focus, attention, and self-regulation) and strengthen critical thinking and decision making for the next generation of leaders (Brown, 2018).

Teaching youth greater compassion and resilience is a foundation for their effectiveness. Educators need support. When teachers are overwhelmed with stress, they are not fully available to their students; educators do best with positive mind-sets and with tools to help youth vision for positivity and an inclusive way forward. Strong educators promote confidence and self-agency, which extends students' strengths. These holdings will lead to learning opportunities designed by healthy adults that are relevant, exciting, and meaningful for students (Barron & Kinney, 2021; Drago-Severson & Blum-DeStefano, 2018; Dueck, 2021; Kaur, 2018).

CFE: THE HOW

To achieve a future that helps our educational system move beyond trauma and suffering will take a multipronged approach. CFE believes that funding, resources, professional development, revisions in teacher education, policy changes, leadership development, technical assistance, and research are needed for the following:

- Youth listening tours and youth leadership development to help education become more meaningful to students and to ignite student learning.
- Ensuring that teacher-preparation programs update their understanding of the psychology of learning to reflect neuroscience, trauma, and heart-mind intelligence.
- Revising educational-administration programs so that administrators' key components and procedures for iterative, research-based visioning and the key components of this proposal.
- Simplifying how we approach social-emotional learning by providing an overarching framework that addresses neuroplasticity, awakening awareness (mindfulness or consciousness), self-compassion and compassion for others, confidence and courage, and community building.
- Revamping education to be more equitable, just, and inclusive. This includes revisions to policies and practices, including revisions to the teaching of history and civics.

- Ensuring self-care and community care for teachers, other school staff, students, and families.
- Collaborating with technology providers to expedite innovation and use of advanced technologies in schools. As we do this, we can help build student skills and interests as well as use technological advances to advance education.
- Ensuring that diverse voices, including marginalized groups, are part of the process of revisioning education and that this new thinking is reflective of innovation, what works, and best practices from many fields.

Ultimately, CFE believes that education cannot be reenvisioned in a silo. Visioning must occur within a broader community that involves families and neighbors and includes a global perspective, with an eye toward not only discovering but also sustaining promising educational practices.

CFE: PASSIONS SHARED

It's important to hear the stories of our underserved schools and the challenges many face as they work hard to educate and meet the needs of their families daily. I think about the stories I heard from aunts and uncles on our reservation about how they were taken out of school and sent to boarding schools, where they were mentally and physically abused in order to eradicate their "Indianess."

Now, reservation schools should be focusing on preserving culture and language and providing quality education to its students. Instead, principals of reservation schools focus on navigating overlapping regulations in order to perform the basic function of purchasing textbooks and school lunches. We must own the conversation that school resources and funding must be distributed equitably so all students have a chance to reach their full potential.

—Tom Payton, Coordinating Committee Member

YOUTH LEADERSHIP

CFE values the voices of youth. We vow to listen to them and help advance their leadership. The future of education should be one that is shaped by youth, one that urges mentoring and scaffolding for young people and that builds on individual self-awareness, metacognition, and self-monitoring. CFE supports a pedagogy that promotes confidence and self-agency and extends students' strengths. By applying principles from neuroscience, we can enhance executive functioning (focus, attention, and self-regulation) and strengthen critical thinking and decision making. It is crucial to teach youth greater compassion and resilience (Brown, 2012; Dueck, 2021; Mason, Asby et al., 2021).

Youth Listening Tours

During the formative work of the coalition, Dr. Chris Mason, CEI researchers, and educators designed intentional experiences and engaged youth in a series of online discussions with several groups of up to 20 participants. Each gathering included a range of diverse middle school, high school, and college-aged youth (Becker & Chen, 2021).

The key learnings for the coalition coordinating committee were the following:

1. Youth valued being asked their opinions and would like to be more involved in planning for and designing their futures, including their course of studies, requirements, and instructional preferences.
2. While many students struggled with online learning, some students thrived. These students appreciated the flexible schedule afforded to them as they worked from home; some students also learned a lot about self-motivation. With practice, they gained new skills that will serve them a lifetime.
3. Many students experienced a profound trauma during the pandemic, missed their social interactions with peers and teachers, and found it hard to stay focused with virtual learning.
4. When considering education in the future, youth want greater use of hands-on learning and more mindfulness to help alleviate their stress and anxiety and create a greater sense of peace, calm, and well-being.
5. Students realized the value of the current focus on equity and diversity and are looking forward to a future where more educators look at them and can relate to them.

Our youth are courageously creating their own journeys each day. Infusing the ideas and voice of our youth into our future planning ensures a value-added approach to doing what's right for the next generations (Brown, 2018; Patschke, 2021).

Design and Execution

Prior to engaging with youth, know what you're going to ask and why. Are you seeking general information about reimagining how we do school, or are you seeking specific feedback on one or two elements? Also consider the following tips:

- When selecting a physical location, consider the value of meeting virtually. Having no travel requirements opens the possibility of easily gathering a mix of voices from a variety of experiences. The time commitment is much smaller from participants and facilitators, and with the use of breakout rooms, students can work in small teams to generate their ideas and explore their contributions in a focus-group-type format.
- No matter their age, youth are busy. We found that it was important to keep the tours to no longer than 75 minutes. This provides participants plenty of time to share their thoughts and ideas while being concise and to the point.
- We suggest framing the process around 20 youth and 5 adult facilitators. This will allow small-group work. We also have discovered that it was important to pull the voices from the small breakout sessions into the whole-group thinking to extend discussion in a larger space.

Mehir Bahir, a Student's Reflections

Voice and opportunity—they go hand in hand. Together, they help ensure that everyone's voices are heard. Listening to everyone's opinions allows us to see others' points of view. In education, it is incredibly important that the voices of students, the teachers and staff, and the administration are heard. Each group needs the others to help schools run in the best way possible. Listening to each group shows that their feelings and views are valued.

Oftentimes, a group may also have insights that others may not be aware of. Youth and teachers often have great ideas that can help improve the school or the district. Listening to students and teachers helps create a positive school environment and helps change happen where it is needed most. During the pandemic, a lot of people are struggling, and if they are finding the strength to speak up, their thoughts should be taken into account as decisions are made.

At our school, we have been fortunate to be able to continue many clubs and activities through the pandemic, and I feel that the collaboration of the students, teachers, and administration has allowed that to happen. I am always grateful at our school's senate meetings (student government) when the class officers and our teachers and principals listen to what we think and help make sure that when we make decisions, everyone feels valued and involved. Having a positive environment and encouraging communication helps to improve the school environment and strengthen a sense of community.

CFE Sample Questions for Youth

- If you could wave a wand and create the perfect educational experience, name the top three things that would be a part of the system.
- What's not working for most youth that we need to change?
- What needs to be created, duplicated, or emphasized to improve education in the future?
- What have been the most impactful experiences about school that helped you become successful?
- What leadership growth opportunities do you wish you had available to you in school?

A VISION FOR THE FUTURE

Visioning is future planning. When we include the voices of our youth, their experiences will be enhanced by opportunities to make their preferences and concerns known. We need to listen to youth, learn from them, and welcome them to the table as partners to move us forward (Becker & Chen, 2021).

Cultures of Courage

Brené Brown (2018) indicates that to be a leader with courage, we need to "write what you need to read." In alignment, the CFE did exactly that. We've taken the language, tools, and ideas of many brilliant youth advocates and educators and synthesized them into words we want to see happen in our schools. Our materials are on the Washington, DC, desks of Dr. Jill Biden and Secretary Cardona. We've seen changes that indicate we've been heard, everything from an emphasis across the country on inclusive practices to youth listening tours popping up in a variety of places.

Our hope is that we've modeled courageous leadership for our profession. By speaking up and advocating for the needs of our schools, children, and communities, we have placed a spotlight on a new direction for reimagining what could be in our future. By listening to our youth and including their voice through our work, our vision becomes real. Courage is contagious. Be brave, listen closely, and use your heart. Elevate the voices that need to be heard, and find your personal courage to say what others need to hear.

VOICES OF YOUTH

Courage is something that everyone possesses. Everyone needs it to keep moving forward. There are many ways that people use courage in their day-to-day lives. For some, it is a simple as mustering up the courage to walk across a busy street, while others use courage to present a big project for their class. It can be finding the courage to fight for what's right in the world, to speak up for something that you know is wrong or something that your passionate about.

Courage can be found all around you. It keeps you going. Courage helps you to step out of your comfort zone, it helps you to push for what is right, or it simply helps you to watch that scary movie you have been wanting to watch. It is never the same for everyone, but it helps us all to simply keep moving forward to pursue our goals in life, no matter what those be.

Keeping It Real: Continuing Angst

As this book goes into publication, the work of the coalition is continuing. In light of serious issues facing school boards, school leadership, and staff within schools, we realize that our list of priorities may need to evolve. Here are a few thoughts:

- Have you conducted a SWOT (strengths, weaknesses, opportunities, and threats)?
- What is the greatest threat?
- Where is the greatest opportunity?
- What are the implications for your action?

Melissa's Leadership

To create safe and equitable schools, Melissa and the Coalition for the Future of Education aim to help educators understand neuroscience, heart-mind connections, and the adverse effects of trauma. They are advocating for revamping how learning is assessed, encouraging equity through antiracist curricula, increasing access to resources, and including the voices of youth. She understands the importance of acknowledging stress and trauma, building self-care and vitality, involving youth and stakeholders to share in the visioning process, and making equity and justice a core part of any solution.

Chapter 13

Preparing New Educational Leaders for Vision-Forward Leadership and the Neuroscience of Purpose

Renee Owen

Renee was the executive director of the Rainbow Community School in Asheville, North Carolina. Renee describes how she has taken what she learned in her role to her current position as a university professor at Southern Oregon University (SOU), including her plans and activities for influencing the administrator-preparation program.

> *To positively affect change for our educational community by listening and responding to needs, cultivating equity, and empowering people to reach their full potential.*
>
> —*Mission statement by Lisa Gilman, administrative licensure student, Southern Oregon University*

One sentence. Powerful. Purposeful. Lisa is a student in the administrative licensure program at Southern Oregon University in Ashland. She was 1 of 25 cohort members who crafted a personal mission statement that captured their core values. In approximately one year, Lisa will likely be starting a position as a principal. Her mission statement will be the guiding light for her and for the school community she will serve.

If our newest generation of leaders are going to transform our educational system toward equity, excellence, and well-being (Fullan & Gallagher, 2020), then universities need to make visioning the foundation of administrative licensure programs, something we are incorporating into the administrative program at Southern Oregon University, where holistic principles guide our School of Education.

Educational leadership, specifically the role of principal, may be the most challenging job in America, which has been exasperated by COVID (Copland, 2001; DeMatthews et al., 2021). The daily onslaught of responsibilities, demands, and conflicts can result in principals spending most of their time trying to cope. Without a clear compass, it's easy for educational leaders to lose their direction.

The pressures and delights of educational leadership are many. This was apparent in a rural charter school I founded and directed in the one of the poorest counties with the highest domestic abuse rate in Colorado. After district consolidation, Paradox Valley no longer had a school, and children spent as much as three hours a day commuting to a district school in another town. As one resident of this community said, "What is a community without a school?"

So a group of committed citizens crafted a vision for a community school, and we opened Paradox Valley Charter School. Though we started out our first year with some of the lowest academic achievement results in the state, within five years, Paradox Valley School was a Colorado School of Excellence, with test scores in the top 10% of the state. Some of those children were the first to graduate from high school in their families, even earning scholarships, and many of them went on to college.

Later, as head of school at a holistic independent school, the Rainbow Community School in Asheville, North Carolina, I found that a shared vision brought similar results. Rainbow was sometimes viewed by the local community as a sweet, nurturing, holistic school but was regarded as being soft on academics.

With the help of appreciative inquiry as a visioning process (Stavros, Torres, & Cooperrider, 2018), Rainbow's reputation transformed as we demonstrated rigorous academic results through various data and through the high performance of our students after they left Rainbow (Owen & Buck, 2020). Within a few years, we went from underenrollment as our main budgetary issue to a long wait list of hopeful families upset at being turned away as one of our biggest challenges.

In both contexts, our accomplishments were directly related to the work our school community did to create a shared vision. A shared vision provides direction during times of conflict and ethical dilemmas, resilience during times of struggle, and inspiration to build the future. Like the sun powers the earth, that shared vision provided the energy for our success.

HOW DOES THE LEADER'S PERSONAL VISION INSPIRE SHARED VISION?

Educators who are dedicated to the service of others often don't like to talk about themselves. But the truth is, my intense passion and my vision were the fire that powered a tenacious drive toward success for our work in schools and therefore the spark that ignited our collective vision. I had a dream—a vision—for education that inspired others to keep their dreams alive, too. Leaders need to hold their *personal* purpose in front of them as a beacon of light if they are to help others create shared vision.

While the words *vision, mission, aim, strategy,* and *purpose* are often intermingled, one can find many definitions for each that vary according to the source. I cluster all these terms as part of *Visioning*, with a capital *V*. To me, a Vision is something that is so huge and so bold that it may not be feasible in concrete terms in this lifetime. Often expressed in present tense, it is an eternal goal—an imagined ideal education to be always working toward. You might think of this Vision as Education Heaven.

Surprisingly, the visions of educators are often narrow. For the most part, their visions still look pretty much like the schools we have, with a few tweaks. Perhaps educators are so practical they don't dare to dream bigger? Or maybe, they are afraid to dream because they don't want to be disappointed about the reality of what's possible? Maybe they have been living in a world of educational compliance for so long that they haven't exercised their imagination muscles enough? Possibly many have forgotten the importance of imagination in education. Their lack of imagination may be due to a combination of all the above.

Einstein said, "Imagination is more important than knowledge. For knowledge is limited, whereas imagination embraces the entire world, stimulating progress, giving birth to evolution." Our current educational system was created by humans. With imagination, we can create an entirely different system, but we must be able to imagine it first.

IS A NEW VISION NECESSARY?

If you believe that education and society reflect one another—that our society is a direct reflection of our educational system and vice versa—then absolutely, it's time for something new. Fullan and Gallagher (2020) report recent data on the radical increase over time in mental health issues, climate change crises, and poverty in our society, and they tie many of our social ills to the massive inequality in our schools and society.

Unless we are satisfied with the results of our current system, we need a new vision. However, consider the changes that are so needed. In Southern Oregon, climate fires are the new normal. We expect smoky skies, polluted air, and being ready to evacuate and run for our lives at any moment as ordinary for "fire season," which is now one-quarter of the year. This is one example of the existential crisis we humans are adapting to but not solving because our schools haven't taught us how to behave differently. We humans haven't learned how to get along well enough so we can work together—across cultures and political boundaries—to solve expansive, complex, multicultural problems.

Throughout society, we can witness that most of our problems are human created—violence, poverty, racism, corruption, and so on—rather than what the Dalai Lama (His Holiness the Dalai Lama, 1999) calls natural phenomenon. Yet most of us continue to live our lives with pretty much the same habits and the same systems that are possibly driving us to extinction without feeling a sense of agency that any of us as individuals can affect enough change to save us. Isn't something better possible? Of course! But only if we *learn* how to live together in harmony with the aim of well-being—*only with education*. We need to teach our children how to live a new way of life in a new world.

Let's remember that humans learn primarily from experience. Delivering content—a unit on well-being, on environmental sustainability, on conflict management—won't result in change. Instead, we need to envision schools where children *live* in a school microculture that mimics the ideal macrosocial culture. If we want a world that is sustainable, peaceful, equitable—a world where everyone is empowered to live their dreams and everyone thrives—then our children need to attend educational communities where that is their day-to-day experience. That needs to be their school culture, or how they know life to be. Children will naturally live what they know when they are adults. Therefore, we need leaders who have a big Vision. If we are going to evolve our educational system toward entirely new results—toward what Fullan and Gallagher (2020) call excellence, equity, and well-being—then we need leaders who can imagine something new.

My Vision Has Been Consistent Since I Entered the Field of Education

For education to be a world of wonder, wisdom, and well-being, where humans learn to thrive.

That Vision has been the Education Heaven of my entire career. Heaven is always there, whispering throughout multiple roles and levels of influence—at the classroom level, in a building leadership role, and now as a teacher of leaders. My current job is to help our new generation of educational leaders to imagine their Vision and grab on to it like they are hitched to a star.

What's My Why?

Our initial and principal administrative licensure (PAL) program at SOU is a cohort model, which lends itself to experiential learning. Before delving into such technical content as policy, data analysis, or instructional leadership, PAL students have opportunities to experience how to create a compassionate cohort community based on core values and visioning. It's important for them to get to know one another, not just on a formal basis, but also to learn about one another's vulnerabilities and dreams (Brown, 2018).

Therefore, before the first day of class, each student watches Simon Sinek's 2009 TED Talk on the Golden Circle, and they each create a screencast video called *What's My Why?* revealing what their Vision for education is and why they are motivated to amplify their influence by becoming a licensed school leader.

Identifying Bone-Deep Core Values and Mission

After defining their Vision, new leaders in our program at SOU articulate a personal mission, such as Lisa's, which opens this chapter. Only with this visioning can leaders be clear enough about their passions and purposes to make a difference while the magnetic swirl of compliance and coping with everyday administrative existence doesn't pull them away from what matters most.

Missions change. They change for organizations, and they change for individual leaders. They change when circumstances change, when roles change, and when new visions come to light.

My Current Personal Mission

To teach, speak, and write to audiences who are empowered to make personal and systemic change toward a world of well-being.

My mission has evolved over the years. At the beginning of my educational career, like many teachers becoming new principals, my mission focused on students—for each child to develop their full potential in life. Later, supporting and developing teachers was my main mission because great teachers positively affect students.

Today, my sphere of influence is expanding out much further with a focus on how education influences our entire society. According to adult developmental theory, as adults develop, we see through a wider and more inclusive lens (Crain, 2005; Kegan, 2000), which explains why my mission statement has expanded over the years.

Identifying Core Values and Writing a Personal Mission Statement

Defining one's core values and writing a mission statement can look deceivingly simple, yet principal licensure students find it surprisingly challenging. Students at SOU are provided with a couple sample lists of core values, such as the one published by Clear (n.d.) or by Faddis (2020, pp. 17–18), and asked to (1) decide on three core values and then (2) write about why and how those values speak to them at their bone-deep core level.

Next, considering their core values, each student writes a personal mission statement. There are plenty of websites with directions for writing a personal mission, such as the one published by the Indeed Editorial Team (2022). It's important for students to discuss their core values and mission statements with one another so that they have the opportunity not only to learn from one another but also to reflect on their inner compass and to develop a habit, as new leaders, of voicing higher values as the guiding principles in their work and their schools (Kolb, 1984).

THE NEUROSCIENCE OF VISION AND PURPOSE

Humans are motivated by only two basic things: to achieve positive experiences and to avoid negative ones. The latter has the brain in constant survival mode, with the older layers of the triune brain constantly working (MacLean, Montefiore, & Winch, 1990). The motivation to avoid negative experiences activates our sympathetic nervous system and a cascade of stress-related chemicals, such as norepinephrine, adrenaline, and cortisol.

When the sympathetic nervous system, sometimes called the stress-response system, in our brain activates, it pulls energy and resources from our neocortex, where our highest levels of cognitive thinking and executive functioning occur (Perry, 2009). Stress-response-system activation lowers our IQ and our ability to perform well. Over time, an overactivated stress response system results in chronic fatigue, otherwise called burnout, and diminishes the capacity of the neocortex.

Avoiding the Negative

At the same time, the reward systems of our brain, which release such chemicals as dopamine and serotonin, activate when we successfully avoid negative consequences and move toward safety. While avoiding the negative can sound, well, negative, the chemical release from successfully avoiding the negative feels good in the short term. This stress/reward cycle describes the addiction of most video games.

For example, while avoiding a car crash during a high-speed video game chase is exhilarating, the shot of dopamine the player receives comes with a price. The adrenaline and cortisol constantly released by the sympathetic nervous system isn't building up resilience, but rather it's draining the brain's capacity while overtapping precious cognitive and emotional resources. Any school principal can relate to school days often feeling like a high-speed chase, running from one crisis to another, trying to stay alive and to save others.

Seeking the Positive

The opposite human motivation is to seek the positive. By making one's Vision, or purpose, the central feature in one's daily life, one is seeking joy rather than simply surviving. The reward systems of the brain make us feel good every time we experience movement toward our purposeful goals, without the negative effects of adrenaline.

Furthermore, in such work as education, which is highly based on relationships, another reward system of the brain activates what neuroscientist and therapist Cameron Allen (n.d.) calls the oxytocin system. Oxytocin is the feel-good chemical, sometimes called joy juice, released in the brain when we experience a positive interaction through a relationship with other human beings (Bailey, 2014; Perry, 2009).

Oxytocin has been largely portrayed in the media as associated with physical sensations, such as sex, giving birth, and breastfeeding. But the yummy sensations of oxytocin, while milder, are also released any time we experience a positive or meaningful relationship with another human, such as when we empathize with someone's story, when we sing or dance together, and even when we learn together. When we create or accomplish something positive together, such as a long-term, shared vision, oxytocin is flooding our system.

Further comparing the two motivations (moving toward the positive and avoiding the negative) and their associated neuro systems, dopamine is released when we reach goals having to do mostly with material gain, while oxytocin is associated more with higher purpose, giving the oxytocin system a spiritual quality. Oxytocin is experienced when we do something good for another human, when we feel a sense of closeness or a relationship to a divine entity or nature, or when we make a sacrifice for the common good.

The brain science of visioning explains why having higher purpose—something meaningful beyond the self—is considered a spiritual gift by philosophers, theologians, and some researchers (Damon & Malin, 2020). All things spiritual are invisible, and *purpose* is the invisible guiding light that feeds our soul and fuels us through challenges.

The Brain Power of Purpose

Consequently, when we are consistently guided by a higher purpose and therefore are experiencing the rewards of oxytocin, we are not only highly motivated, but we are also building resilience. Oxytocin is a stress buffer, telling us we can trust other humans and we can trust ourselves; the world is a safe place, and we are going to be okay (Perry, 2009). When operating from the higher centers of our brain, we are open to curiosity (which only operates when we are feeling safe and trusting), and our creative and cognitive abilities are unleashed (Robinson, 2010).

When our abilities are unleased, we become unstoppable—capable of achieving our highest potential. Our energy becomes an irresistible force field that people want to be around, which is why leaders who have a passion for purpose are so charismatic and capable of rallying an entire community toward a shared vision.

As a point of clarification regarding the brain science, let's return to the triune brain (MacLean, Montefiore, & Winch, 1990). The previous explanation of the brain science behind motivation is extremely oversimplified in that it portrays positive purpose as seated in the neocortex of the brain and negative motivations, such as the drive to survive, as seated in the lowest and oldest center of the brain. However, both types of motivation also live in the limbic system, the emotional aspects of the brain sometimes thought of as the middle brain.

The limbic system stores emotional memories in the physical recesses of our brain. When we experience something negative, such as a trauma, our limbic system recognizes anything that looks like a similar situation and tells us to avoid it. Likewise, when we experience the high from the reward systems of the brain, our limbic system remembers it, and we crave more of that experience.

One system, the dopamine/norepinephrine stress-response system, promotes emotions and attitudes of skepticism and distrust: Every situation and person is potentially dangerous. The other system, the oxytocin system associated with our higher purpose, promotes emotions and dispositions of curiosity, openness, and optimism: Every situation is potentially an opportunity for learning, growth, and movement toward our Vision. Even challenges and conflicts are seen as opportunities when we are operating with our oxytocin system.

The more we experience the sensation of moving toward positive purpose, the more our positive intentions become habituated, and the more productive and successful we become. A basic principle of neuroscience is that neurons that fire together wire together (Rechtschaffen, 2014; Siegel, 2010). That's why part of my mission, in the context of administrative licensure, is to make visioning a habit for rising educational leaders.

Helping Students Find a Sense of Purpose

Even without knowing the brain science of why leaders need Vision to be happy and effective, students in the administrative licensure program are intuitively drawn to developing their inner core and identifying their purpose. Most of these people identify themselves as lifelong learners, making them curious about themselves, others, and the world around them. Identifying Vision and purpose is a pleasurable activity for these motivated learners, and visioning can revitalize their passion for education.

Of course, passion and purpose are not enough. Rising leaders also need to develop the skills, knowledge, and dispositions to manifest their purpose effectively—all of which they will spend the next year of practicum and courses learning and developing. But because we first take the time in the administrative licensure program to ensure our rising leaders have used visioning to define a higher purpose, they build the necessary internal resources needed to power them through the challenges of public service and to build communities that share meaningful and motivating visions.

Keeping It Real: Assessing What's Needed

- What are the requirements for certification for administrators and teachers in your state?
- Do they include requirements for learning about trauma, neuroscience, and mindfulness? If not, what could be done?

Who Am I? Why Do I Exist?

These are life's eternal questions and arguably education's ultimate quest. When educational leaders place their purpose for life at the center of their career, they give those around them permission to pursue lives of higher purpose, too. Together, my purpose, your purpose, our purpose create shared purpose. Together, we make a difference.

Renee's Leadership

Renee aims to empower people to make personal and systemic changes toward a world of well-being and to guide and inspire change. Diving into the neuroscience of vision and purpose, Renee shares how positive purpose can habituate positive intentions, productivity, and success. By encouraging people to identify "bone-deep" core values and mission, she espouses the value of leading with heart and hope, recognizing that your vision and plans will evolve over time.

Chapter 14

Youth Leadership

Julia Murphy

At the core of civic youth development, there is an inherent focus on building trust, relationships, and group cohesion so that youth are prepared to enter political and civic spheres. Civic youth development requires action. Young people can't just talk about issues; they must be provided with the invitation and support to act on the things that they find most meaningful. The embodiment of "lived citizenship" and, at the very least, the intentional welcoming of young people into certain spaces, bodies, communities, and roles are the first step toward changing the limitations that society has used to confine our youth.

BUILDING LEADERSHIP CAPACITY IN YOUTH

During the fall of my senior year, I took a class called Mapping Youth Leadership as an elective. The first exercise we did as a group was to create a list of stereotypes and commonly used descriptions of young people. *Lazy, entitled, arrogant, self-centered,* and *unmotivated* were all words that came to mind for myself and my peers—as young people ourselves.

Thinking about how the world and society perceives young people is essential to understanding how young people perceive the world. From there, the ever-important question was posed by our class facilitator and my personal mentor, Nick Longo: "How can we expect youth to be engaged, active citizens and leaders in their communities if people see them in a negative light?"

As a society, the negative connotations and descriptions that are associated with youth are detrimental to young people and their perceived capacity for leadership. In the political world, I quickly became familiar with the real-life application of these attitudes. When young people bring their ideas to the table (if they are offered a seat at all), they are often met with such responses as, "You haven't experienced enough," "You don't know how the world works," or "You're not ready to do meaningful work yet." I was discouraged to say the least when my first campaign assignment was to collect signatures in the freezing cold instead of taking on (or at least learning how to take on) more advanced projects.

When young people enter spaces where they believe they can be or aspire to be agents of change, the lack of agency they are given can be a direct hindrance on their self-esteem, goals, and motivation. Through personal reflection and in-class learning, I came to understand how disempowering perceptions of youth really can be.

If young people aren't viewed as being capable of contributing or offering a crucial point of view, then they will opt out of participating in certain endeavors when the time comes. If we are to prime and prepare the next generation of leaders, then we must start offering young people a seat at the table and, more importantly, listening to them when they get there.

Positive Youth Development Framework

The framework of positive youth development offers a promising starting point for us to restructure the discussion around building youth leadership. Emerging from an uptick in negative connotations about young people in the 1980s and 1990s, positive youth development redefines young people as resources instead of problems. As a result, young people are encouraged and invited into decision-making spaces, where they know that their voice is being heard and valued (Cammarota & Romero, 2011).

The result of the positive-youth-development theory and its subsequent critiques was the emergence of civic youth development. At the core of civic youth development, there is an inherent focus on building trust, relationships, and group cohesion so that youth are prepared to enter political and civic spheres. Civic youth development requires action—young people can't just talk about issues; they must be provided with the invitation and support to *act* on the things that they find most meaningful.

The embodiment of "lived citizenship" and, at the very least, the intentional welcoming of young people into certain spaces, bodies, communities, and roles are the first step toward changing the limitations that society has used to confine our youth.

How Schools Can Help

When it comes to building leadership capacity in youth, our education systems can serve as built-in infrastructures to tap into. What if, just as multiplication tables and punctuation rules are ingrained into pupils' minds, students are given the chance to learn about different styles of leadership and how they can thrive as a leader and apply skills they've obtained in a school setting? I often think of all the children who probably thought they weren't cut out to be leaders because they were shy or didn't speak up in class and therefore aren't considered for certain opportunities to get involved. What if we taught them that quiet leadership is a concept entirely of itself and that you don't have to be the most outspoken to positively influence others?

Positive youth development, civic youth work, and the idea of bringing young people to the table all stem from the same thing: demonstrating to young people that they are valued. Of course, the key here is that every student, regardless of race, gender, or socioeconomic status, feels valued so that they can recognize their own ability to be an informed, involved, and active member of whatever communities they belong to. You need not look further than the current climate movement to find an example of why valuing young people now is important to our success and survival as a society.

AN INTERNATIONAL YOUTH MOVEMENT

The Organisation to Decolonise International Schools (ODIS) started in 2020 with the goal to create a movement within *all international schools* and the expat community at large to expand the scope of international education beyond current Western values and to be intersectional and inclusive of all marginalized groups. Former international school students Clara Reynolds and Xoài David are the two youth who started ODIS. As International Baccalaureate (IB)–educated students, they took up a huge piece of much-needed work on accountability and amplification of diverse voices in the world of international education. They are part of a generation who are not going to accept lip service.

Clara, Xoài, and others are asking hard questions of leadership and boards. They initiated many conversations and public statements on Black Lives Matter and antiracist policies posted by international schools and organizations. They started a petition that stated,

> In the current climate it is now more obvious than ever that reforms are needed in educational institutions ensuring the teaching of Black, Indigenous and people of colours' (BIPOC) stories are taught to its students. This petition implores

the International Baccalaureate to hold itself accountable, because despite supposedly championing intercultural respect and open-mindedness, the IB has failed to make a stand on these issues. (Reynolds, n.d.)

Young people feel an obligation to fight for this because their lives in many ways depend on it; the need is much more urgent than it may be for people who are decades their elder.

CAPITALIZING ON YOUTH AGENCY AND VIGOR

As young people have diligently rallied around this cause, they have not only shed light on an important issue but also have created a ripple effect that spans beyond activism. Young people are getting involved in political campaigns to elect climate-centered candidates, they are focusing on environmental studies in school, they are taking up local fights in their hometowns to reduce litter and plastic waste, and they are challenging *all* of us to recognize the urgency of the moment.

We may not know who or when young people were officially incorporated into the climate-change discussion as key stakeholders or if they persistently worked to incorporate themselves so that they couldn't be ignored, but the agency that they have been given has completely changed the game. While they might not know everything—as no one truly does—they are working to make our world a better place because they believe that they have the capacity to do so.

It is long past time to ensure that young people are considered valuable players in any space where decisions are being made. While their perspectives may not be all-encapsulating, they are undoubtedly invaluable. In the realm of education, we would certainly be remiss if the voices and experiences of students were not at the heart of every discussion, as they are the ones for whom the system needs to work. Including and incorporating youth shows them that they are important and inspires them to seek out future opportunities for change making, big or small. By extending invitations to youth and involving them in important visioning work, we can engage in the cycle of creating a stockpile of quality, engaged, and passionate leaders who can one day make the choices that greatly impact our lives.

It is equally important to note that singular representation is rarely sufficient; young people are at their best when they are united, forming coalitions around causes that mean the most to them. Allow them to bring more people in, and as a result, your cause will be revitalized, challenged, and transformed for the better by the perspectives that young people so beautifully possess.

From Aiden Cardwell, Student

From the days of the first single-room schoolhouse, students' opinions on school matters have been largely swept under the rug. The prevailing belief of wisdom only being granted through age has historically refused us a voice. In the modern era, however, growing movements both within the student body and out have allowed students to speak on the issues that affect them most.

Growing up with educators as parents, it's plain to me that teachers and administrators have the best interests of their students eternally at heart. Yet, input from the student body is vital to proper policy and overall cohesiveness of any school. Staff and students are two sides of the same coin. Students feel heard now more than ever, and above all, they *care*. The ability to exercise that care through our voices has minimized that former feeling of powerlessness. For this, we have foundations such as the coalition to thank.

Building Youth Leadership Capacity at Your School

- In what ways are you building leadership capacity in youth?
- List places where students are offered an opportunity to lead. What is missing? Where are places for growth where students can be invited to the table?
- Ask your parents and students for their ideas and suggestions for increasing youth leadership.

Julia's Leadership

To build leadership capacity in youth, Julia argues we must intentionally welcome young people into certain spaces, bodies, communities, and roles to foster their civic development. By urging leaders to invite and capitalize on youth agency and vigor, Julia acknowledges the power of inviting a wider group to share in the visioning process as we strive for sustainable and intergenerational change.

Chapter 15

Visioning at Peace at Home Parenting Solutions

Ruth E. Freeman

Peace at Home Parenting Solutions' vision is to make digital parenting education available to larger numbers of diverse vulnerable families by working with our corporate partners' social responsibility programs.

"Courage is to tell the story of who you are with your whole heart," according to popular sociologist Brené Brown. Peace at Home Parenting Solutions is as close a manifestation of who I am as I can possibly imagine. So let's give this story a try.

I was raised by a mother whose mother lost most of her family in the Holocaust. When I was two years old, my mom went back to work and hired a full-time caregiver—an African American woman from the South whose ancestors were enslaved. My mother, my grandmother, and my caregiver Mildred were all good, loving, hard-working women. And they were all traumatized by the aggression visited upon them and their ancestors. Trauma comes down through both genes and behaviors. It is passed on insidiously, even in families like mine whom we might call "looking good."

My first hint about my past with trauma and aggression should have been the way I gravitated toward and loved caring for children and how even as a child I wanted to protect kids and make them happy. The most glaring hint came when my daughter, Andrea, finally decided to sit on the potty, and I could never wait in the bathroom with her. This is a milestone that most parents joyfully look forward to. It signals the end of diapers. However, I always called on my husband, Joe, to help.

I would usually feel queasy, get a stomachache, or experience that antsy sensation when you just want to run away when I was in the bathroom with Andrea. Only after some reflection and a conversation with an older brother and a former therapist did I realize how Mildred's emotional pain had not only affected me at an early age but had also left an emotional scar.

WHAT IS ALEXITHYMIA?

Psychiatrists call this phenomenon alexithymia—Greek for not having words for feelings. Many traumatized children and adults simply cannot describe what they are feeling because they cannot identify what their physical sensations mean. They may look furious but deny that they are angry; they may appear terrified but say that they are fine. Not being able to discern what is going on inside their bodies causes them to be out of touch with their needs, and they have trouble taking care of themselves, whether it involves eating the right amount at the right time or getting the sleep they need.

Alexithymics might substitute the language of action for that of emotion. When asked, "How would you feel if you saw a truck coming at you at 80 miles per hour?" Most people would say, "I'd be terrified," or "I'd be frozen with fear." An alexithymic might reply, "How would I feel? I don't know. I'd get out of the way." They tend to register emotions as physical problems rather than as signals that something deserves their attention. Instead of feeling angry or sad, they experience muscle pain, bowel irregularities, or other symptoms for which no cause can be found (Van der Kolk, 2014, p. 100).

Leaving her two young sons with her mother, Mildred came up North to make some money to support her family. One way Mildred expressed her grief and anger about her children, her family, and her ancestors was the anger she expressed because I wasn't potty trained. Mildred used the only tools she had to "train" me—threatening, yelling, and hitting.

When I tried to help my own toddler with toilet training, my body remembered, even as I had forgotten Mildred's rage and corporal punishment. Our bodies remember our losses and our fears. Our bodies remember the terror. We use a lot of strategies—food, substances, sex, technology, work, exercise, aggression—anything to get away from the disturbing, inconvenient, and confusing story our bodies sometimes try to tell us.

What about you? How have you come to learn about traumatic experiences from family members, friends, and colleagues, as well as from students at your school, and supported them through their journeys?

AN UNREASONABLE MISSION

A year or two before our daughter was born, I attended a workshop with Joe. We were asked to stand up in front of the group and declare our mission. I volunteered to share without actually knowing what I was going to say. Yet this powerful energy seemed to be coming up from my solar plexus, and something inside me wanted to be spoken out loud.

The following words came out of my mouth: "My mission is to eliminate aggression visited upon children in their homes." The language seemed so archaic; the mission way too big. And only later did I discover how my personal history was driving those words.

That mission has guided my career as a clinician and parenting educator to this day. I invite parents to talk about their children and then tell them I'll give them tools to improve discipline. US parents seem to measure their worth as parents based on compliance: "Do my kids do what I want when I want it?" Sadly, the emphasis on following directions often drives parents to use approaches that can steal important assets from children, like courage, confidence, curiosity, and positive attachment.

I started out teaching in schools, churches, and nonprofit organizations. I expanded this work to include "lunch and learn" sessions in corporate conference rooms. These popular sessions were organized by an inspiring wellness program coordinator at a large insurance company with more than 50,000 employees working across the United States. I switched to webinars under her guidance after the success with this company. This proved to be a more sustainable platform, and more parents began connecting with us in the process. Within a few months, there were 200–300 parents on waiting lists. This was the first turning point in my career that led to the creation of our company, Peace at Home Parenting Solutions.

THE POWER OF PROGRAM EVALUATION

Another powerful moment came when a young University of Connecticut professor asked if she could evaluate our program to determine if we were actually affecting parent behavior through digital classes. At the time, there wasn't much evidence about the impact of webinars on parent learning. One corporate client agreed to participate in the research. We had received nearly 100% overall satisfaction among those corporate participants, but changing parent behavior seemed like a much bigger challenge.

At the end of the process, our researcher published two articles and declared over lunch that I had achieved the "gold standard of parenting"

(Russell & Lincoln, 2017). Parents reported, after just one 1-hour webinar, decreased hostile and dysfunctional parenting practices—screaming, yelling, threatening, harsh punishment, and hitting. I almost burst into tears—here was evidence that indeed we were making progress on the mission that called me decades earlier.

A Response from a Parent

I've taken a few of your online parenting sessions, and I always walk away feeling more empowered as a parent to make better decisions and approach my two children. They are 1½ and 4 years old and both very strong willed, and I mean that in the very best way. The self-regulation session you offered has given me actionable steps and a new frame of mind around how to best help them "self-regulate" without squelching their will, independence, spirit, or personality.

—Heather, Connecticut

Parenting during the Pandemic

While pandemic parenting challenges are without precedent, the essential features of what helps children and their parents thrive remain unchanged. Initial research findings related to pandemic stressors for families indicated that parental support and increased perceived control are promising interventions (Brown et al., 2020). In addition to reducing dysfunctional discipline practices, the evaluation found the following outcomes among our class participants:

- increased feelings of being supported in parenting goals
- increased sense of control and competence with their children

That evaluation not only got us started, but it also helped keep us on course as the pandemic unfolded. We recognized that our classes gave parents what they needed during these difficult times—a sense of support and control.

Another Parent's Comments

Now that my daughter is 31 months, I find things more challenging as I find my parents coming through (I'm not interested in my daughter growing up in the same environment I did). . . . I feel as though you've given me a life raft (I'm so emotional about it really) because what I heard last night makes sense to me, just like I knew not to let her cry. I think it's so hard and scary being a parent, especially now, and no one really talks about that. . . . I think our inner child lives on and tugs at us a bit more when we become parents.

—Jessica, Massachusetts

BECOMING A BUSINESS: A TEAM TRANSFORMS MY PERSONAL MISSION

The final important step in the creation of Peace at Home Parenting Solutions was a nudge from that same daughter whose potty training I tried to avoid. Andrea is a director of digital marketing analytics in a major advertising company. She patiently guided me toward imagining an online company. Andrea; my husband, Joe, who is also a social worker; and a small group of wise and deeply caring colleagues and friends came together as a leadership team to guide the formation of Peace at Home Parenting Solutions.

This team met regularly, asked important questions, and strategically guided our direction. The company was named after a response that parents inserted on their class feedback forms under the question, "Any other comments?" Several parents noted that they were now experiencing more "peace at home." This idea made my heart sing.

My personal mission of eliminating aggression was transformed by our team into a more positive purpose. Our mission is now to connect parents with inspiring experts and each other so they can gain the skills and support they need to build positive, peaceful, and joyful families. The importance of felt support from the surrounding community cannot be discounted.

Parents Want Help with Parenting

It was not only our corporate wellness coordinator and our leadership team who inspired us, but well-respected organizations also were documenting the need for parenting support, ideally online. In October 2015, ZERO TO THREE conducted a national survey called, "Tuning In: Parents of Young Children Tell Us What They Think, Know and Need." Here is what they learned from parents who responded:

- 58% find the importance of the first five years both "motivating and terrifying."
- 42% do not want to yell as quickly as they do.
- 30% say, "I spank even though I don't feel okay about it."

- 48% don't feel they are getting the support they need when they feel stressed.
- 54% want information from a "special website or blog from child development experts."

Parenting educators love to get our hands on parents in those first five years, when parent-child interactions are shaping the brain so powerfully. Behaviors, beliefs, capacities, and relationship styles are forming in ways that will likely last a lifetime. We also know that as children get older, challenges can be more complex. Dealing with adolescence brings many parents to their knees. Mark Brackett (2019), founder and director of the Yale Center for Emotional Intelligences, notes in his popular book *Permission to Feel* that US youth are in the bottom quarter of developed nations, with stress levels higher than adults:

- Our teens are the world leaders in violence, binge drinking, marijuana use, and obesity.
- More than half of college students experience overwhelming anxiety.

Parents have made it clear to us that they want and need support, knowledge, and tools through every stage of child development.

A Question for You: Parent Involvement

How is your school communicating and sharing resources with parents, caregivers, and family members of your students?

CORPORATE PARTNERS AS OUR GUIDES

The need was clear: Our corporate wellness colleagues were increasingly acknowledging that parenting can be especially challenging for working parents. We did not anticipate, however, the degree to which wellness coordinators and diversity and inclusion professionals would guide our development.

Even beyond our first "angel" who insisted we go digital, several corporate partners chose to go beyond their basic packaged parenting classes and offer our classes developed with the expertise of our teachers, all of whom hold advanced degrees and have years of experience with parents and children. Organizations quickly recognized the power of our experience and expertise in helping parents understand developmental stages and evidence-based approaches that often solve challenges on the spot.

OUR CORPORATE PARTNERS HELPED US BUILD PEACE AT HOME BY HELPING TO

- make our classes interactive through inviting parents to submit specific questions in the chat, "raise their hands," engage in a live conversation with the teacher, and participate in frequent polls;
- define which data points we should collect to meaningfully contribute to their company assessment and planning processes;
- host our early classes through their own WebEx systems and encourage us to develop our own platform and learning management system to make it easier for parents to connect directly with us;
- expand our content in important ways by requesting classes and roundtable conversations on current issues, such as talking with kids about racism and protest, raising LGBTQ+ children, and responding to mental health issues among children and teens since the pandemic; and
- shape the way we deliver content, including the development of Flash Classes (focused recorded videos, about 15 minutes long, that parents can access on the run); one-on-one brief online coaching sessions to help parents solve specific, persistent challenges; monthly Q&A sessions where parents can get help applying ideas they learn in class; and a private, monitored Facebook group of 1,000+ parents and professionals to talk about challenges and share resources.

GATHERING OUR PEACE AT HOME TEACHERS

Peace at Home Parenting Solutions has created an opportunity to work with diverse specialists who have the answers that parents need. As a parenting educator, I was a generalist, but when parents asked about infants, toddlers, children with ADHD or autism, or how to motivate kids in school, I was out of my league. Our contracts with corporate and nonprofit organizations gave us the budget needed to recruit experts in their fields who were grounded in both research and practical experience. Our staff is excited to challenge ourselves to translate research into practical tools that diverse parents across the country can use to solve problems and build the nurturing families they really want.

Our teachers meet quarterly to discuss new ideas and current parenting challenges. We home in on key themes that we want to use across classes, such as:

- the power of playfulness and the ways it calms the brain and invites cooperation and learning
- the role of parents as children's "calm center" as well as applying self-regulation and coregulation
- the importance of recognizing the way that behavior often shows us what children need—reaching out rather than acting out

Outcomes and Plans for the Future

In 2020, we had the privilege of serving 8,382 class participants in 156 public classes and 105 corporate classes, with a 97% overall satisfaction rate. We have built 27 Solutions Libraries—collections of 5–10 Flash Classes focusing on specific topics like birth-to-5 development, special needs, and mental health literacy.

In addition to members of the public, parents came from a wide range of companies, such as CVS Health, LEGO Systems, and Yum! Brands, as well as such nonprofit organizations as Big Brothers Big Sisters and Beacon Health Options of Connecticut. We also serve the professors and staff at Massachusetts Institute of Technology (MIT), all Medicaid members living in Connecticut, and community members in 12 Connecticut towns.

We have a few specific projects we hope to launch:

- One program will focus on increasing safe birth outcomes for women of color through education and support.
- We want to expand our focus on increasing parent mental health literacy and child therapists' engagement of parents in the therapeutic process through effective parent assessment and targeted integration of parenting education into the treatment process.
- We want to build our program for Spanish-speaking parents and reach a larger audience with culturally sensitive content and delivery.

In all these programs, we will seek funding to continue having researchers evaluate our work, and we will partner with parents from diverse backgrounds to help us to come closer to our vision for all children to grow up in families who help them thrive, reach their potential, and live in peace.

Keeping It Real: Parent Involvement

Even though these are tremendous ideas and programs, it can be challenging to capture the interest of schools. Here are a few considerations:

- How interested are schools in helping parents with parenting?

- Where will the funding come from to access programs such as these?
- Who in the school or district will be a parent liaison, and what role will that person play in supporting parents and staff as parents go through programs like these?
- How can this be implemented so that there is follow-up and support from school staff?

Ruth's Leadership

To better support parents and eliminate aggression visited on children in their homes, Ruth and Peace at Home Parenting Solutions are working to make parenting education accessible to larger numbers of diverse vulnerable families. Driven by her urgent personal mission, Ruth understands the power of leading with heart and hope and acknowledging that your vision and plans will evolve over time. She urges us to acknowledge stress and trauma and build resilience, self-care, and vitality, and she fully embraces putting equity and justice at the center of her vision.

PART VI

Scalability and Sustainability

THE INTEGRAL ROLE OF ADVOCACY, SELF-CARE, AND COLLECTIVE EFFICACY

Ultimately, after all the effort to lead transformational changes, we want to reach many—many educators, many schools, and many students—and we want these essential practices to stand the test of time. If you are like us, when you reflect on the number of hours it will take and the many hours you have already invested in change, you want to be able to look back and see lasting results. To arrive at scalability and sustainability, leaders will need to persevere. You can expect that, as you conquer one obstacle, another will appear, almost like clockwork.

In Part II we explore trauma, racism, and injustice, as our contributors explain their visions and journeys for schools to play a significant role in bringing healing to so many. What if we created space for dialogue and discussion around systemic inequities, structural racism, and antiracism? There are so many layers to the needed healing, and in order to heal, we need to address these inequities head on.

HEALING

The needed healing involves so much. Here are a few considerations:

- Instead of reacting with frustration and punitive measures, what if schools embraced students with compassion and understanding?

- What if we focused on increasing protective factors, increasing resilience, and giving students the tools to succeed?
- What if we destigmatized self-care, reframing it as a necessary maintenance activity instead of a self-indulgent luxury?
- How might we come together to support, encourage, and strengthen each other so we might achieve what once seemed impossible—remodeling the education system to better serve *all* students?

ADVOCACY

A crucial component that is absent from many leadership texts is advocacy. We know about the importance of connectedness and belonging; however, a closely related variable, advocacy, has received little attention. Yet we all appreciate the support of others, be they mentors, peer mediators, fellow team members, family, or friends.

The word *advocacy* also connotes the support for ideas—advocating for change—and changing legislation to advance a cause as well as serving as an advocate for someone who may need additional support or resources. Earlier in this book, Hawkins (Chapter 4), Kohler (Chapter 9), and Liabenow and Domagalski (Chapter 11) reference the work they are doing to advocate for change, including how they are supporting others to advance healing, overcome racism, and alleviate trauma.

Dan Siegel (2010) in *Mindsight* describes the "neurobiology of we" and the importance of becoming advocates for one another, saying, "[T]he brain is a social organ and our relationships with one another are not a luxury but an essential nutrient for our survival" (p. 211). As he says, "we must look inward"; we must know ourselves before we can "become receptive" to knowing others. We are suffering in part, according to Siegel, because when we cannot identify with someone else; "we see others as objects, as 'them' rather than 'us'" (p. 257).

In essence, many have shut off neural "circuits of compassion." Further, when we see threats, we may distort what we see in others, "putting our humanity at risk" (Siegel, 2010, p. 258). When we consider how difficult it has come to bridge our political and ideological differences, Siegel's words ring true. For the great teamwork that will be needed in the months and years to come, we must strive for harmony.

SELF-CARE

Siegel (2010) explains not only the need for advocacy but for self-care. Self-care can be enhanced when we understand our brains and how we can help our brains heal, not only healing wounds and overcoming trauma, but also increasing our own sense of vitality and well-being. A part of this is our mind-set. However, there is a bodily component to our well-being. We can "up" our efficacy by our own self-care. Our self-care begins with considerations for diet and nutrition; adequate sleep exercise; and the intentional work of yoga, breath work, and meditation (Mason, Asby, et al., 2021; Mason, Donald, et al., 2021; Mason, Rivers Murphy, & Jackson, 2019; 2022).

EQUITY

While everyone can benefit from self-care, people of color face systemic challenges that others do not. Wanting to address this, Kevin Simpson shares in Chapter 16 how he established the Association of International Educators and Leaders of Color (AIELOC) to amplify the work of international educators and leaders of color and create a space for antiracist conversations and systems to take place. The group regularly asks, "What will it take to end racism and discrimination in the international school ecosystem?" AIELOC invites all past, present, and future educators and leaders around the world to speak up, learn, and advocate for change.

PEAK PERFORMANCE AND COLLECTIVE EFFICACY

In *The Leading Brain: Neuroscience Hacks to Working Smarter, Better, Happier*, Friederike Fabritius and Hands Hageman (2018) reference "collective peak performance," describing the joy that is palatable when not only individuals but also a team experience a sense of being in the flow (Csikszentmihalyi, 1997). Fabritius and Hageman provide numerous examples to help readers understand the efficacy of this collective "social" flow.

Some components of achieving this social flow and collective peak performance are challenges and clear goals, extraordinary communication that involves "real-time interactions" that almost parallel a jazz performance, and flexible teamwork that contributes to optimal collaboration. As Fabritius and Hageman remind us, with optimal collaboration, our egos stand aside as the group moves ahead.

Imagine such energizing—such vital—teamwork. As we know all too well, we are facing significant challenges. If your team has been engaged in visioning, you are likely to have clear goals. When educators band together and dare to believe, they can positively affect their own lives and the lives of their students as they foster transformational change (Donohoo & Hite, 2021). Peter DeWitt (2021) explains that we build collective leadership efficacy by

- understanding one another,
- truly collaborating, and
- understanding the impact we want to make.

Effective groups include diverse voices and perspectives, and they focus on developing the leadership capacity of others.

BUILDING COLLECTIVE EFFICACY

- What are you doing to support diversity and collective efficacy?
- What are the barriers?
- Are you seeing progress?

In Chapter 17, Christine Mason and Martha Staeheli share how the New England Mental Health Technology Transfer Center is relying on collective efficacy to promote compassionate school practices and support staff and student well-being. In forming the Childhood-Trauma Learning Collaborative (C-TLC), they sought to build leadership capacity in New England and focused on eliminating punitive school discipline, enhancing interactions with students and families, and fostering resilience and self-care in order to eradicate stigma, reduce inequity and injustice, and "help each other ride the inevitable waves of joy, sorrow, setbacks, and success that we each experience."

CHANGING OUR PRACTICES, POLICIES, AND PROCEDURES

In Chapter 18, Victoria Romero, coauthor of *Race Resilience* (Romero, Warner, & Hendrickson, 2022), asks us to reflect on why our mission statements continue to promote a vision of educational equity that schools in our nation rarely achieve. Victoria explores what school communities might look like if educators are intentional about mitigating the impact of structural racism in education.

When educators are conscious of barriers that impede the social-emotional and academic growth of their students, they change their practice, policies, and procedures and can improve student outcomes. How might we all learn from Victoria and implement intentional change to create race-resilient school cultures in our communities?

LASTING CHANGE

Let's be clear: The work we are doing requires much from many. It is no small task! It will require collective action, visionary leadership, and self-care at each step of the long and arduous journey. Along the way, we will see the benefits in the elevation of a sense of well-being, efficacy, and purpose. And there are no guarantees; there is uncertainty and the looming presence of yet another initiative. Our internal and external worlds will evolve as we are in the midst of these changes. However, we have significant knowledge and tools. And many ready to join us—yet there is substantial hope—hope for today and for the future.

Chapter 16

Advocacy and Equity for International Educators

Kevin Simpson

The vision for the Association for International Educators and Leaders of Color (AIELOC) is to create a space where Black, Indigenous, and people of color (BIPOC) are centered and where BIPOC can come and be their authentic selves. We are devoted to sharing opportunities for educators and leaders of color interested in serving globally and ensuring our work reflects the diversity of the world.

In 2007, after working at Vientiane International School in Laos, I returned to the United States and vowed to work in education globally. Returning to the Washington, DC, area seemed the right choice, as there are many international organizations in the city. Through research, volunteer work, and connecting with a plethora of folks, I discovered that I needed to create what I did not see.

GOING GLOBAL

Education entrepreneurs can be nonprofit or for-profit; for the folks we talk to every day, mission is the most important thing, and few expect to end up rich. . . . Increasingly, education entrepreneurs are seen as vital to wider change.

—Jonathan Schorr, NewSchools Venture Fund, 2012

I focused on sharing my new love for global education and learning about cultures. During that same year, I would set up a company called KDSL USA. The vision was to partner with organizations worldwide to increase student achievement, teacher knowledge, and education leadership. How this would be done? Who would be involved? What would work look like?

An international opportunity arrived. This work was the result of attending several education events, reading, and meeting people who served as guides. The goal was to align with people and organizations who had similar ambitions and look beyond what others were doing.

One such group was the Student Support Center in DC, where I met Dr. Christine Mason. This group focused on provided high-quality professional development in the form of coaching and more to local charter schools. They hired me as an education consultant after facilitating professional development with a new teacher cohort. This work and being selected to collaborate as a senior associate on a new project seeking to transform math teaching and learning in Maryland (connected with a focus on math practices from Asia) allowed me to focus on education locally.

In addition, I set up an education and innovation group that met monthly around Virginia and Washington, DC. This was a space for entrepreneurs, educators, and leaders to assemble, learn from each other about local and global topics, and collaborate. This group grew as others shared with colleagues via word of mouth. My vision was still to work in education globally.

EXPERIENCES IN THE MIDDLE EAST

More than a year later, two opportunities in the Middle East would lead me back abroad. The first was an opportunity to mentor teachers in Doha, Qatar, who were working on transforming teaching and learning. The second was an opportunity to teach and lead at a new International Baccalaureate School in Dubai, United Arab Emirates. Dubai allowed time and space after each workday to continue to create the vision for KDSL USA. This had not been fully done because we had taken on new local projects. At this time, the vision remained the same, as I sought ways to increase our work globally.

After returning to the United States, it was apparent that my head and heart were tuned into working globally. At the end of 2011, I worked as a freelance consultant in the United Arab Emirates, splitting time between DC and Dubai, before setting up a company in 2013. Working with two schools led to invites to other schools, and we set up the first EdCamp overseas. A large publishing company hired me to be an exclusive trainer on projects in the Middle East, Europe, and Africa, and I was invited to give talks and workshops at several conferences and schools in Asia, Central America, South America, and the Caribbean.

THE EVOLUTION OF OUR WORK

After nine years of collaborating with education organizations around the world, KDSL USA transformed into KDSL Global in 2016 to rethink the previous work. I had started in 2007 in the Washington, DC, area and then moved to Dubai, United Arab Emirates, in 2013. Year 10 needed to be different. I shifted to a leading learning organization focused on empowering educators and education businesses globally.

A RESTART AND REBRANDING

The restart meant a rebranding with a new logo and new tagline and informing previous clients. Everyone was supportive of this move and onboard with the vision. Work over three months was completed before the launch at the 2016 GCC Association for Supervision and Curriculum Development (ASCD) MENA Teacher Summit. This was widely attended by educators and leaders from around the Middle East, Asia, and Africa.

To garner support, we aligned with people and organizations who had similar visions to the work we were doing and seeking to do. We also

- listened to what people and organizations needed and provided it at a high level of delivery;
- remained open and willing to change (transition from KDSL USA to KDSL Global);
- offered something new and unique (conferences for American curriculum educators in Dubai); and
- worked with a wide range of stakeholders, such as freelancers, education service providers, publishing companies, government agencies, associations, international schools, foundations, and technology companies.

ADDRESSING DISCRIMINATION

At some point when you have proven yourself and fought your way into institutions that were not built for you, when you've proven you can compete and excel at the highest level, you have to decide that you are done forcing yourself in.

> *For too long, powerful people have expected the people they have mistreated and marginalized to sacrifice themselves to make things whole. The burden of working for racial justice is laid on the very people bearing the brunt of the injustice, and not the powerful people who maintain it. I say to you: I refuse.*
>
> —Nikole Hannah-Jones

We created AIELOC in 2017 because a highly qualified colleague of color shared that she was turned down for an interview as head of an international school because they were seeking a British person. The American organization with whom she was registered claimed to have a nondiscriminatory policy, which states that they do not discriminate on the basis of race, religion, gender, sexual orientation, national origin, age, or on any other basis. In January 2020, we evolved AIELOC to an association open to all past, present, and future educators and leaders around the world committed to speaking up, learning, advocating for change, taking action in addressing racism and discrimination in the international school ecosystem, amplifying the work of BIPOC, and researching topics of our own interest.

BIPOC educators are not just adjusting to the global pandemic of COVID but also the global "permanence of racism" (Pollaert, 2020). The intersectionality of the privileges of White international school educators is evident when you consider how well they continue to move from school to school. These educators take advantage of the neocolonial international education system by making large salaries, hiring local individuals to take care of their chores and watch their children, and get away with behavior that is literally illegal in their passport countries of the United States or the United Kingdom.

The main reason BIPOC educators remain committed to this racist system is the marginalized students. Marginalized educators know what it is like to feel oppressed, to jump through hoops to survive in a system that is not made for them, and to work twice as hard to get half as far. The Hippocratic oath as educators is to prioritize our students; marginalized educators live that commitment. If international schools were originally created for colonizers' children, then are they colonizing institutions?

The short answer is yes. Many international schools promote internationalism on the surface but employ oppressive systems daily. Recruitment, the school board, vendors, accreditation agencies, curricula, student activities, professional development/learning, and even daily conversations center and uplift one group of people.

AIELOC wants the anti-racist conversations and systems to take place.

VISIONS IN CONVERSATIONS

Here are some examples of what we vision in conversations:

POC EDUCATOR: Mrs. X, my supervisor just threw a microaggression at me this morning.

HUMAN RESOURCES (HR) REPRESENTATIVE: Oh no. Are you okay? Please take the next three days to heal. Because we do not yet have a trauma-informed therapist internally, here is an external agency that you can talk to while you are working on self-care. The school will cover the copay, will find coverage for you, and will start the 10-step antiracist intervention plan for Mrs. X right away.

POC EDUCATOR: I don't know who to talk to. My supervisor just threw a microaggression at me.

COLLEAGUE: That is awful. Are you okay? Our HR director is a member of the school diversity, equity, and inclusion (DEI) team and certified in antiracist human resources. They can advise you on what to do next. Thank you for trusting me with your truth.

POC EDUCATOR: I do not feel safe being myself at work.

SCHOOL LEADER: Oh dear. It sounds like we need to continue to grow. Thank you so much for trusting me with your perspective. I hear you. I will call an emergency meeting with the leadership team in an hour so we can analyze what aspects of your day could have been unsafe for you. We especially prioritize the well-being of teachers of color. If you have any tips for us, we are ready to listen. Thank you again for sharing your expertise. We are so lucky to have you.

ACCREDITING ORGANIZATION/RECRUITMENT FIRM/EDUCATIONAL AGENCY: We are impressed with your DEI work. Would you be able to present at our conference on antiracism?

WHITE EDUCATOR: Thank you for acknowledging my work. However, my experience with antiracism cannot compare to the expertise of people of color. Here is a list of POC that you can contact. They deserve the recognition for their work. Your organization should also look into hiring only POC for antiracism issues, unless the session has to do with White accountability.

WHITE LEADER: You are considered White passing, so why do you support BIPOC agenda?

WHITE-PASSING POC: The privilege I have had by being able to pass as a White person is real. I feel very lucky. However, I am a person of color and prefer to be referred to as such. I am proud of my heritage and ancestry.

A truly diverse, equitable, inclusive, and just international school cannot survive in this White-body-supremacist ecosystem. Our vision for AIELOC has been to create a space where BIPOC are centered and where BIPOC can come and be their authentic selves.

Educators come to AIELOC abused and traumatized by these institutions that were built against them. AIELOC welcomes them with open arms and hearts. As the organization picks out the true believers, it is strategically spreading out to organizations. We are devoted to sharing opportunities for educators and leaders of color interested in serving globally and ensuring our work reflects the diversity of the world.

SELF-CARE TO SUSTAIN

Self-care means taking care of yourself so that you can be healthy, you can be well, you can do your job, you can help and care for others, and you can do all the things you need to and want to accomplish in a day.

—*Moira Lawler*

At AIELOC, we have a group who focuses on self-care. Each month, they invite our members to assemble at a dedicated time and space where their well-being is prioritized. This may be meditation, physical activity, or reading and reflection, among other things. The beauty is that this group is quite eclectic, with a physical education leader, a counselor, a teacher, and a service and learning coordinator. They each bring a unique perspective based on their roles.

Part of our work at AIELOC is devoted to fighting racism and discrimination. There is an emotional impact this work will have on one's being. Our work is centered on humans who many times are tired of being viewed as inhuman. In order to take care of others, our team sees it as necessary to take care of ourselves. Sustaining and enduring change will not happen if we do not take care of ourselves. It says a lot about who an organization is and it values when it makes this a priority. At AIELOC, we value individuals who are well and who get to be their full selves.

Monthly Community Visioning

"What will it take to end racism and discrimination in the international school ecosystem?" is one question we address monthly in our community visioning sessions. These virtual forums started in 2021 and are open to all stakeholders in the international school ecosystem. It will take all of us to make the necessary changes that some believe will take a long time. Schools, individuals, and organizations are invited to share their work with diversity, equity, inclusion, and justice (DEIJ).

AIELOC is not an organization that needs the DEIJ labels. It is diverse, inclusive, equitable, and just. This has been a long time coming. There is too much White comfort and performance. We are going to continue to amplify the voices of BIPOC who are committed to continuing the work toward liberation. AIELOC will continue to grow and thrive.

Put Vision into Action

One way the AIELOC leadership team ensures their vision is ever present is their pledge, the International Educator Equity Statement, which, drives the work to disrupt inequitable practices in the international school ecosystem. The pledge is shared with any new member to the organization. It is comprised of the tasks members will engage in and is posted weekly on social media and reviewed by the team.

Head of School in Finland Kathleen Naglee retweets and shares excerpts from the pledge on Twitter, the Principal's Training Center embedded it as part of their summer courses, and the AIELOC Team collaborated with the International Educator to create a call to action using language from the pledge. The goal is for the entire international school ecosystem to adopt the statement and put the words into action.

The following is a sample from the pledge:

We Pledge To:
- Not wait any longer but to speak up now about racism and all forms of discrimination in international education.
- Be students of our host cultures and to actively work toward understanding and engaging our local communities.
- Counter xenophobia and long-standing cultural biases that place certain countries or cultures above others.

Keeping It Real: Racism and Global Communities

- How much do you know about international systems of education?
- When we consider our global communities, it is likely that the racism explore in this chapter is the tip of the iceberg. Racism likely runs deep across many global businesses. If we are interested in the global healing described in Chapter 4, then what role might schools, districts, and organizations play in helping to advance the needed healing?
- How important is it to see leaders of color in positions of influence both in the United States and globally?

Kevin's Leadership

After a highly qualified colleague of color was turned down for a job due to her nationality, Kevin dedicated himself to creating space where BIPOC can collaborate, empower each other, and simply be their authentic selves. He understands the importance of beginning with a sense of urgency, leading with heart and hope, embracing equity and justice, and sharing in the visioning process.

Chapter 17

The Collective Efficacy of Compassionate School Practices

Christine Mason and Martha Staeheli

We envision a growing network of caring, compassionate schools where the school community (students, staff, and families) support the mental health and well-being of each other, moment by moment, day by day, year after year. We envision a network of school leaders who support each other, sharing and problem solving, with compassionate practices that eliminate punitive school discipline, enhance interactions with students and families, and foster self-care.

From a compassionate, heart centered base, we eradicate stigma, reduce inequity and injustice, empower staff and students, develop caring relationships, and help each other ride the inevitable waves of joy, sorrow, setbacks, and success that we each experience. With compassionate practices, we believe schools can reduce the fears, concerns, and stigma of children and youth facing the most serious emotional and behavioral challenges.

By increasing mental health literacy and collaborating with mental health providers while educators implement compassionate protocol and practices, members of school communities will help alleviate the impact of childhood trauma, build protective factors and resilience, and further the well-being of all members of school communities. In compassionate schools, children and youth will flourish; find joy; and build positive, protective relationships as they learn skills that will help them transform our culture to one of kindness, understanding, and caring.

Chapter 17

OUR CHARGE

In 2018, the Program for Recovery and Community Health (PRCH) at Yale University was notified that the Substance Abuse Mental Health Services Administration (SAMHSA) was providing extra funds to 10 regional mental health centers, including the one at Yale. (See Mental Health Technology Transfer Center, 2021, for more about these regional centers.) The goal was to extend services that improved the mental health of adults in order to address the mental health challenges of youth.

The funds were allocated to disseminate best practices to school staff and to more actively engage schools in addressing the mental health concerns of children and youth. When we designed the Childhood-Trauma Learning Collaborative (C-TLC), we were told that funds might last one year. What could be done in one year? We thought about the importance of a network of supports for adults who would undertake the challenge of transforming their school cultures.

In many ways PRCH and the Center for Educational Improvement (CEI) were perfect partners for this undertaking. Our underlying philosophies and belief systems are similar, and it was in a sense a marriage of understanding mental health and education, both relying on a strengths-based approach based on peer supports, evidence-based practices, and systemic change.

The Program for Recovery and Community Health

PRCH was established in 2000 and is based in the Yale School of Medicine Department of Psychiatry. Co-led by Larry Davidson, PhD, and Chyrell Bellamy, PhD, MSW, PRCH has become an internationally recognized center for research, evaluation, education, policy development, consultation, and technical assistance aimed at transforming mental health systems to provide strength-based, culturally responsive, and person- and family-centered care to people living with psychiatric disability, their loved ones, and their communities.

To carry out this work, PRCH has received funding from state agencies, most prominently from the Connecticut Department of Mental Health and Addiction Services, and from such federal research institutions as the National Institute of Mental Health, the Patient-Centered Outcomes Research Institute, the US Substance Abuse and Mental Health Services Administration, and the National Institute on Drug Abuse.

In addition, PRCH contracts with public and nonprofit organizations seeking evaluation and programmatic consultation in the areas of recovery, person-centered care, health disparities, and community inclusion. At the center of our work remains our commitment to supporting individuals in their own recovery process and in promoting their pursuit of their own aspirations and interests, beyond the illness- and deficit-based paradigm from which the mental health system has historically operated.

The Center for Educational Improvement

CEI, established in 2009, works largely with a network of school principals for outcomes similar to those of PRCH but with a focus on school leaders and children and youth to increase their sense of empowerment and well-being through what we term Heart Centered Learning (see Chapter 10). Heart Centered Learning and its Five Cs (consciousness, compassion, confidence, courage, and community) provide a concrete way to infuse compassion into schools.

However, given the extent of societal violence, when we implemented the C-TLC in 2019, we realized that this was a huge undertaking, that the needed transformational change would take years, and that most efforts to improve social-emotional health were far too fragmented. We realized the needed changes would not come about with social-emotional learning (SEL) as an optional after-school activity or through isolated lessons delivered one or two days a week over a few years. With the impact of COVID-19, racial unrest, and divisiveness in the United States, the need for extensive and intensive compassion-oriented supports has grown.

In contrast to many other approaches, CEI provides resources to help schools embed the Five Cs throughout the academic school day (Mason, Rivers Murphy, & Jackson, 2019, 2020). Over the course of the last decade, CEI has offered webinars and monthly e-newsletters, presented at national and state conferences, conducted research, and provided technical assistance to schools. By 2018, CEI had conducted pilot projects in four schools and developed the School–Compassionate Culture Analytical Tool for Educators (S-CCATE) and an accompanying assessment measure, and they had evidence from educators that student and teacher self-care, compassion, and resilience had improved with our practices.

Some of the unique features of our approach are its intentional inclusion of understanding neuroplasticity and the neurobiology of trauma, including consciousness, or mindful awareness, of self and others as an essential component to our model. It also focuses on building equity, courage, and resilience as well as enhancing self-care and strengthening the competency of caring school leaders (see also chapter 7).

Self-Care Is Crucial

As time passes and COVID extends its long reach into our days, our nights, and our futures, the importance of self-care becomes all that more clear. While Heart Centered Learning began with a premise that teacher and administrator self-care sets the stage for compassionate school cultures, each day it becomes more and more crucial that we elevate self-care. Our initial premise was that we couldn't teach what we didn't understand, and if we were to help others come to a place of compassion and confidence using mindfulness tools, then we needed to walk the walk.

How is self-care supported in your school and in your classrooms? Is it enough? When we are feeling more stress and trauma, we must increase our self-care practices to maintain an equilibrium. Think of it as a scale: we must offset our stress and trauma with greater self-care. As we become weary of masks, of quarantines, of uncertainty, we can maintain strength and courage through spending more time with some of the primary tools of self-care: breath work, yoga, exercise, mindfulness, and meditation, along with enhanced sleep, nutrition, and opportunities to show support for and encourage others. We also find time to celebrate even small gains, share our concerns and fears, and find our way forward.

Years 1 and 2 of the Childhood-Trauma Learning Collaborative

When PRCH and CEI joined forces, our vision was to build leadership capacity in the New England region so that a growing network of educators would understand and implement practices in schools that could alleviate mental health challenges of children and youth. We realized that trauma and stress in children are manifested in many ways, including heightened fear, anxiety, and depression, and that early intervention could be a key to improving the mental health and well-being of children (see Figure 17.1).

These beliefs formed the basis for the initial goals of the C-TLC:

1. **Goal 1:** Foster alliances to address the needs of children and youth who have experienced or are at risk of experiencing significant trauma
2. **Goal 2:** Provide publicly available, free training and technical assistance to early childhood, elementary, and secondary teachers, principals, school psychologists, and other school staff
3. **Goal 3:** Accelerate adoption and implementation of evidenced-based mental health practices through the C-TLC for New England

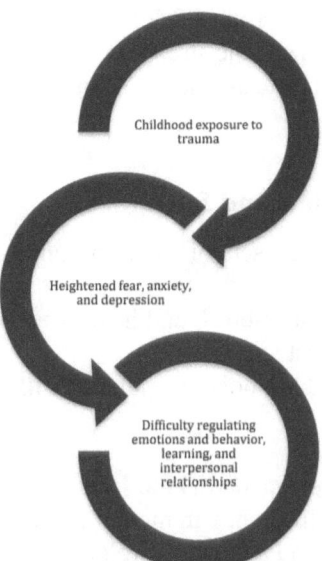

Figure 17.1. Impact of Childhood Trauma on Emotions and Learning

Initially believing we might have only one year to implement this work, in Year 1, we recruited and prepared a group of 24 C-TLC fellows, including an assistant superintendent and several school principals, assistant principals, psychologists, and social workers. Our intent was that the fellows would be our eyes and ears on the ground and that they could help us understand more about community needs, successes, and concerns.

We learned a lot in the first year from our fellows, as we grew to understand more about the dearth of mental health services in remote rural areas, the cultural needs and concerns that prevent some families from seeking or securing mental health supports, and the barriers to achieving the radical change we sought.

CONSENSUS REGARDING THE VISION FOR THE C-TLC AND MENTAL HEALTH SUPPORTS FOR SCHOOLS IN NEW ENGLAND

As we worked with fellows, schools, and other educational leaders, not only in New England, but also as a part of the national network of regional centers, we were able to clarify our vision and advance our leadership. We discussed our vision with our fellows, and we learned about their visions and the barriers to implementation. We secured their consensus for our vision during the first few months of the project. Tools, such as administering S-CCATE, helped to secure a database of the strengths, areas of emerging strengths, and areas in need of additional technical assistance to realize what became our collective vision.

Keeping It Real: Barriers and Successes

- How much does your school or community understand about mental illness?
- What is the system of referral, and how effective has it been?
- Who are your greatest supporters?
- What will you do if schools are not yet willing to go the full mile in implementation?

One of the barriers we found was the lack of understanding about mental illness, another was the difference in mental health protocol in medical communities and in schools, and a third was related to habits and practices. Many schools and communities were used to a system of mental health referrals, which might mean a significant delay in youth receiving the advice, counseling, mediation, and other supports they needed.

Customized Implementation to Meet Local Needs

We also found that schools were experiencing some successes and that most of our fellows were already well informed and implementing innovative and effective practices. New England is blessed with a wealth of medical facilities and hospitals that had implemented significant programs to improve children's mental health. However, these programs alone are inadequate to meet children's mental health needs.

When we initiated the project, we found the fellows had implemented "bridge" programs to help youth in crisis transition from mental health units back into schools, that some had counselors conducting groups to improve social-emotional well-being, and that some counselors and social workers were coteaching to help improve self-care. In addition, some of our fellows were implementing such evidenced-based SEL programs as Conscious Discipline, and others were following the Collaborative for Academic, Social, and Emotional Learning's (CASEL) recommendations (see Chapter 10) for improving self- and social awareness, self-management, and responsible decision making.

Based on input from our fellows, during the first year, we held a series of webinars on such topics as children's mental health, the neurobiology of trauma, self-care, mindfulness, and how Heart Centered Learning had been implemented in pilot schools. Fellows were expected to participate in a certain number of these, and they were open to the general public (for our materials, see Mental Health Technology Transfer Center, 2021).

Fortunately, SAMHSA saw the potential and impact of its 10 regional programs, and in 2019, funding for the program was extended. With a second year of funding, we worked with our fellows to expand the depth of their knowledge and understanding. During that year, we also wrote a book, *Compassionate School Practices: Fostering Children's Mental Health and Well-Being* (Mason, Asby, et al., 2021), which tells the story of our vision and has many examples of how fellows have implemented our program.

To explain compassionate school practices, we devised a schema showing the four quadrants of support that we believe are essential for schools to be fully engaged in providing needed mental health supports for children and youth. Figure 17.2 shows how prevention, school and community support for youth who are identified as most in need, protective factors, and building resilience can be the four cornerstones for positively influencing youth, homes, communities, and schools.

The HEART Collective: Its Origins

The COVID-19 pandemic illuminated both the need for increased mental health supports within the school setting and the lack of funding and staffing available to provide mental health supports for all students who required them. At the same time, many community health care centers were already providing mental health care to youth and had more capacity to meet this growing need.

In 2020, the C-TLC was asked by New England's SAMHSA regional administrator's office and HRSA's regional office of operations to convene a group of educators and community health providers to problem solve

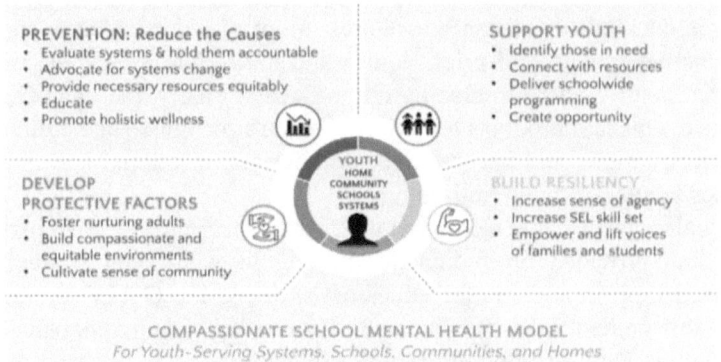

Figure 17.2. Compassionate School Mental Health Model

about collaborations between schools and community health providers. Both groups were challenged by the demand for services and some barriers that make effective collaborations difficult. The HEART Collective initial group convened in September 2020 as a group of education, behavioral health, and lived-experience leaders in the New England region who believe school mental health services are enhanced through intentional collaboration between schools and community health providers.

In the first several months of meeting, the HEART Collective used input from members to revise and improve the Compassionate School Mental Health Model, identified barriers and best practices for school mental health collaborations, and created an action plan to deliver training and resources to support collaborations. In the next phase of the HEART Collective, the group will convene a Student Advisory Council to inform all aspects of the HEART work from the perspectives of students. The HEART Collective will also begin facilitating learning sessions and webinars to address some of the challenges in collaboration and to promote best practices. Additionally, HEART Collective members will begin convening meetings with regional and state leaders and promote a public mental health awareness campaign.

Using these discussions and a robust evidence base, the C-TLC will create a brief, friendly online course to disseminate best practices around and beyond the New England region to better support the need for school-based mental health supports.

Additional Activities in Years 3 and 4

As the COVID-19 pandemic made the Fall 2020 return to school unpredictable, the C-TLC shifted its focus to supporting educators and school mental health staff through an increased need for student support, burnout, and trauma. C-TLC fellows entered mentoring relationships and joined affinity groups to address specific concerns but also participated in continued virtual training and technical assistance to address more systemic concerns surrounding collective trauma and grief, equity and antiracism strategies, mindfulness, and identifying and reducing trauma. Additionally, the C-TLC created wellness events and products to help school staff recognize and address their compassion fatigue and burnout and promote organizational and individual strategies to support their well-being.

They also began the Compassionate Conversations in Schools initiative, which provided brief didactic training in well-being strategies and peer-based drop-in support for educators. Finally, the C-TLC produced an online, self-guided, and free course, Cultivating Compassionate School Communities That Respond to Trauma Effectively.

In 2021, the fourth year of the project, the New England Mental Health Technology Transfer Center (MHTTC) School Mental Health Initiative offered expanded C-TLC activities in addition to the HEART Collective, collaborations with the national MHTTC network on mental health literacy and comprehensive school mental health best practices, and technical assistance to SAMHSA's Project AWARE grantees. These initiatives, along with the C-TLC, were focused on creating more opportunities for resource dissemination, amplifying local capacity in school mental health, and creating connected communities.

VISIONING FOR COMPASSION

Visioning for compassionate school practices, dare we say it, almost becomes addictive—however, in the positive sense, such as a "runner's addiction." One way to stay uplifted is to create a sense of flow, where the positive possibilities seem to almost float in front of our eyes, appearing magically. Even in the midst of so much negativity, the basic principles of compassionate school practices are so fundamental, so we must ask, Who wouldn't be in favor?

Who wouldn't want to propel others forward by daring to dream and to put thoughts into motion? So much can be done with so little. The compassionate practices we suggest are not expensive. We would suggest that you show up with your heart and then ride the wave, perhaps imagining that hundreds of others are joining with you, as you truly focus on enjoying the journey.

Reasons to Turn to Compassionate School Practices

Schools can do much to alleviate trauma and stress for youth. Our approach, which relies on what Peter Senge terms an "organic" approach, building on readily available resources, is viable. With the current shortage of mental health staff and the huge need to address mental health concerns in schools, Compassionate School Practices provides a relatively low-cost solution that has many advantages over other procedures. It reduces stigma, provides supports early without a waiting list, and builds important life skills and supports.

Christine and Martha's Leadership

To disseminate compassionate school practices, eliminate punitive school discipline, foster self-care, and eliminate the stigma around mental health, Christine and Martha aim to increase mental health literacy, collaborate with mental health providers and educators to implement more heart centered practices, and build resilience and protective factors. They urge us to acknowledge stress and the impact of trauma; build self-care and vitality; and take action to help students, families, and staff deal. They recognize that embracing equity and justice is crucial, and leading with heart and hope can bring about powerful change.

Chapter 18

When Visioning, Educational Equity, and Educator Emotions Matter

Victoria E. Romero

In my vision, striving for equity involves having a process for fostering emotional resilience to challenge the assumptions, beliefs, and values we attach to our racial identities and how we see others.

INEQUITIES AND ACHIEVEMENT

There are schools in our country that successfully educate Black and Brown students from low-income families (Bradley, 1996; Edmonds, 1979; Parrett et al., 2011; Sizemore, Brossard, & Harrington, 1983). The educators in these schools, regardless of their racial identities, lead and teach in ways that all students benefit (McKinley, 2010; Stronge, 2018). Yet these schools are far too few.

Asking Some Hard Questions

We must ask ourselves, why do we continue to have an achievement gap between Black and Brown students and their Asian and White counterparts despite evidence to the contrary? Why are Black and Brown students disproportionately represented in special education programs for behavior and emotional disorders? Why do our mission statements continue to promote a vision of educational equity that schools in our nation rarely achieve? Is there more that we can do?

In *Race Resilience*, I describe the need to assume ownership for bringing about significant changes:

> Faculty in high-performing high-poverty schools that work with predominantly BIPOC students are racially aware, sensitive, and attuned to how racism impacts their students. Staff, of whom a significant number are racially different from the students they teach, have transformed their mindsets. They collectively agree that the social-emotional development and academic achievement of their students are in their professional locus of control. (Romero, Warner, & Hendrickson, 2022)

Schools have a significant role to play in improving race relationships. In the late 1970s, Dr. Ron Edmonds published the first research on effective schools for Black and Brown students living in poverty. This body of research continues to grow and now defines the attributes any school should strive to attain if we still believe in our ultimate mission: All students *will* learn.

But first, educators need to develop the stamina to have authentic conversations about the role race has come to play in our beliefs and expectations. In this chapter, readers explore visioning what educational equity can be in practice, by understanding the following:

- Every American is racialized, and we are acculturated based on our racial positioning to hold certain beliefs about ourselves in relation to "others."
- For educators in particular, racialization cannot be a fixed state of being in our practice.
- Our educational system is racially inequitable by design.
- Fostering a race-resilient school culture is second-order change. Systems change when the people in them change.

UNDERSTANDING THE ROOTS OF RACISM AND RACE RESILIENCE

Race resilience begins with looking inside ourselves. It is not another initiative or strategy. It is about how we can begin to respond when talking about race and its impact on our profession. When we understand how racialization influences our perceptions and how perceptions affect our interactions and mind-sets, we have begun the process of cultivating race-resilient behaviors (Romero, Warner, & Hendrickson, 2022, p. 7).

Race resilience is cultivated by learning about and understanding our own biases as well as the more generic roots of racism. We must each take responsibility; however, the process will be uncomfortable, and it will sometimes take a while to understand each other. Even with the inevitable discomfort, we need to speak honestly and strive to hear each other. This means learning, understanding, and having examples of what racial positioning, internalized racism, stereotypic threats, micro- and macroaggressions, cultural (mis)appropriations, and historical trauma related to racism look like in school settings.

Understanding these concepts is essential in developing a culture that promotes positive well-being for all racial groups (Romero et al., 2022). This doesn't happen if only a few staff take on this charge. Our collective efficacy is a key factor, and it will take both intentionality and commitment to build this shared understanding and support collective well-being, especially when there is resistance. One of the major attributes of staff in high-performing/high-poverty schools is their collective sense that student achievement is within their locus of control.

For race resilience to become a reality, authentic communication is needed—even when it is difficult. "The school's culture must be one where staff can have authentic conversations about racialization, discuss how their perceptions of other racial groups were shaped, and brainstorm ways to bring all these divergent experiences together to support racial diversity" (Romero et al., 2022, p. 46). To become race resilient will require time, reflection, discussion, and effort. Conscious awareness of self in relationship to the students we serve and a conscious effort to increase our understanding and empathy of each other are vital. This process is a crucial step forward in reviewing and revising school policies to ensure they are welcoming and inclusive and taking time to celebrate and embrace our differences.

Toxic, Emotionally Cold School Cultures: My Own Experiences

Looking back at the start of my career, I taught in schools where the culture was either toxic or just emotionally cold. This is in sharp contrast to the vision I formed earlier. In many settings, as a Black woman working in predominately White spaces, I had to deal with microaggressions and assumptions. I was told that I was articulate, very smart, and never angry. I was lionized instead of being recognized. Because of my own internal messaging, I didn't have the self-awareness to realize that I was actually okay being categorized as different if it meant fitting in better. Yet all this was having an impact on my well-being. I didn't know how distressed I was until my dentist asked if I grinded my teeth at night, a condition that could be caused by stress, frustration, or anger. If I knew then what I now know, I would have understood that as racialized people, my colleagues and I had distorted perceptions of each other.

If we are genuinely honest about achieving the equity in education that our mission statements promote, then we need to understand that racialization—subjecting others to different and/or unequal treatment based on race—can be blinding, in that we may be unconscious of what we are doing and its impact. For example, in a racially mixed school, what group is more likely to be in AP/gifted programs? What group is more likely to be in special education classes for students with emotional and behavioral disorders? Then and only then, can we use this awareness to mitigate implicit biases, eliminate inequitable barriers, foster respect, and care for each other to transform the cultures within our school so they can support the social and emotional well-being for staff and students.

SAVAGE INEQUALITIES: WHY HAVE INEQUALITIES ENDURED?

If asked to name a book that had a profound impact on changing some of my perceptions as an educator, it would be Jonathan Kozol's *Savage Inequalities* (2005). In this book, Kozol masterfully details his reasoning why the opportunity gap in our educational system persists. Contrasting the differences in the funding of suburban and low-income urban and rural schools, what curriculum is taught or not taught, and teacher expectations of who can learn and who cannot, he explains why in 1991 there was achievement gap between suburban White youth and the rural and urban poor. While all the points Kozol makes are valid, they raise such questions as, Why is this still true 30 years later?

Keeping It Real: We May Be a Part of the Problem

As educators, when will we (or why can't we) begin to reckon with the possibility that we may be part of the problem? Perhaps we need to take a deep dive and examine our perceptions about our students' academic capabilities, regardless of who they are or the families they happen to belong to. When will we ask ourselves, "Do we play a role in failing to provide an adequate education for all students?"

I must confess, as a Black woman, it did not readily occur to me throughout my 36 years, first as a classroom teacher and then as a principal, that our perceptions as racial groups might offer a possible explanation for our systemic failures. For me, it took the political years of 2016–2020, a pandemic, the worldwide protest after the murder of George Floyd, and the January 6,

2021, insurrection to truly actualize how deeply polarizing our country is about race.

As a person of color, my family taught me that life would not be easy. I had to work harder and smarter just to get a sliver of the American dream. I was successful as a classroom teacher in schools that served students of color because I emphasized that they, too, could make it if they worked hard. When former 6th-graders as teens or young adults would tell me I was their best teacher, I thought they were just being nice.

At that time, we didn't know that a student who was at grade level after finishing their 6th-grade year could lose those academic gains. Conceptually, most of us did not understand it was a systemic failure. It took the culminating events of 2016–2021 to fully recognize that in our profession, our racial identities, as White and people of color, matter in our perceptions of the students we serve.

SYSTEMIC FAILURES AND ARTIFICIAL HIERARCHIES

Systemic failure has created what Isabel Wilkerson in her book *Caste* (2020) describes as an artificial hierarchy that predetermines who gets benefit of the doubt and who doesn't. In our field, we have fixed assumptions about who will learn and who will not. We continually message ourselves subliminally by always comparing the achievement gap in the dichotomy of Black versus White. We rarely talk about or scrutinize the fact that by 5th grade, Asian students, even when they come from poorer families, outperform White students (Morin, 2014). We fail to attend to research on high-poverty, high-performing schools that began in 1978 and continues to evolve (Chenoweth, 2013; Edmonds, 1979). Our mission statements continue to promote a vision of educational equity that schools in our nation rarely achieve. If our institutions were a corporation that continued decade after decade to not meet its mission goals, then our business wouldn't last its first 10 years. Race, and all our explicit and implicit perceptions about racial identity, how we see ourselves and others, are always in the classroom.

My First School as Principal

Race matters. My first school was in a predominantly White, upper-middle-class community. However, approximately 40% of my students were bused in to attend an English language learning (ELL) program. They were from Vietnam, Laos, Cambodia, Ethiopia, Eritrea, Nigeria, and Ukraine. Most of their parents worked hard to provide the bare essentials for their families.

I had studied the school's data to prepare for my first state-of-the-union speech—which I'd hope to be celebratory. As an aggregate, the data looked decent. Disaggregated, it was not. The achievement gap was a Grand Canyon between White and the students at the highest ELL level, Level 4. More revealing, though, was the trend that as our middle-class White students matriculated from kindergarten to 5th grade, they lost academic gains. There wasn't much to celebrate.

My first meeting with staff began well. I shared how, as a classroom teacher, I had worked with great principals and some who were not so great and that my goal was to be for them the principal I would want to work for. I knew before beginning this job that the teachers were notorious for filing the most grievances in the district against the former principal, a White male who'd been there for seven years before he was reassigned to a district position. So I was pleased that as they introduced themselves, the temperature in the room felt comfortable.

It didn't get hot until we took a deep dive into the disaggregated data. Several teachers were insistent that the data were the "bilinguals' fault." When I shared the data about the decline in the academic achievement of our White students, they still blamed it on the "bilinguals." I continued to challenge this perception, and the more vocal staff continued to push back. It took the PE teacher, a White male, to stop the madness, and he used a few expletives to bring us back to reality. The mostly female staff heard him but were resistant to receive the same information from me—and I did not use swear words.

The locus of control was in our hands as professionals, and together, we had the power to change our situation. We committed to know each child by name and need. We were able to move forward in our planning, and I was able to say, "We will not refer to our children in language that was pejorative. Words matter." A few days later, however, it was race déjà vu all over again.

Segregation within the School

Visiting all the classrooms on the first day of class, I noticed the rooms were not balanced racially. Some classes were mostly to all White, while others were mostly students of color. I returned to my office to collect my thoughts and feelings. These were the first days as a leader in a school where the staff had worked together on average for 10 years. When I was working on my administrative credentials, we were advised by our instructors not to make momentous changes our first year.

As a Black woman who happened to be the principal in a school where staff knew their contractual agreements forward and backward, I knew changes needed to be made before the end of the first week, and it literally made me feel queasy. Where to begin? There were several White parents on my interview team, including the president of the very active parent association. That was my first call. In that conversation, I learned many parents were not comfortable with how students were assigned to classrooms. Some had voiced their concerns to the previous principal, to no avail.

The PTA president said they would activate the phone tree and call all the families to let them know children would be reassigned to different rooms starting the following week. With the support of the district's bilingual services, the families of students in the ELL program were also notified. My second and third calls were to my immediate supervisor and the superintendent. It became clear that some parents would not be happy about this decision and subsequent actions and would likely complain to my superiors before coming to me. The biggest group of resisters turned out to be some members of an all-White-classroom staff. I called an emergency meeting after our first day.

The more vocal teachers expressed their outrage. They explained that the classes had been set up that way because the students in our ELL program needed to learn at a slower pace. What was interesting about their argument was that just a few days before, we seemed to be all on the same page, concerned that all our children, White and students of color, were not achieving as they matriculated through our system. We appeared to have the same dream.

However, perception differed from reality. A few days before, we had brainstormed together to create a list of our collective professional-development needs in terms to ensure all our children made academic gains. We had even changed the master schedule so grade-level teams had joint planning time during their workday, and all morning, lunch, and recess duties were taken off their plates. I had to remind them that these accommodations were made so they could focus their attention on our students and care for our students.

My next step was to figure out how well our support services aligned with classroom instruction. It didn't because our classroom instruction was not progressive. Teachers within grade levels were using different textual materials to teach the standards, and I wasn't about to shake that tree.

Shifting Focus

The focus of staff meetings shifted from covering logistical and managerial topics to calibrating the standards at each grade level and then analyzing student work within and across grade-level teams. These sessions turned out to be the best "aha" moments and figuring out next steps as a collective, as teachers began to share pedagogical strategies. Teachers continued to use their favorite text but agreed on which standards they would cover within a four- to six-week period to ensure we would be able to create common assessments and compare apples to apples.

Teachers were beginning to feel they had more autonomy in making decisions about their work. This process, providing time to work together as a K-to-5th-grade team, made it easier for the literacy and math coaches as well as the teacher who provided ELL instruction to align supplemental support with what was happening in real time for students needing additional academic support.

The teacher specialist who taught all the kindergarten through 5th-grade students receiving ELL support was a master teacher who happened to be Filipina. She taught me a lot about the progression of how students learned language. Being the exceptional teacher she was, she recommended a prescriptive, repetitive series, and it did not take the general education teachers long to note and share in our meetings the progress they were seeing in our students.

Changing Perceptions, However Inequities Continued

By November and December of my first months, the teachers' perceptions about who could learn and who could not were shifting. In a short period of time, we had established a sense of collective teacher efficacy in terms of academic achievement, but that did not change the discipline data. However, even as teachers were seeing their students more equitably in terms of their intellectual capacity to learn, race was still in the classroom. Students of color were more likely to be sent to the office for behavior than their White classmates. Because I was now doing all their recess duties, I was not seeing those behaviors on the playground or during lunch times.

Our building leadership team, which was composed of representatives from each grade level, specialists, the family support worker, and a representative from the PTA, reviewed that school discipline data. One teacher on that team suggested that we should create a list of behavior expectations to share with the staff and then commit to teaching these expectations to all our students. This teacher shared her idea at a staff meeting and asked for volunteers. The best emoji that represented our collective reaction to the document they presented would be the exploding head—it was that brilliant. They gave us the three Rs of well-being for the adults and the students.

Prior to my arrival, the school had adopted the Second Step Program, a social-emotional curriculum. However, not all teachers integrated the curriculum into their daily practice with students. Not all teachers used the curriculum. The committee had embedded the Second Step curriculum into defining the three Rs: responsible, respectful, and reasonable behaviors the adults and students should all strive to adhere to.

Before the long winter break, we planned together to begin the new year teaching our students the behavioral three Rs. We coupled this with incentives that included students earning a three-R button that earned them a few extra benefits—like not needing to use a hall pass. They could earn a three-R button for a day or for months—it all depended on their daily behavior. All staff members, including our custodial engineer and cafeteria personnel, were given "Gotcha" tickets that they could give to students demonstrating three-R behaviors.

During those first few months back at school, we initiated a Monday and Friday routine of focusing everyone's attention on one of the details in the three Rs that we would be looking for in individual and classroom exemplars. The best part was hearing the claps and squeals from students when the name of a classmate was called out or classroom winners were announced.

Students learned to celebrate each other. Discipline referrals became less frequent and aligned better with our demographic numbers. When behaviors needed redirecting, we could ask students to identify which of the three Rs they needed to improve. And although we never discussed what was happening to change perceptions, our data would soon indicate how invaluable this committee's efforts were in minimizing how we reacted to the intersectionality between race and behavior.

PARENTS AND PREJUDICE

Although most days were personally rewarding, a few were not—like the day a parent came into my office at the start of the school day. No appointment scheduled ahead of time, she came and sat down in the school office with her Starbucks cup. Parents knew I had an open door, and most understood that meant scheduling an appointment. I stopped what I had planned to do to give her my full attention.

She had a concern about our three-R program, as she called it, and began to explain how she thought it was prejudicial, an example of discrimination, and that the school was becoming a place where some students were treated like second-class citizens. Her expression and body language suggested she knew her wording would be emotionally triggering. And below my calm exterior, inside I was exploding. In one sentence, she had managed to fire the best volleys she could about issues of equality impacting my racial group. I managed to maintain emotional control as she whipped through all her microaggressions.

I apologized for her feelings and invited her to come to the next meeting of our building leadership team and share her concerns, but she was not through. With that issue resolved, she started complaining about something else. This pattern went on for several rounds. She was not going to be happy or leave satisfied. She had a lot of stuff she felt was wrong.

Where was this coming from? I was genuinely puzzled. When I tried to insert some levity into the conversation, even though my gut was churning, I said something to the effect, "It seems like I am not going to please you today." She then added, "You need to know we're watching you!"

And in a blink of an eye, it became crystal clear. It was my racial identity that she was not happy about. I thought, "Some days, I leave at night. How closely are you watching me? Are you going to slash my tires or hurt me?" I may have said it out loud; that memory is now a blur. Things had escalated quickly as I rose from my chair and abruptly ended the meeting. Her expression was one of shock as I opened the door and asked her to leave. I called my supervisor.

CENTRAL OFFICE ADMINISTRATION SUPPORT

At that point, I was crying and felt like I really wanted to vomit. My supervisor asked for the parent's name and number. She would tell her from that day forward that she would handle all this parent's concerns directly. She informed this parent that she would be allowed on school property with access to her child's classroom only. This parent was not to come into the office or in any space, like the playground or cafeteria, if I was there. If she refused to comply, the superintendent would file for a restraining order. The superintendent called to reiterate the message and offer support. With this level of support, I was able to continue working at this school knowing my superiors valued me.

Our Efforts Paid Off

We all worked very hard during my rookie year, and those efforts paid off when our students took the district and state performance-based assessments. We were ranked 1 of 10 schools in the state that made significant academic growth considering our demographic population. Our Level 3 and 4 students in our ELL program boosted those scores by making the greatest gains (Engel, 1999).

At the end of my second year, we were ranked number 1 in our district for demonstrating value-added instruction systemically. Our staff was happy and liked working together. The parents and community were pleased. The reader board on the local supermarket congratulated us, and the community newspaper did an article sharing our turnaround.

Yet Trauma Keeps on Coming

However, within two years, I would have to support my school community, staff, students, and their families through two traumatic events: the death of a beloved staff member and the crash of Alaska Airline 261. In education, emotions matter.

Our music teacher, at 32, was the youngest member of our staff. She was vibrant and vivacious, and her sense of humor was infectious. It was a joy to visit her classroom. However, the summer between my first and second year, she was diagnosed with ovarian cancer. She worked as long as she possibly could, with the support of all us veteran teachers allocating some of sick leave time on her behalf until the day came when she could not work anymore. I would become the liaison to share how she was doing with the school community, to recount all our fond memories of her at her memorial, to care for our school community, and to lead us through our loss.

Later the same year, Alaska Airlines flight 261 crashed returning from Hawaii. This happened at the end of our spring break. On board were families returning to Seattle from vacation. Although the children on board attended the only other elementary school in our area, our families and students knew them from playing sports.

Two schools were leaning on each other in grief. In these moments, academics are secondary and social-emotional support is primary for all. The district reassigned counseling staff to come into both schools to support our grieving communities. This was my first exposure to learning about trauma and how it affects behavior. It was also the first time I heard about ways to foster resilience and had exposure to the concept of self-care to alleviate or minimize the lingering impact of trauma.

The assignment at my first school transformed my thinking about how schools needed to be sacred spaces where the adults could challenge their perceptions to get at the head and heart of teaching and learning. At this school, we grew together. We were able to change our thinking and stop blaming our students receiving ELL support for things we were responsible for professionally. Together, we significantly reduced race-based discipline referrals by explicitly teaching all students behavior expectations. In two years, not only was a once-fractured staff able to work more collaboratively together, but we also liked pushing ourselves to be professional exemplars by focusing on things within our control. We invited our parents to share their hopes, dreams, and culture with us. Nearly half our PTA meetings were held near a school where our ELL students boarded a bus to come to our school. After each PTA meeting, a teacher and parent representative would share with staff what they learned from these meetings. The parents of students who were bused felt valued and that they were an integral part of our school community.

And not once did a staff member file a grievance against me.

Keeping It Real: Race at Your School

- How is race discussed at your school? In the classroom?
- What are some leadership takeaways from this chapter?

BEING ACTIVE PARTICIPANTS AS WE VISION FOR EQUITY

After the experience in my first school, I believed second-order change, which involves challenging our assumptions; changing our values, language, and goals; and restructuring our organizational systems of delivery to give instructional staff more autonomy, are crucial. At this school, we worked smarter, not harder, to make our mission statement a movement and not a monument. We were active participants in having a collective vision of what educational equity could be.

My hope is that with this chapter, you will understand the necessity of examining our beliefs in order to improve outcomes for all students. My early experience helped me to realize that I was a member of the staff who needed support and that my social-emotional well-being was also a key to our success. However, I had support from our staff, students, parents, my supervisor, and superintendent.

As a staff, our successes accelerated a need to also look at our systems and share strategies to address inequities. Our schoolwide three Rs gave us a common language to also redirect student behaviors. We no longer labeled our kids or made assumptions about who could meet academic or behavioral expectations. A once-fractured staff was now whole and focused on ensuring all children made gains, had fun, and felt a sense of connection.

Our resilience is dependent on our collective well-being. To be prepared and act with integrity, even in the midst of the next round, will take a definitive culture; heightened awareness of the social and emotional needs of others; and deep caring for our students, our staff, and ourselves.

Victoria's Leadership

To address the achievement gap between Black and Brown students and their Asian and White counterparts, Victoria urges us to examine systemic inequities and implicit biases. When educators are conscious of barriers that impede the social-emotional and academic growth of their students, they can change their practices, policies, and procedures accordingly. By making equity and justice central to our vision, Victoria shares how we can uplift lives, further learning, and create real and meaningful change.

Chapter 19

Scalability and Sustainability

Leadership and Paths to Enduring Change

Paul Gilbert and Pema Choden (2015) begin their book *Mindful Compassion* with a statement about "waking up" our minds:

> For all the challenges we face in the world, from the injustices of rich versus poor; the need to address global warming and nurture our planet; the need to reduce exploitation of young, weak, and poor; to the need to develop universal health care systems—the common denominator in all of these is our minds. It's our minds that will create grasping selfishness, pitting group against group, or an open, reflective, cooperative, and sharing approach to these difficulties. And of course, it is our minds that are the source of our own personal experiences of happiness and joy, or anxiety, misery, and despair. (p. 14)

Gilbert and Choden go on to explore how we—including our minds—are affected by relationships: "[E]verything emerges through patterns of relationships" (p. 25).

While this book is about leadership, it is also about connecting, supporting, and caring as we seek enduring change. It is about building community, building up and out, achieving milestones over time, and knowing that adequate is not enough. Our work today must be more than adequate—the trauma is too great and the stakes are too high to be satisfied with anything less than what is truly needed.

Chapter 19

GETTING PRACTICAL

On the practical side of our coin, we must consider scalability and sustainability, two crucial components for lasting change. Now that you have heard from our 20 contributors, let's review a few key steps that many of us followed:

1. We began by understanding ourselves, reflecting on our lives, and wanting to make a difference.
2. Wanting to keep our visions alive, we created records and shared our visions with others.
3. We shared widely through many common tools today: books, articles, e-newsletters, websites, webinars, workshops, presentations, and social media.
4. Often, we found colleagues with like passions who brought diverse thinking to our landscapes and challenged us to improve and refine our thoughts and actions.
5. Sometimes we even sought legislative changes and support.
6. We continue to network, to guide others in implementing our visions, sometimes revisiting and perhaps even revising, adjusting, or clarifying our visions.

In Chapter 3, we describe visioning as an inner and outer journey and urge leaders to vision with a conscious awareness of their mind, body, and heart intelligence. In times when many are stressed out and even traumatized by unfolding life events, many are making decisions that may be constrained by our limited mind-sets and our stress. Your visions may be stronger, clearer, and perhaps even wiser if you vision from a place of vitality, with some vision of being victorious (the three Vs).

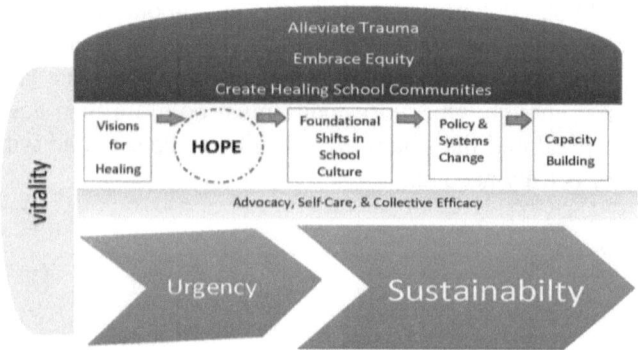

Figure 19.1 Our Model for *Leading with Hope and Vitality*

Figure 19.1, first presented in the preface, shows that you should begin with a sense of vitality. This may take some inner work—some stress relief.

Leading with Hope to Greater Hope, with Vitality to Greater Vitality

Missie Patschke, in describing the work of the Coalition for the Future of Education, shares the foundational visions for their work:

Vision for the World:

We envision a world that leans in with heart and compassion for self, others, and our environment, where people and institutions are dedicated to expanding conscious acts of caring, building resiliency, and advancing equity and justice.

Vision for Education:

We envision education that serves as the foundation for our humanity; it is flexible and empowering, where there is room for adventure, students drive their own learning, learning is celebrated, and communities support their individual and collective self-care, resiliency, and well-being.

You may notice that these visions have much in common with the visions in this book. Compassion and conscious awareness are underlying themes, as are empowerment; alleviating trauma; building capacity and networks; and advancing resiliency, equity, and justice. Consider for just a moment how you might feel if we were to achieve these visions? Would you feel a greater sense of hope, vitality, and vibrance?

A WORD ABOUT EVALUATING OUR/YOUR IMPACT

We haven't said much about the yardsticks we use to measure progress as we implement our visions. However, we certainly have them, including the number of subscribers, the number of members, invites to participate with others, feedback from our trusted advisors, our productivity (webinars, books, articles, e-newsletters), encouragement from others to keep going forward, and advice from those who implement the practices we suggest.

Scalability and sustainability are about impact. At a certain point in time, if you aren't making an impact, support will diminish. As you look at these two Ss, we suggest you review your impact, not only in terms of what you know at this moment, but also in terms of how in the future you will measure the significance of your work. Then use this feedback for continuous improvement, considering whether to scale back, throw your support behind a related initiative, make some minor course corrections, or start anew.

Your Impact

- How are you measuring your impact?
- Are there other measures you might use?
- Who are your collegial check-ins with along the journey? Never underestimate the power of critical friends who will listen and challenge your thinking.
- Are these data informing your continuous improvement through your cycles of planning, doing, and implementing?

Key Elements

As you consider scalability and sustainability, reflect on the world's current needs, our knowledge, and the key elements from these visions:

- Heart and compassion for self, others, and our environment
- Expanding acts of caring
- Building resilience
- Advancing equity and justice
- Education as the foundation for humanity
- Flexible and empowering education
- Room for adventure
- Elevation of student voice
- Students driving their own learning
- Celebrations of learning
- Community support for collective self-care, resilience, and well-being

Review this list of elements. Which are part of the vision you have?

The Back Story

To create these visions at the Center for Educational Improvement (CEI), a small group of board members, staff, and representatives from CEI's network of supports met several times virtually. During our sessions, we began with sharing a mindful meditation moment. We created a space where we could be mindfully aware of our collective circumstances and the larger, more global needs of the planet.

We also spent time reflecting on the visions over a period of weeks, giving people opportunities to edit and revise our statements. We brought our whole selves—mind, body, and heart—to our visioning. It was only over a period of weeks, as we reflected on the successes and failures of education and of humanity, that we landed on these visions. We'll see if these visions will endure the test of time or if they will be useful guideposts on our journey over the next few years.

Looking back on the chapters written by some entrepreneurs with diverse interests and concerns, what can we learn about how they have visioned?

- Some, such as Jeff Ikler, have partnered with one other person (his cohost) and stayed open to their evolving visions as they learn from those around them.
- Some, such as Martha Staeheli, Michele Rivers Murphy, Missie Patschke, and Chris Mason, have collaborated with a group of others, reflecting on their input and comparing and contrasting possibilities as they arrived at their final versions.
- Some, such as Orinthia Harris, have reflected on their own lives and the lives of others, turned to such sages as Ibram Kendi, and considered fundamental, underlying ways of being that must change.
- Some, such as Jesse Kohler, have linked up with others and used their own experiences and their own pain and to be part of a movement that seeks change.
- Some, such as Renee Owen, have used their cumulative experiences to broaden a vision of what to do with one school to a vision of what needs to happen in a broader venue. In Renee's case, she, like Chris Mason, moved from one job to another to tackle the work that needs to be done.

Reflecting on Visions and Leadership

When it comes to scalability and sustainability, reflect on the vision you have:

- Was it developed with mindful awareness?
- Does it reflect your inner and outer journey?
- Were you coming from a place of inner vitality and celebration (imagining victory)?
- Are you still developing your vision?
- How has your vision influenced your leadership? And how has your leadership influenced the lives of others?

The Test of Time

Will your vision last the test of time? Not all visions will endure. Not all visions are meant to endure. Whether your vision endures may not be the most important thing. Instead, there is the importance of the journey, of being on the road together with fellow travelers.

An Enduring Vision: A Personal Experience

The vision for Heart Centered Learning began years before CEI was formed. While Michele Rivers Murphy and Chris Mason share the vision and visioning process for Heart Centered Learning in Chapter 5, there is the back story of our lives and our personal journeys. Like many of our contributors, Chris had always wanted to make a difference and particularly to help those who have had more than their fair share of burdens to carry.

When Chris took a hiatus from her life as a researcher and returned to teaching, working in an inner-city environment with teens from more than 80 countries speaking 50 different languages, she learned from them as she tried to help them heal. She looked for laughter, she sought to understand more about their passions and their dreams, and she tried to help them experience fun and joy and to improve their sense of self and well-being. A part of her dream was to someday write a book about "healing in the classroom." Fast-forward a few dozen years, and she has written six recent books (including this one) and three recent e-books, all related to this story.

In 2005, as Chris embarked on another part of her journey: She became director of professional development for the Student Support Center in Washington, DC. In this position, she guided professional-development experiences for mentors and teachers who were brought in to teach under an alternative certification program. In this position, Chris and her team worked with 90% of the city's charter schools, which at that time served approximately 45% of the city's children and youth. Most of these schools were in the poorest and crime-ridden areas of DC. As a White woman, Chris learned a lot about navigating as a minority among schools where most staff and students were Black.

Her vision for how to help others heal, how to address racism and injustice, and how to help with individual and collective self-care also expanded during this time, and like Victoria, she turned to Kozol's *Savage Inequalities* (2005) to help her understand the full extent of the problems faced by youth in DC.

As Chris was doing this, she also was becoming more immersed in her passion of teaching yoga, and she became the chair of the Education Committee for an international boarding school in India where yoga and meditation were integrated throughout the days and lives of the students. She learned from these international students and teachers over the next five years, traveling to India in 2007 and 2008. In 2009, she became the interim principal at the school. This helped to cement her dream to somehow bring yoga, meditation, and "heart-centeredness" philosophy and practices to schools around the globe, particularly the United States.

In short, Chris's dreams and visions have endured. Her latest book, *Cultivating Happiness, Resilience, and Well-Being through Meditation, Mindfulness, and Movement* (Mason, Donald, et al., 2021), epitomizes the realization of combining her passion and understanding of yoga, mindfulness, and meditation with her dreams of improving schools. Even in the midst of global upheaval, planetary unrest, strife, and panic, she has continued to work with an evolving group of supporters to help alleviate trauma and, in essence, to help children, youth, families, and educators to heal.

Missie and Kevin have similar stories. Perhaps you do, as well.

Upper Providence Elementary School in Royersford, Pennsylvania

As the principal of Upper Providence Elementary in southeastern Pennsylvania, Missie Patschke's personal spotlight has always focused on creative ways to support and grow a culture of leaders, teachers, learners, and stakeholders to elevate a positive school climate while offering a range of strong instructional practices. Together, they find ways for students to be successful. Often, this is individualized and unique to the individual. Success is personal and unique to each child.

Across 20 years and many changes of staff, resources, and leadership, their common vision has always been heart centered, empathetic, and core kindness. The vision of the school is to take care of humans, lift each other up, and take opportunities to positively contribute to its success. This is done daily through collegial exchanges, flexibility, and the underlying motivation to focus on what's right for our kids.

Through the first year of the pandemic, they were affected just as many other schools across the country and world. Everyone was sent home. Tomorrow didn't feel guaranteed. They flipped to a virtual setting and struggled to find their way as a school community. Yet they did it, and they did it well. Using all forms of communication, they reached out and showed how much they cared about their students, their families and each other.

One of the first things Missie did as a principal was to connect with each family through their teachers, social workers, or the local police. At the same time, Missie contacted each staff member to do a personal check in, to ask, "Are you okay?" She listened and offered help where she could.

What Missie found warmed her heart and confirmed her belief in the power of our school culture. She learned that most staff had already been checking up on each other. They were connected and supported. Not only were they already 10 steps ahead of her with planning for virtual instruction, but they were also ready with information to share about each of their students. This was amazing.

When the adults in a system care for each other, it matters. Staff want to be a part of a school they believe in and they know works. There is a huge element of personal satisfaction when you know you are part of something much greater than yourself.

Their school continues to grow and improve because of the sum of all the parts. Teamwork is important, but this supersedes typical collaboration. The synergy is based on trust, experiences, and having the confidence to do what's right. This collective efficacy defies roles or titles. This is the glue of their vision in operation. What keeps that moving ahead is every human, every staff member, and every teammate who believes in this momentum. It's such an honor to be a part of this collective mastery.

Keeping It Real: Our Advice about Leadership, Scalability, and Sustainability

- Follow your heart, and pursue your dreams and your passions as best you can.
- Sometimes opportunities for growth come from left field; not everything is planned. Be open to serendipity, and use care not to easily dismiss or miss an opportunity.
- Listen carefully to others, and involve a broad community of stakeholders, including children, youth, and family, as appropriate.
- Listen deeply—beyond words—checking your own vitality and listening for your own inner wisdom.
- Persevere and focus on those in your circle of influence, wherever that might be. Your work matters. Never lose sight of its impact.
- Check the data.
- Reach out to others.
- Build leaders and coleaders, empowering others as leaders.
- Apply the evidenced-based principles that should increase visibility and viability of your ideas—research, writing, presenting, and dissemination.

As you travel on your journey, keep the following in mind:

- Start with vitality and images of victory, celebrating the potential of what might be.
- Realize the joy of the journey and help structure activities so others will be uplifted and enjoy the visioning and its implementation.

- Consider what people need to implement the vision—awareness, training, and technical assistance. In education, this may mean new standards and expectations for teachers, administrators, and other educators.
- Keep listening to your heart, and continue to dialogue with peers and supporters, growing your circles of support. This is an ongoing process.
- Realize that everything may not happen with the timeline and sequence that you had planned. Have patience.
- As you continue with implementation, also continue your self-care, advance the collective efficacy, and look at options and alternatives. Consider the pros and cons of alternatives, including such practical factors as finances and resources, likely arenas of support, and barriers.
- Keep seeking to understand your role, and humbly find ways to be the wedge, supporting those working with you.
- As you implement, continue acknowledging your community and the shared leadership.
- As new barriers emerge, be flexible, consider options, and find support for ways to persevere.
- Be the optimist in the room. You can do much to uplift and support others with optimistic leadership.

Our final piece of advice: Whoever you reach and whatever the outcome, trust that it is what was meant to be. Be grateful and trust. Have confidence and courage as you build communities of kindness and caring. Not every dream will result in lasting, enduring success. Not every dream is meant to endure. However, be grateful for whatever small improvement you can bring to others, whatever happiness you can support, and whatever you have learned.

LEADERS LEARN ALONG THE WAY

If you are scaling up your leadership, turn to trusted colleagues for advice; be humble; admit when you need to change; realize that you, too, are human; and continue to lead and learn.

Visioning Is Not a Destination: It Is a Journey

Some visions have lasted for centuries. Consider the vision for our democracy, a vision for public education, a vision for living a good life. Others have been more immediate—perhaps a vision for a cell phone, for YouTube, for Netflix. The journey is one that started with the designers and continues with the implementers. Implementation is something that involves cocreation, and sometimes it is only as good as those doing the implementation.

Abuses and misuses, exploitation, selfishness, greed, and other factors can impede progress. Leadership is needed; we encourage you to continue visioning, realizing that the visioning does not end with a vision. We hope that the wisdom of our contributors has inspired you on your path and helped to strengthen your visioning and your community.

References

Abbott, J., & MacTaggart, H. (2010). *Overschooled but undereducated: How the crisis in education is jeopardizing our adolescents.* Continuum.

Allen, R., Shapland, D. L., Neitzel, J., & Iruka, I. U. (2021, Summer). Viewpoint: Creating anti-racist early childhood spaces. *Young Child, 76*(2). https://www.naeyc.org/resources/pubs/yc/summer2021/viewpoint-anti-racist-spaces

American Indian Science and Engineering Society (AISES). (2018). *About AISES.* https://www.aises.org/about

Anda, R. (2013). *What are adverse childhood experiences (ACEs)?* Centers for Disease Control and Prevention.

Andrew, N. T. (2020). *What is resilience?* Center for Native American Youth. https://www.cnay.org/what-is-resilience/

Association for Supervision and Curriculum Development (ASCD). (2005). *Characteristics of high-poverty, high-performing schools.* https://www.ascd.org/publications/researchbrief/v3n06/toc.aspx

Bailey, R. A. (2014). *Conscious discipline: Building resilient classrooms.* Loving Guidance.

Bandura, A. (1977). *Social learning theory* (Vol. 1). General Learning.

Barron, L., & Kinney, P. (2021). *We belong: 50 strategies to create community and revolutionize classroom management.* Association for Supervision and Curriculum Development.

Beach, H., & Strijack, T. (2020). *Reclaiming our students: Why children are more anxious, aggressive, and shut down than ever—and what we can do about it.* Page Two.

Becker, W., & Chen, C. (2021, July). CEI's youth listening tour: What we learned and the pathway forward. *CEI's HeartMind eNews, 1*(7).

Bolman, L. G., & Deal, T. E. (2013). *Reframing organizations: Artistry, choice, and leadership.* Wiley.

Brackett, M. (2019). *Permission to feel: Unlocking the power of emotions to help our kids, ourselves, and our society thrive.* Celadon Books.

Bradley, A. (1996). Barbara Sizemore stresses test preparation to help poor Black children. *Education Week on the Web.* https://nuatc.org/articles/pdf/sizemore.pdf

Bristow, J. (2019). Mindfulness in politics and public policy. *Current Opinion in Psychology, 28*, 87–91.

Brown, B. (2012). *Daring greatly.* Penguin Random House.

Brown, B. (2018). *Dare to lead: Daring greatly and rising strong at work.* Penguin Random House.

Brown, S. M., Doom, J. R., Lechuga-Peña, S., Watamura, S. E., & Koppels, T. (2020). Stress and parenting during the global COVID-19 pandemic. *Child Abuse and Neglect, 110*, 104699.

Cajete, G. (1994). *Look to the mountain: An ecology of Indigenous education.* Kivaki Press.

Cammarota, J., & Romero, A. (2011). Participatory action research for high school students: Transforming policy, practice, and the personal with social justice education. *Educational Policy, 25*(3), 488–506.

Campaign for Trauma Informed Policy and Practice (2017, June). Trauma-informed approaches need to be part of a comprehensive strategy for addressing the opioid epidemic. *CTIPP Policy Brief, 1*. https://www.opioidlibrary.org/wp-content/uploads/2019/08/Strategy-four-Final-CTIPP_OPB.pdf

Canfield, J. (2015). *The success principles: How to get from where you are to where you want to be.* 10th anniversary ed. Mariner Books.

Center for Educational Improvement. (2021). *Heart Centered Learning and CASEL crosswalk.* https://www.edimprovement.org/post/crosswalk-heart-centered-learning-and-casel

Center for Educational Improvement. (2022). *Our initiatives.* https://www.edimprovement.org/

Chenoweth, K. (2013). *How high-poverty schools are getting it done.* Association for Supervision and Curriculum Development. https://www.ascd.org/el/articles/how-high-poverty-schools-are-getting-it-done

Clear, J. (n.d.). *Core values list.* https://jamesclear.com/core-values

Coates, T. (2019). *The water dancer.* Penguin Random House.

Collaborative for Academic, Social, and Emotional Learning (CASEL). (2021). *What is the CASEL framework?* https://casel.org/fundamentals-of-sel/what-is-the-casel-framework/

Comenius, J. A. (1638). *The great didactic of John Amos Comenius.* Adam and Charles Black.

Copland, M. A. (2001). The myth of the superprincipal. *Phi Delta Kappan, 82*(7), 528–533.

Covey, S. R. (2013). *The 7 habits of highly effective people: Powerful lessons in personal change.* Simon and Schuster.

Crain, W. (2005). Kohlberg's stages of moral development. In *Theories of development: Concepts and applications.* Pearson Prentice Hall.

Csikszentmihalyi, M. (1997). *Flow and the psychology of discovery and invention.* Harper Perennial.

Damon, W., & Malin, H. (2020). The development of purpose. In L. A. Jensen (Ed.), *The Oxford handbook of moral development: An interdisciplinary perspective* (p. 110). Oxford University Press.

DeMatthews, D., Carrola, P., Reyes, P., & Knight, D. (2021). School leadership burnout and job-related stress: Recommendations for district administrators and principals. *The Clearing House: A Journal of Educational Strategies, Issues, and Ideas*, 1–9.

DeWitt, P. (2012). Rigor, relevance and relationships: An interview with Bill Daggett. *EducationWeek.* https://www.edweek.org/education/opinion-rigor-relevance-relationships-an-interview-with-bill-daggett/2012/01

DeWitt, P. (2021). *Collective leader efficacy: Strengthening instructional leadership teams.* Corwin.

di Giacomo, E., Krausz, M., Colmegna, F., Aspesi, F., & Clerici, M. (2018). Estimating the risk of attempted suicide among sexual minority youths: A systematic review and meta-analysis. *JAMA Pediatrics, 172*(12), 1145–1152.

Dintersmith, T. (2018). *What school could be: Insights and inspiration from teachers across America.* Princeton Press.

Dobkin, P., & Hutchinson, T. (2013). Teaching mindfulness in medical school: Where are we now and where are we going? *Medical Education, 47*, 768–779.

Domenech, D. (2016). *Personalizing 21st century education.* Jossey-Bass.

Donohoo, J., & Hite, S. A. (2021). Addressing inequity with the power of collective efficacy. *Educational Leadership, 78*(6). https://eric.ed.gov/?id=EJ1288237

Drago-Severson, E., & Blum-DeStefano, J. (2018). Building a developmental culture of feedback. *Journal of Professional Capital and Community, 3*(2): 62–78.

Dueck, M. (2021). *Giving students a say: Smarter assessment practices to empower and engage.* Association for Supervision and Curriculum Development.

Edmonds, R. (1979). Effective schools for the urban poor. *Educational Leadership, 37*(1), 15–24.

Ellis, W. (2017, March 20). *When a picture tells the story: The pair of ACEs tree.* Moving Health Care Upstream. https://www.movinghealthcareupstream.org/when-a-picture-tells-the-story-the-pair-of-aces-tree/

Engel, D. (1999). Scores on standardized tests don't tell the whole story. *The Seattle Times.*

Fabritius, F., & Hageman, H. (2018). *The leading brain: Neuroscience hacks to working smarter, better, happier.* Penguin.

Faddis, T. (2020). Adhere to ethical and legal parameters. In *The ethical line: 10 leadership strategies for effective decision making.* Sage. https://www.doi.org/10.4135/9781071801031.n4

Faircloth, S. C. (2020–2021, Winter). The education of American Indian students: A brief history. *American Educator.* https://www.aft.org/ae/winter2020-2021/faircloth_sb1#:~:text=In%201969%2C%20the%20US%20Senate%20issued%20a%20report,sense%20of%20academic%20ability%20among%20some%20Native%20children

Felliti, V. J., Anda, R. F., Nordenberg, D., Williamson, D. F., Spitz, A. M., Edwards, V., & Marks, J. S. (1998). Relationship of childhood abuse and household dysfunction to many of the leading causes of death in adults. *American Journal of Preventive Medicine, 14*(4), 245–258.

Fergus, E. (2017). *Solving disproportionality and achieving equity: A leader's guide to using data to changing hearts and minds*. Corwin.

Fixico, D. L. (2003). American Indians in Kansas. *Kansas History, 26*(4), 272–287.

Fullan, M. (2020). *Leading in a culture of change*. John Wiley and Sons.

Fullan, M. (2021). *The right drivers for whole system success*. Centre for Strategic Education.

Fullan, M., & Gallagher, M. J. (2020). *The devil in the details*. Corwin.

Fullan, M., & Scott, G. (2014). *Education PLUS*. Collaborative Impact SPC. http://www.michaelfullan.ca/wp-content/uploads/2014/09/Education-Plus-A-Whitepaper-July-2014-1.pdf

Gailor, J., Addis, S., & Dunlap, L. (2018). *Improving school outcomes for trauma-impacted students*. National Dropout Prevention Center. http://dropoutprevention.org/wp-content/uploads/2018/10/Trauma-Skilled-Schools-Model-Final-I.pdf

George, B. (2007). *True north: Discover your authentic leadership*. John Wiley and Sons.

Gilbert, P. (2017). *Compassion: Concepts, research, and application*. Routledge.

Gilbert, P., & Choden. (2015). *Mindful compassion: How the science of compassion can help you understand your emotions, live in the present, and connect deeply with others*. Robinson.

Goleman, D., & Senge, P. M. (2014). *The triple focus: A new approach to education*. More Than Sound.

Grummitt, L. R., Kraske, N. T., Kim, S. G., Platt, J., Keyes, K. M., & McLaughlin, K. A. (2021). Association of childhood adversity with morbidity and mortality in US adults: A systematic review. *JAMA Pediatrics, 175*(12), 1269–1278.

Guild. (2020, June). *Why compassion matters*. https://guildservices.org/why-compassion-matters/

Gupta, M. (2020). *The art of joy, resilience, and movement*. Center for Native American Youth. https://www.cnay.org/the-art-of-joy-resilience-and-movement/

Gustafson, B. (2017). *Renegade leadership: Creating innovative schools for digital-age students*. Corwin.

Halliwell, E. (2014, May 23). *Can mindfulness transform politics?* Mindful. https://www.mindful.org/can-mindfulness-transform-politics-2/

Hammond, Z. (2014). *Culturally responsive teaching and the brain: Promoting authentic engagement and rigor among culturally and linguistically diverse students*. Corwin Press.

Hanson, R. (2013). *Hardwiring happiness: The new brain science of contentment, calm, and confidence*. Harmony Books.

Hargreaves, A., & Shirley, D. (2012). *The global fourth way: The quest for educational excellence*. Corwin.

Harvard University Native American Program. (2022). *About us*. https://hunap.harvard.edu/about-us

Hatcher, S. M., Agnew-Brune, C., Anderson, M., Zambrano, L. D., Rose, C. E., et al. (2020). COVID-19 among American Indian and Alaska native persons—23 states, January 31–July 3, 2020. *Morbidity and Mortality Weekly Report, 69*(34), 1166.

Hawkins, K. (2017). *Mindful teacher, mindful school: Improving wellbeing in teaching and learning.* Sage.

Hawkins, K., & Burke, A. (2021). *The mindful teacher's toolkit: Teaching and embedding awareness-based wellbeing in school.* Corwin.

Heath, D. (2020). *Upstream: The quest to solve problems before they happen.* Simon and Schuster.

Helliwell, J. F., Layard, R., & Sachs, J. (Eds.). (2015). *World happiness report 2015.* Sustainable Development Solutions Network. https://worldhappiness.report/ed/2015/

His Holiness the Dalai Lama. (1999). *Ethics for a new millennium.* Riverhead.

Holzer, A., Bradley, C., Fernandez-Berrocal, P., & Patti, J. (2020). The relationship between emotional intelligence and leadership in school leaders: A systematic review. *Cambridge Journal of Education.*

Hughes, M. (2018). *Happier hour with Einstein.* The Andrick Group.

Ikler, J., & Richert, K. (2021, July). How do you stay focused on what matters? [Audio podcast episode]. In *Getting Unstuck: Educators Leading Change.* https://shift2getunstuck.libsyn.com/174-how-do-you-stay-focused-on-what-matters-update

IllumiNative. (n.d.a). *About IllumiNative.* https://illuminatives.org/about-us/

IllumiNative. (n.d.b). *Reclaiming Native truth.* https://illuminatives.org/reclaiming-native-truth/

Indeed Editorial Team. (2022, May 24). *How to write a personal mission statement (40+ examples).* Indeed. https://www.indeed.com/career-advice/career-development/personal-mission-statement-examples

Indian Country Today. (2022). *2020 census: Native population increased by 86.5 percent.* https://indiancountrytoday.com/news/2020-census-native-population-increased-by-86-5-percent

Indian Health Service. (2018, October). *Urban Indian health program.* https://www.ihs.gov/newsroom/factsheets/uihp/

Indigenous Education. (2021, April 16). *2021 Cobell Graduate Summer Research Fellowship recipients announced.* https://cobellscholar.org/wp-content/uploads/2021/12/2021-Cobell-Fellowship-Recipients-Announced-Press-Release-Final.pdf

International Center for Leadership in Education. (2021). *Theory of action and our approach.* https://leadered.com/theory-of-action-and-our-approach/

Jackson, Y., & McDermott, V. (2012). *Aim high, achieve more: How to transform urban schools through fearless leadership.* Association for Supervision and Curriculum Development.

Jorgensen, C. (2005). The least dangerous assumption: A challenge to create a new paradigm. *Disability Solutions, 6*(3). http://www.uwosh.edu/coehs/cmagproject/readings/documents/Least_Dangerous_Assumption.pdf

Kabat-Zinn, J. (2003). Mindfulness-based interventions in context: past, present, and future. *Clinical Psychology: Science and Practice, 10*(2), 144–156.

Kafele, B. K. (2021). *The equity and social justice education: Critical questions for improving oppotunities and outcomes for Black students.* Association for Supervision and Curriculum Development.

Kalibatseva, Z., Bathje, G. J., Wu, I. H., Bluestein, B. M., Leong, F. T., & Collins-Eaglin, J. (2022). Minority status, depression, and suicidality among counseling center clients. *Journal of American College Health, 70*(1), 295–304.

Kaur, K. (2006). *Y.O.G.A. for Youth: Teacher's manual and curriculum guide*. Y.O.G.A. for Youth. www.yogaforyouth.org

Kaur, K. (2022). *Y.O.G.A. for Youth*. https://yogaforyouth.org/

Kaur, S. (2018, June 14). *When youth speak the world should listen*. Global Partnership for Education. https://www.globalpartnership.org/blog/when-youth-speak-world-should-listen

Kegan, R. (2000). What "form" transforms? A constructive-developmental perspective on transformational learning. In J. Mezirow and Associates (Eds.), *Learning as transformation: Critical perspectives on a theory in progress*. Jossey-Bass.

Kendi, I. X. (2019). *How to be an antiracist*. One World.

King, J., Masotti, P., Dennem, J., Hadani, S., Linton, J., Lockhart, B., & Bartgis, J. (2019). The culture is prevention project: Adapting the cultural connectedness scale for multi-tribal communities. *American Indian and Alaska Native Mental Health Research, 26*(3), 104–135. http://dx.doi.org/10.5820/aian.2603.2019.104

Kirtman, L., & Fullan, M. (2016). *Leadership: Key competencies for whole-system change*. Solution Tree Press.

Kolb, D. (1984). *Experiential learning: Experience as the source of learning and development*. Prentice-Hall.

Kozol, J. (2005). *Savage inequalities: Children in America's schools*. Broadway Paperbacks.

Kroger, J. (2007). *Identity development: Adolescence through adulthood*. Sage.

Krol, D. U. (2018, October 6). Refocusing on Indigenous knowledge. *AISES Winds of Change*. https://woc.aises.org/content/refocusing-indigenous-knowledge

Lauter, D. (2021, October). Researchers asked people worldwide about divisiveness. Guess where U.S. ranked. *Los Angeles Times*. https://www.latimes.com/politics/newsletter/2021-10-15/us-most-divided-nation-in-worldwide-survey-essential-politics

Leeb, R. T., Bitsko, R. H., Radhakrishnan, L., Martinez, P., Njai, R., & Holland, K. M. (2020). Mental health–related emergency department visits among children aged < 18 years during the COVID-19 pandemic—United States, January 1–October 17, 2020. *Morbidity and Mortality Weekly Report, 69*(45), 1675–1680.

LeFevre, M. L., & US Preventive Services Task Force. (2014). Screening for suicide risk in adolescents, adults, and older adults in primary care: US Preventive Services Task Force recommendation statement. *Annals of Internal Medicine, 160*(10), 719–726.

Love, B., & Hayes-Green, D. (2018). *The groundwater approach: Building a practical understanding of structural racism*. The Racial Equity Institute. https://racialequityinstitute.org/groundwater/

MacLean, I., Montefiore, A., & Winch, P. (1990). *The political responsibility of intellectuals*. Cambridge University Press.

Mason, C. (2021, September). Stress, vitality, and our thoughts. *HeartMind eNews, 1*(10). https://myemail.constantcontact.com/HeartMind-e-News--Stress

--Vitality--and-Compassion--September-2021-.html?soid=1103736720061&aid=h-kRFONL1S4

Mason, C., Asby, D., Wenzel, M., Volk, K. T., & Staeheli, M. (2021). *Compassionate school practices: Fostering children's mental health and well-being.* Corwin.

Mason, C., Donald, J., Khalsa, K. K., Rivers Murphy, M. M., & Brown, V. (2021). *Cultivating happiness, resilience, and well-being through meditation, mindfulness, and movement.* Corwin.

Mason, C., Liabenow, P., & Patschke, M. (2020). *Visioning onward: A guide for all schools.* Corwin.

Mason, C., Rivers Murphy, M., Bergey, M., Sawilowsky, S., Mullane, S., & Asby, D. (2018). *School compassionate culture analytical tool for educators.* Center for Educational Improvement. https://s-ccate.org/static/media/manual.782a06fb.pdf

Mason, C., Rivers Murphy, M. M., & Jackson, Y. (2019). *Mindfulness practices: Cultivating heart centered communities where students focus and flourish.* Solution Tree.

Mason, C., Rivers Murphy, M. M., & Jackson, Y. (2020). *Mindful school communities: The five Cs of nurturing heart centered learning.* Solution Tree Press.

Masotti, P., Dennem, J., Hadani, S., Banuelos, K., King, J., Linton, J., Lockhart, B., & Patel, C. (2020). The culture is prevention project: Measuring culture as a social determinant of mental health for Native/Indigenous peoples. *American Indian and Alaska Native Mental Health Research, 27*(1), 86–111.

McInerney, M., & McKlindon, A. (2015). *Unlocking the door to learning: Trauma-informed classrooms and transformational schools.* Education Law Center. https://www.elc-pa.org/wp-content/uploads/2015/06/Trauma-Informed-in-Schools-Classrooms-FINAL-December2014-2.pdf

McKinley, J. (2010). *Raising Black students' achievement: Through culturally responsive teaching.* Association for Supervision and Curriculum Development.

Meckler, L., & Rabinowitz, K. (2019). America's schools are more diverse than ever. But teachers are still mostly white. *The Washington Post.* https://www.washingtonpost.com/graphics/2019/local/education/teacher-diversity/

Mental Health Technology Transfer Center (MHTTC). (2021). *New England MHTTC.* https://mhttcnetwork.org/centers/new-england-mhttc/home

Merrick, M. T., Ford, D. C., Ports, K. A., & Guinn, A. S. (2018). Prevalence of adverse childhood experiences from the 2011–2014 behavioral risk factor surveillance system in 23 states. *JAMA Pediatrics, 172*(11), 1038–1044.

Morin, M. (2014, May 5). Study examines achievement gap between Asian American, White students. *Los Angeles Times.* https://www.latimes.com/science/sciencenow/la-sci-sn-why-do-asian-american-students-perform-better-than-whites-20140505-story.html

Murray, T. C. (2019). *Personal and authentic: Designing learning experiences that impact a lifetime.* ImPress.

National Congress of American Indians. (2022). *State of Indian nations.* https://ncai.org/about-ncai/state-of-indian-nations

National Indian Council on Aging. (2019). *American Indian suicide rate increases: Native communities experience higher rates of suicide compared to all other racial* and ethnic groups in the U.S. https://www.nicoa.org/national-american-indian-and-alaska-native-hope-for-life-day/

National Indian Education Association. (n.d.a). *ESSA implementation*. https://www.niea.org/essa-implementation

National Indian Education Association. (n.d.b). *Native education by the numbers*. https://www.niea.org/

National Indian Education Association. (n.d.c). *NIEA mission statement*. https://www.niea.org/missionvision

Norris, T., Vines, P. L., & Hoeffel, E. M. (2012, January). *The American Indian and Alaska Native population: 2010*. https://www.census.gov/history/pdf/c2010br-10.pdf

O'Donnell, S., Meyer, I. H., & Schwartz, S. (2011). Increased risk of suicide attempts among Black and Latino lesbians, gay men, and bisexuals. *American Journal of Public Health, 101*(6), 1055–1059.

Owen, R. L., & Buck, J. A. (2020). Creating the conditions for reflective team practices: Examining sociocracy as a self-organizing governance model that promotes transformative learning. *Reflective Practice, 21*(6), 786–802.

Parrett, W. H., & Budge, K. M. (2020). *Turning high-poverty schools into high-performing schools*. Association for Supervision and Curriculum Development.

Patschke, M. (2021, May). A heart centered community: "You are valued, and you belong!" *CEI's HeartMind eNews, 1*(6). https://myemail.constantcontact.com/HeartMind-e-News--Teach--Learn--Lead--May-2021--Leading-with-Heart--Connecting-with-Youth.html?soid=1103736720061&aid=k7CgGgwIIKA

Payne, R. K. (2018). *Emotional poverty in all demographics.* aha! Process.

PBS Wisconsin Education. (2020, January 30). *Wisconsin First Nations: Exemplar Profile: David O'Connor* [Video]. YouTube. https://www.youtube.com/watch?v=aCF-pfV5i0g&t=1s

Perry, B. (2009). Examining child maltreatment through a neurodevelopmental lens: Clinical applications of the neurosequential model of therapeutics. *Journal of Loss and Trauma, 14*(4), 240–255.

Perry, B. D., & Szalavitz, M. (2007). *The boy who was raised as a dog*. Basic Books.

Perry, B. D. & Winfrey, O. (2021). *What happened to you? Conversations on trauma, resilience, and healing*. Flatiron Books.

Pinto, A. (2020, July 15). American spirit: Why school dropout rates among Native American students are higher than any other ethnic group. *MEAWW*. https://meaww.com/american-spirit-native-american-school-drop-out-rates-high-than-any-ethnic-group-education-issues

Pollaert, E. (2020, July 2). *Racism is not a pandemic*. Lilith. https://www.lilithmag.nl/blog/2020/7/2/racism-is-not-a-pandemic-hate-is-not-a-disease

The Positivity Project. (2021). *Character strengths*. https://posproject.org/character-strengths/

Purbasari Horton, A. (2020, March). *Why you find it so difficult to be nice to yourself*. Fast Company. https://www.fastcompany.com/90468300/why-is-self-compassion-important-and-difficult-to-practice

Rechtschaffen, D. (2014). *The way of mindful education: Cultivating well-being in teachers and students.* Norton.

Reynolds, C. (n.d.). *Call to decolonise the International Baccalaureate curriculum.* Change.org. https://www.change.org/p/decolonise-the-international-baccalaureate?recruiter=375518752&recruited_by_id=caf9c190-53e5-11e5-9e2f-f1db7be04d6b&utm_source=share_petition&utm_medium=copylink&utm_campaign=petition_dashboard

Richert, K., Ikler, J., & Zacchei, M. (2020). *Shifting: How school leaders can create a culture of change.* Corwin.

Robinson, K. (2010, February 4). *Changing paradigms* [Video]. YouTube. https://www.youtube.com/watch?v=mCbdS4hSa0s

Romero, V. E., Warner, A. N., & Hendrickson, J. (2022). *Race resilience: Achieving equity through self and systems transformation.* Corwin Press.

Russell, B. S., & Lincoln, C. R. (2017). Reducing hostile parenting through computer-mediated parenting education. *Children and Youth Services Review, 73,* 66–73. https://doi.org/10.1016/j.childyouth.2016.11.036

Sanfelippo, J., & Sinanis, T. (2016). *Hacking leadership: 10 ways great leaders inspire learning that teachers, students, and parents love.* Times 10 Publications.

Schank, R. C., & Cleave, J. B. (1995). Natural learning, natural teaching: Changing human memory. In *The mind, the brain, and complex adaptive systems* (pp. 175–202). Routledge.

Schorr, J., & McGriff, D. (2012). Blending face-to-face and online learning. *The Education Digest, 77*(5), 30.

Schwartz, P. (1996). *The art of the long view: Planning for the future in an uncertain world.* Currency.

Senge, P. M. (1990). *The fifth discipline: The art and practice of the learning organization.* Currency.

Senge, P. M., Cambron-McCabe, N., Lucas, T., Smith, B., & Dutton, J. (2000). *Schools that learn (updated and revised): A fifth discipline fieldbook for educators, parents, and everyone who cares about education.* Currency.

Sharp, F. (2021). *NCAI state of Indian Nations 2021 address: A new dawn, an eternal promise, a courageous future.* National Congress of American Indians. https://www.ncai.org/conferences-events/ncai-events/NCAI_StateofIndianNations_2021_Address_AsDelivered.pdf

Shear, S. B., Knowles, R. T., Soden, G. J., & Castro, A. J. (2015). Manifesting destiny: Re/presentations of Indigenous peoples in K–12 US history standards. *Theory and Research in Social Education, 43*(1), 68–101. https://doi.org/10.1080/00933104.2014.999849

Sheninger, E., & Murray, T. (2017). *Learning transformed: 8 keys to designing tommorrow's schools, today.* Corwin.

Siegel, D. J. (2010). *Mindsight: The new science of personal transformation.* Bantam.

Sinek, S. (2009). *How great leaders inspire action* [Video]. TED. http://www.ted.com/talks/simon_sinek_how_great_leaders_inspire_action.html

Sizemore, B., Brossard, C., & Harrington, B. (1983). *An abasing anomaly: The high-achieving predominantly Black elementary school.* https://files.eric.ed.gov/fulltext/ED236274.pdf

Smylie, M. A., Murphy, J. F., & Louis, K. S. (2020). *Stories of caring school leadership.* Corwin.

Snowshoe, A., Crooks, C. V., Tremblay, P. F., Craig, W. M., & Hinson, R. E. (2015). Development of a cultural connectedness scale for First Nations youth. *Psychological Assessment, 27*(1), 249–259. http://dx.doi.org/10.1037/a0037867

Stavros, J. M., Torres, C., & Cooperrider, D. L. (2018). *Conversations worth having: Using appreciative inquiry to fuel productive and meaningful engagement.* Berrett-Koehler.

Stronge, J. H. (2018). *Qualities of effective teachers.* Association for Supervision and Curriculum Development.

Substance use-disorder prevention that promotes opioid recovery and treatment for patients and communities act or the SUPPORT for patients and communities act. Public Law No: 115–271 (2018, October 24). https://www.congress.gov/bill/115th-congress/house-bill/6

Suicide Prevention Resource Center. (2021). *Racial and ethnic disparities.* https://sprc.org/scope/racial-ethnic-disparities

Tough, P. (2016). *Helping children succeed: What works and why.* Haughton Mifflin Harcourt.

United National Indian Tribal Youth (UNITY) & Office of Juvenile Justice and Delinquency Prevention. (2022). *Healing Indigenous lives: Native youth town halls.* https://ojjdp.ojp.gov/programs/native-youth-town-halls-report

United Nations Youth. (n.d.). *Culture and youth development.* https://www.un.org/esa/socdev/documents/youth/fact-sheets/youth-cultureasavector.pdf

United South and Eastern Tribes. (2022). *Reclaiming Native psychological brilliance.* https://www.usetinc.org/event/bhecho-2022-02-22-2022-03-22/2022-04-19/

University of Alaska, Fairbanks. (n.d.). *Indian Self-Determination and Education Assistance Act (ISDEAA) 1975.* https://www.uaf.edu/tribal/112/unit_3/indianselfdeterminationandeducationassistanceactisdeaa1975.php

US Department of the Interior, Indian Affairs. (2022). *Tribal leaders directory.* https://www.bia.gov/bia/ois/tribal-leaders-directory/

US Department of the Interior, Office of Congressional and Legislative Affairs. (2021, April 28). *COVID-19 impact on Native education.* https://www.doi.gov/ocl/covid-19-impact-native-education

US National Library of Medicine. (n.d.). *1972: The Indian Education Act empowers parents; funds student programs.* https://www.nlm.nih.gov/nativevoices/timeline/530.html

Van der Kolk, B. (2014). *The body keeps the score: Brain, mind, and body in the healing of trauma.* Viking.

VanOrman, A., & Jarosz, B. (2016). *Suicide replaces homicide as second-leading cause of death among US teenagers.* PRB. https://www.prb.org/resources/suicide-replaces-homicide-as-second-leading-cause-of-death-among-u-s-teenagers/

Wagner, T., & Dintersmith, T. (2015). *Most likely to succeed: Preparing our kids for the innovation era.* Scribner.

West-Ed. (2019). *Creating trauma-informed learning environments.* https://www.wested.org/wp-content/uploads/2019/03/TIP-K-3-TIP-SHEET.pdf

White House. (2021, November 15). *Fact sheet: Building a new era of nation-to-nation engagement.* https://www.whitehouse.gov/briefing-room/statements-releases/2021/11/15/fact-sheet-building-a-new-era-of-nation-to-nation-engagement/

Wilkerson, I. (2020). *Caste: The origins of our discontents.* Random House.

Youth.gov. (n.d.). *American Indian and Alaska Native (AI/AN) youth.* https://youth.gov/youth-topics/american-indian-alaska-native-youth

Zacarian, D., Calderon, M., & Gottlieb, M. (2021). *Beyond crises: Overcoming linguistic and cultural inequities in communities, schools and classrooms.* Corwin.

ZERO TO THREE. (2015). *Tuning in: Parents of young children tell us what they think, know, and need.* https://www.zerotothree.org/document/765

Acknowledgments

First and foremost, we want to recognize all the great educators who show up day after day to teach and lead other educators in schools and districts, nationally and globally. Our thanks particularly to those who continue to serve children even in the midst of escalating violence, school shootings, pandemics, and the myriad issues that add to our children's trauma and are destroying the long-held visions of schools as safe havens. May we see a day soon when the physical and psychological safety of our children becomes an essential concern and priority of adults.

Also, our thanks to educational pioneers, those who are willing to step out and lead, those with insights into what could be, and those who strive to serve not only our children but also our planet. Among those pioneers, we list our 17 contributors—individuals who lead with heart and compassion as well as passion and a conviction that we can contribute to the collective good. May we all be stronger and wiser as we, in a spirit of unity, work together, seeking to inspire others and achieve our goals for transformational change.

On a personal level, my love and thanks to my family, the CEI board and staff, and those who network with us on CEI's journey to help our world become more heart centered.

—Chris Mason

My belief in the power of collective efficacy and the crucial significance of SEL practices have been operationally confirmed many times over by many of the remarkable educators I've worked with across my career. It has been a privilege to grow alongside them. I am extremely grateful to Dr. Chris Mason for her contributions to the health and well-being of educational communities. The opportunity to share my insights on the importance of her work is a great honor. Finally, I extend my deepest gratitude to my daughters, Victoria and Olivia. The love, laughter, and joy they bring to my life is immeasurable.

—Missie Patschke

I would like to acknowledge the ongoing support of education colleagues of the global majority who work around the world. We are committed to ensuring you are seen, heard, valued, and affirmed. Nayoung Weaver and Rama Ndiaye, you are radical dreamers reimagining what international schools could be like for all. Thank you to my mother, Paulette Simpson, for her ongoing advocacy, support, and encouragement.

—Kevin Simpson

And on a final professional note. Our thanks to Meghan Wenzel, a senior writer and researcher at CEI; CEI intern Mishel Alexandrovsky; and CEI research assistant Margaret Bass for your help in finalizing documents and preparing this manuscript for publication. At CEI, we can do more because of your expertise, your accuracy, and your dedication. In a similar vein, we are blessed that the team at Rowman & Littlefield led by Tom Koerner, sensing the urgency of our authors and the needs in education, found ways to bring this publication to print within a matter of months. We are grateful to Tom, Kira Hall, Carlie Wall, and Andrew Yoder for their attention to both the big ideas and details in the preparation of our manuscript.

Index

Note: Page numbers in *italics* refer to tables and figures.

Abbott, John, 38–39
ACERT Program, 97
adverse childhood experiences (ACEs): deaths from, xiii; educators' roles in, 101–3; original study of, 95; tree image, *100*. *See also* trauma
advocacy, 158
AIELOC. *See* Association of International Educators and Leaders of Color (AIELOC)
AIHEC (American Indian Higher Education Consortium), 65
Aim High, Achieve More (Jackson & McDermott), 69
AISES (American Indian Science and Engineering Society), 68
Alaska Natives. *See* Native youth
alexithymia, 148
Allen, Cameron, 137
Allen, Rosemarie, 52
Alvord, Lori Alviso, 68
American Indian Higher Education Consortium (AIHEC), 65
American Indians. *See* Native youth
American Indian Science and Engineering Society (AISES), 68

American Rescue Plan (ARP), 64
Andrew, Nyché Tyme, 61
antiracism: about, 7–8; compassion and, 49–50, *51*, 52–53; diversity, equity, and inclusion, 50, 114, 115; in early childhood education, 50–53; encouraging equity through curricula, 124; policies for, 143–44; vision of, 47–48
ARP (American Rescue Plan), 64
The Art of the Long View (Schwartz), 11
Asby, D., 49, 83, 177
aspirational leaders, 13
assessment, 124, 187–88, 190
Association of International Educators and Leaders of Color (AIELOC): about, 159, 163; addressing discrimination, 165–66; background, 163–65; community visionings, 168–69; conversation examples, 167–68; self-care, 168
assumptions, 40–41, 185. *See also* racism
Australian education, 44

Bachelder-Giles, Stacy, 82
Bahir, Mehir, 128
Bandura, Albert, 3
Be a Mr. Jensen video, 13

"Becoming Visible" report, 66–67
behavior expectations for
  students, 188–89
Bhutan government, 43
BIE (Bureau of Indian Education), 64
Black, Indigenous, and people of
  color (BIPOC), 163, 182. See also
  antiracism; race resilience
Bolman, Lee, xii
Boynton, Paul S., 20
Brackett, Mark, 152
briefs after meetings, 110
Brown, Brené, xiii, 129, 147
Bureau of Indian Education (BIE), 64
Burnett, Richard, 45
Busteed, Brandon, 44

Cajete, Gregory, 15–16, 26, 27
Campaign for Trauma-Informed Policy
  and Practice (CTIPP): about, 91–92,
  95–103; educators' roles, 101–3;
  hope for the future, 102–3; policy
  role, 96–97; stories of trauma and
  healing, 96, 97–101
Canfield, Jack, 13
Caraballo-Suarez, Liza, 122–23
Cardwell, Aiden, 145
caring practices, 4
Caste (Wilkerson), 8, 185
caste systems of India, 8
CEI (Center for Educational
  Improvement), 17, 33–34, 75, 121,
  172, 173, 198
celebrations, 28–29
Center for Educational Improvement
  (CEI), 17, 33–34, 75, 121,
  172, 173, 198
change, 92, 161, 192
Cheeshahteaumuck, Caleb, 65
Childhood-Trauma Learning
  Collaborative (C-TLC): about, xiv–
  xv, 160; Heart Collective and, 177–
  79; initial goals, 174–75; origins,
  172–73; vision consensus, 175–79
Choden, 195

circle meetings, 86–87
Clear, J., 136
Cleave, J. B., 38
climate-change discussions, xiv, 144
Coalition for the Future of Education
  (CFE): about, xiv–xv, 121–22;
  focus of, 119, 123–25; future vision
  of, 129–30; members of, 122–23;
  multipronged approach to, 125–26;
  reasons for, 123; valuing youth
  leadership, 126–29; visions for, 196–
  97; voices of youth on issues, 33–34
Coates, Ta-Nehisi, 1
Cobell Scholarship Program, 67–68
Collaborative for Academic and Social
  Emotional Learning (CASEL): about,
  75, 76, 78; comparing to HCL, 78,
  82; recommendations of, 174
collective efficacy, 9–10, 201–2
collective peak performance, 159–60
collective vision, 15, 20–21, 31–32
colleges, 43–44, 65
Comenius, John Amos, 38–39
Common Core, 49
community, 92. See also five Cs
compassion: healing trauma with, 71,
  102; mental health model, 177,
  177–78; mindfulness and, 49–50,
  51; origins of Center for Educational
  Improvement, 173; vision of
  school practices for, 171, 179. See
  also Childhood-Trauma Learning
  Collaborative (C-TLC); five Cs;
  Heart-Centered Learning (HCL)
Compassionate School Practices
  (Mason, Asby & et al.), 49, 177
connectedness, 58–60, 92
consciousness, 71–72. See also five Cs
corporate partners, 152–53
courage, 10, 129–30. See also five Cs
COVID-19 pandemic: connections
  and support during, 177–78, 201;
  effects of, xi, 63–64, 119; healing
  from, 6–7; mental health and, 108–9;
  parenting during, 150; post-pandemic

challenges, xi–xii; self-care and, 174; trauma and injustice of, 102, 123
Crouch, Tracey, 45
CTIPP. *See* Campaign for Trauma-Informed Policy and Practice (CTIPP)
Cullen, Chris, 45
Cultivating Happiness, Resilience, and Well-Being Through Meditation, Mindfulness, and Movement (Mason, Donald, Khalsa, Rivers Murphy & Brown), 30, 49, 88, 200–201
cultural connectedness, 58–60
Cultural Connectedness Scale (CCS), 59
Culture is Prevention project, 59

Daggett, William, 76–83, *78*
dance and movement, 57
David, Xoài, 143–44
Deal, Terrance, xii
denial and racism, 48
DeWitt, Peter, xii, 5, 9–10, 160
dialogues, 41–42
diversity, equity, and inclusion (DEI), 50, 114, 115
Dobkin, P., 44
Domagalski, Michael, *17, 23,* 92, 113–20
Donald, Jeff, 6, 85–90
Donohoo, Jenni, 9
dopamine/norepinephrine stress-response system, 138–39
dreams, 10
Drucker, Peter, xiii
Duckworth, Angela, xiii
Duke University, 44
Durbin, Senator, 97

Echo-Hawk, Holly, 36, 55–69
EdCamp model, 6–7, 164
Edmonds, Ron, 182
educational focus, 39–41
equity and justice: in access to education and resources, 124; in early-childhood spaces, 51;

embracing, 7; hard questions about, 181–82; IllumiNative, 66; importance of, 7; mindfulness and, 85–86. *See also* antiracism; diversity, equity, and inclusion (DEI)
Every Student Succeeds Act (ESSA), 64

Fabritius, Friederike, 159
Faddis, T., 136
The Fifth Discipline (Senge), 40
five Cs, 73, 76, 80–84, 173. *See also* community; compassion; consciousness; courage
Fixico, D. L., 56
Flanders, Jillayne, 35, 47–53
flow, 159–60
focus groups, 21
focus of education, 39–41
Freeman, Ruth E., *19, 23,* 120, 147–55
Fullan, Michael, 5, 8, 11, 12, 17, 19, 76–83, *78,* 133, 134

Gallagher, M. J., 133, 134
Gallup research, 44
George, Bill, 8–9, 11, 25
George Mason University, 44
Getting Unstuck podcast, 75, 92, 105–10
Gilbert, Paul, 27–28, 71, 195
Gilman, Lisa, 131
The Global Fourth Way (Hargreaves and Shirley), 10
Goleman, Daniel, 39
government's approach to mindfulness, 44–45
grief, 191
"Gross National Happiness," 43
Groundwater Approach, 86
Gupta, Madeline, 56–57
Gustafson, Debra, 105, 111

Hageman, Hans, 159
Hammond, Zaretta, 7
Hanson, Rick, 28
Harf, Daniel, 88
Hargreaves, Andrew, 10

Harris, Orinthia, 35, 47–53, 199
Harvard University, 65
Hawkins, Kevin, *18, 23,* 27, 35, 37–46
healing, 6–7, 71, 73–74, 98–99, 102, 157–58. *See also* Heart Centered Learning (HCL)
Heart Centered Learning (HCL): about, *79,* 79–80, 173, 174; background, 199–200; communities' needs, 73–74; comparing and contrasting to other frameworks, 76–78, *78,* 81–83; development of, 74–75; five Cs, 73, 76, 80–84, 173; uniqueness of, 75–80
Heath, Don, 20
Heitkamp, Senator, 97
"Hello!" meetings, 110
Hendrickson, J., 160–61, 182
historical traditions, 26, 49–50, *51*
Hite, Stefani Arzonetti, 9
hope. *See* vitality and hope
How to Be an Antiracist (Kendi), 7–8
Huchinson, T., 44
humanized systems of education, 38–39
Ikler, Jeff, xv, 9, 28, 75, 92, 105–11, 199
IllumiNative, 66
Indeed Editorial Team, 136
"Indian Education" (Kennedy Report), 62, 63
Indian Education Act, 62, 63
Indian Self-Determination and Education Assistance Act, 62, 63
Indigen(i)ous Education, 67–68
inequality. *See* racism
injustice. *See* racism; trauma
Intentional School of Prague (ISP), 39–40
International Center for Leadership in Education, 76
International Educator Equity Statement, 169
international educators. *See* Association of International Educators and Leaders of Color (AIELOC)
ISP (Intentional School of Prague), 39–40

Jackson, Yvette, 7, 21, 69, 85
Johnson, Melanie, 36, 55–69
Johnson-O'Malley Act, 62
Jorgenson, Cheryl, 101
justice. *See* equity and justice

Kabat-Zin, Jon, 45
KDSL, 164
Kendi, Ibram, 7–8, 48, 53, 199
Kennedy, Edward, 62
Kennedy, Robert, 62, 63
King, Jeff, 56
King, Martin Luther, Jr., 122
Kirtman, L., 5, 8
Kohler, Jesse, 28, 75, 91–92, 95–103, 199
Koru Mindfulness, 44
Kozol, Jonathan, 184, 200

Lawler, Moira, 168
leadership: considerations for, 5–11; courage in, 10; finding time for, 12–13; heart-centered and compassionate, 17, 19; strategies for, 4; styles of, 8–9. *See also* vision; visioning; vitality and hope; youth leadership
Leadership (Kirtman and Fullan), 5
The Leading Brain (Fabritius and Hageman), 159
"The Least Dangerous Assumption" (Jorgenson), 101
LGBTQ+ youth, xiv
Liabenow, Paul, xv–xvi, xviii, xix, 10, 15, *17, 23,* 92, 113–20
limbic system, 138
Lincoln High School, 100–101
long-term plans, 11

MacTaggart, H., 38
marginalized communities, 7
Mason, Christine, xv–xvi, xviii, xix, 6, 10, 15, 21, 28, 35, 47–53, 72, 73–84, 85, 127, 160, 164, 171–80, 199–201.

See also Coalition for the Future of Education (CFE)
Mastery Charter Schools, 101
McDermott, V., 7, 69
meditation, 30, 200
MEMSPA. *See* Michigan Elementary and Middle School Principals Association (MEMSPA)
mental-health-related issues of children, xiii–xiv
Mental Health Technology Transfer Center, xiv–xv
mentors, 13
MHTTC (New England Mental Health Technology Transfer Center), 160, 179
Michigan Elementary and Middle School Principals Association (MEMSPA): about, 92, 113; expanding visioning, 117; Positivity Project, 116–17, *117*; strategic planning, 113–15
Mindful Compassion (Gilbert and Choden), 195
mindfulness: beyond the classroom, 43–45; community considerations, 46; compassion and, 49–50, *51*; connectedness and, 45–46; coordinator of, 85–90; development of program for, 87; exercises, 42–43; focus on reflective exploration, 41–43; increasing vitality, 30; MEMSPA programs, 115; shifting focus to, 39–41; teaching, 41–42
Mindfulness Practices (Mason, Rivers, Murphy, & Jackson), 21
Mindful Teacher, Mindful School (Hawkins), 41
The Mindful Teacher's Toolkit (Hawkins & Burke), 41
Mindsight (Siegel), 158–59
Mindwell Education, 35, 37–46
mission statements, 135–36
Monash Medical School, 44
moral purpose, 17, 19

multiple traumas, 100
Murphy, Julia, 120, 141–45

Naglee, Kathleen, 169
Nanakuli-Waianae School, 99–100
National Congress of American Indians (NCAI), 62, 65–66
National Indian Education Association (NIEA), 58, 60, 62–66
National Trauma Campaign, 97
Native youth: advocacy of educational rights for, 61–67; damaging narratives, 68–69; fostering cultural connectedness, 58–60; identifying brilliance of, 56–58; population growth, 60, 69; reservation schools, 126; resilience of, 61; suicide risk, xiv; supporting public education for, 67–69; suspension and expulsion rates, 60–61; underestimating brilliance of, 36, 55
NCAI (National Congress of American Indians), 62, 65–66
NEAR sciences, 101–3, 124, 136–39. *See also* Campaign for Trauma-Informed Policy and Practice (CTIPP)
Neff, Kristin, 71
neuroscience, epigenetics, ACEs, and resilience (NEAR) sciences, 101–3, 124, 136–39. *See also* Campaign for Trauma-Informed Policy and Practice (CTIPP)
New England Mental Health Technology Transfer Center (MHTTC), 160, 179
NIEA (National Indian Education Association), 58, 60, 62–66
No Child Left Behind, 49

O'Connor, David, 58–59
ODIS (Organisation to Decolonise International Schools), 143–44
opioid use disorder, 96–97

Organisation to Decolonise International Schools (ODIS), 143–44
Overschooled but Undereducated (Abbott & MacTaggart), 38
Owen, Renee, 119, 131–40, 199
oxytocin system, 137–39

PAL (principal administrative licensure) program, 135
pandemic. *See* COVID-19 pandemic
Paradox Valley Charter School, 132
Patschke, Melissa, xv–xvi, xviii, xix, 10, 15, 20, 45–46, 119, 121–30, 196–97, 199, 201
Peace at Home Parenting Solutions: background, 147–49; becoming a business, 151–53; evaluating programs, 149–51; experts recruited for, 153–54; future plans, 154–55; trauma passed to others, 147–48
Pennsylvania Educational Leadership Summit, 6–7
Permission to Feel (Brackett), 152
Perry, Bruce D., 48, 98–99
personal vision, 19, 20. *See also* vision; visioning
planet, sharing, 37–39
podcasts, 75, 92, 105–10
positive-youth-development theory, 142
Positivity Project, 116–17, *117*
PRCH (Program for Recovery and Community Health), 172–73
principal administrative licensure (PAL) program, 135
Program for Recovery and Community Health (PRCH), 172–73
Pulver, Clint, 13
"purposeful change," 92

Quetico Leadership and Career Coaching, 106
quiet leadership, 143

race resilience, 182–84

Race Resilience (Romero, Warner, & Hendrickson), 160–61, 182
Racial Equity Institute, 86
racism: dismantling, 35–36, 48; fighting. *See* antiracism; healing trauma of, 48–50; inequalities and systemic failures, 184–89; parents and prejudice, 189–90; trauma and legacy of, 101; understanding roots of, 182–84
radical empathy, 8
Rainbow Community School, 132
Reclaiming Native Truth survey, 65–66
reflection, 39, 43–45. *See also* mindfulness
Reframing Organizations (Bolman & Deal), xii
relationships, 76, 77, *78,* 195
resilience, 138–39
Reynolds, Clara, 143–44
Rickert, Kirsten, xv, 9, 105–10
RISE from Trauma Act, 97
Rivers Murphy, Michele, 21, 72, 73–84, 85, 199
Romero, Victoria E., *18, 23,* 160–61, 181–93

SAMHSA (Substance Abuse Mental Health Services Administration), 172, 177, 179
Savage Inequalities (Kozol), 184, 200
scalability and sustainability: advice about, 202–3; elements, 198; implementing for, 10–11; visioning steps to, 195–96, *196*
scales for visioning-vitality-victory, 29, *29*
S-CCATE (School Compassionate Culture Analytical Tool for Educators), 74, 76, 80–82, *81,* 84
Schank, R. C., 38
School Compassionate Culture Analytical Tool for Educators (S-CCATE), 74, 76, 80–82, *81,* 84
Schools That Learn (Senge), 40–41

Schorr, Jonathan, 163
Schwartz, Peter, 11
Scott, Geoff, 76–83, *78*
Second Step Program, 188
SEL. *See* social-emotional learning (SEL)
self-care, 76, 84, 89, 159, 174. *See also* Heart-Centered Learning (HCL)
self-compassion, 71
Senge, Peter, xiii, 39, 40–41, 179
shared visions, 10–11, 12, 119–20
Shifting (Rickert, Ikler, & Zacchei), xv, 9, 75, 91, 107, 111
Shirley, Dennis, 10
Siegel, Dan, 158–59
Simpson, Kevin, 22, 159, 163–70
Sinek, Simon, xiii, 135
six Cs, 76, 77, *78*
Snowshoe, Angela, 59
social-emotional learning (SEL): all learning as social learning, 3, 49; evidenced-based programs, 174; focus on, 41, 42; with MEMSPA, 114, 117. *See also* Collaborative for Academic and Social Emotional Learning (CASEL); Heart-Centered Learning (HCL); TRAILS curriculum
social justice. *See* equity and justice
social system, education as, 3, 49
societal issues, xiii–xiv. *See also* adverse childhood experiences (ACEs); COVID-19 pandemic; racism; trauma
Southern Oregon University (SOU) administrator-preparation program: mission statements, 135–36; need for big vision, 133–36; neuroscience of vision and purpose, 136–39; personal and shared visions, 131–33
Staeheli, Martha, 160, 171–80, 199
State of Indian Nations address, 63
St. Clair Middle School, 92, 116–17, *117*
Stone, Andrew, 45

storytelling, 108–9
stress, 5, 28, 29–30, 174
stress-response system, 136, 138–39
STRONG Support for Children Act, 97
substance abuse, 96–97
Substance Abuse Mental Health Services Administration (SAMHSA), 172, 177, 179
success. *See* healing; scalability and sustainability; vision; visioning; vitality and hope
The Success Principles (Canfield), 13
suicide, xiii–xiv
SUPPORT Act, 97
suspension and expulsion rates, 60–61, 99–101

Tallchief, Maria, 57
teamwork, 8–10, 21, 159–60, 201–2
technology, 124
Thich Nhat Hanh, 45
three Rs of Daggett, 76, 77, *78*
three Rs of well-being for student behavior, 188–89, 192
Tough, Paul, 1–2
TRAILS curriculum, 92, 114
trauma: acknowledging, 5; collaboratives for alleviating, xiv–xv, 75; COVID-19 and, 102, 123; grief and, 191; healing, 6–7, 71, 96, 97–101, 102; impact on learning, *175*; passed to others, 147–48; personal story of, 97–99; racism and, 48–50, 101; RISE from Trauma Act, 97; school culture redesign needed for, 3. *See also* Campaign for Trauma-Informed Policy and Practice (CTIPP); Childhood-Trauma Learning Collaborative (C-TLC); Heart-Centered Learning (HCL); Peace at Home Parenting Solutions; Yale's Childhood Trauma Learning Collaborative
Tribal Communities in Schools project, 65

Triple Focus (Goleman & Senga), 39
triune brain, 138
True North (George), 8–9, 11, 25
Tulsa race massacre, 47

United Kingdom government, 44–45
United National Indian Tribal Youth (UNITY), 58
United Nations, 43
UNITY (United National Indian Tribal Youth), 58
universities, 43–44, 65
University of Montréal, 44
University of Rochester, 44
Upper Providence Elementary School, 201–2
Upstream (Heath), 20
urgency, sense of, 5
U.S. Congress, 96–97

vision: baseline for, 26; bringing whole self to, 27–28; commonalities and differences among, 22, *23*; emotion and, 27; as enduring, 199–200; examples of, 16, *17, 18–19*; focus on visionary leadership, 108; genesis of, 21–22, *23*; reflecting on, 15–16, 31, 199; sharing, 10–11, 12, 119–20; statements of, 37–38; vitality, victory, and, 28–32. *See also* leadership; Southern Oregon University (SOU) administrator-preparation program; teamwork; vitality and hope
visioning: barriers to, xviii; evaluating, 197–203; as journey, 203; as step to scalability and sustainability, 195–96, *196*; techniques for, 88–89; uses of, 110–11; without limit, 120. *See also* vitality and hope

Visioning Onward (Mason, Liabenow, & Patschke), xv–xvi, xix, 10, 15, 113, 117
vitality and hope: assessing, 31; increasing, 30–31; inward and outward journey to, 25, 27; leading and, *xvi,* xvii–xviii, *xviii*; paths to, 32, *33*; Upper Providence Elementary School, 201–2; vision, victory, and, 28–32. *See also* visioning

Warner, A. N., 160–61, 182
The Water Dancer (Coates), 1
webinars. *See* Peace at Home Parenting Solutions
Wenzel, Meghan, 73–84
West-Ed report, 78–79
What Happened to You (Winfrey & Perry), 48
What's My Why? (video), 135
Wheatley, Margaret, xiii
Wilkerson, Isabel, 8, 185
Williams, Mark, 45
Winfrey, Oprah, 48
"wisdom of imperfection," 88

Yale's Childhood Trauma Learning Collaborative, 52–53
"yes" actions, 20
yoga, 30, 87, 200
Y.O.G.A. for Youth, 85
youth leadership: activism of, 144–45; building, 141–43; CFE valuing, 126–28; elevating voices, 32–34; international movement, 143–44; listening tours and, 127; questions for, 129

Zacchei, Margaret, xv, 9
ZERO TO THREE survey, 151–52

About the Editors and Contributors

ABOUT THE EDITORS

Christine Y. Mason, PhD, is the executive director of the Center for Educational Improvement and an assistant clinical professor at Yale University's Department of Psychiatry with the Program for Recovery and Community Health. She is also lead author of five recent books and two e-books on education, mindfulness, visioning, and well-being and a cohost of the podcast series *Cultivating Resilience: A Whole Community Approach for Alleviating Trauma in Schools* (with Jeff Ikler and Jesse Kohler). Christine has experience as the principal investigator, director, or evaluator of more than 18 proposals funded primarily by the US Department of Education and National Institutes of Health, resulting in more than $40 million in federal and state funding.

During her career, Christine has taught students at the elementary and middle school levels, served as an interim principal at an international boarding school in India, and served as an assistant and associate professor at three universities. Her expertise has also been honed as a director of innovation, senior director and associate executive director of research and development, senior scientist, and director of professional development for several national organizations; her leadership at the Student Support Center in Washington, DC; her ongoing experience as a yoga instructor since 2001; and her global work in education in India, Dubai, England, and Finland.

Melissa D. Patschke, EdD, is principal of the Upper Providence Elementary School in Royersford, Pennsylvania, and a national principal leader and coauthor of *Visioning Onward: A Guide for all Schools*. She is also an adjunct professor at Wilkes University, Neumann University, and Immaculata University and serves on several national leadership initiatives.

Kevin Simpson is founder and CEO of Global KDSL and Association for International Educators and Leaders of Color (AIELOC). Kevin is also transformative social-emotional learning (SEL) specialist in Dallas, Texas, where he helps implement a newly designed SEL professional-development program by leading online learning activities and providing clinical support on SEL practices for 30 novice teachers in urban schools.

ABOUT THE CONTRIBUTORS

Michael Domagalski is the principal at St. Clair Middle Schools in the East China School District in Michigan and president of the Michigan Elementary and Middle Schools Principals Association.

Jeffrey Donald, MS, has served as an educator and instructional leader for the past 16 years. He is the mindfulness coordinator for Montgomery County Public Schools, Maryland. Jeffrey holds a master of science degree in educational administration and supervision from Hood College and is a certified 500-hour master yoga and meditation teacher and reiki master. Mr. Donald has held international wellness retreats in Mexico and Costa Rica, has been featured on such national news as *PBS Newshour*, and has coauthored two school-based mindfulness books.

An advocate for social justice and systemic change, Mr. Donald believes that the fundamental application of yogic practices and philosophy is essential to lifelong success and satisfaction and that everyone deserves free access to these practices and lifestyle. To this end, Jeff serves on several yogic-based boards of directors and regularly in restorative truth and reconciliation commissions and, most importantly, consistently teaches the science of Kundalini yoga, Vipassana meditation, and mindfulness to populations who historically have not had free access or opportunity.

Holly Echo-Hawk, a member of the Pawnee Nation, has spent decades working in the field of behavioral health and has been honored to use her experience to assist Native communities develop services to support the innate capacity of Indigenous people. She is a tribal behavioral health subject matter expert and serves as a board member of the International Initiative for Mental Health Leadership. She is also a member of the Wharerātā Group, an international network of Indigenous behavioral health experts.

Jillayne Flanders is the deputy executive director of the Center for Educational Improvement and an education consultant with a long and successful career as an elementary principal and teacher. Upon retirement from the public education system, she was principal of Hadley Elementary School (pre-K–6) in Hadley, Massachusetts. In that role, she oversaw a growing learning community with an average enrollment that doubled from 200 to 400 students during her tenure. She is a tireless advocate for early childhood education, and she has served on a number of related policy-driven committees, including her appointment to the advisory committee of the Massachusetts Department of Early Education and Care as its elementary principal representative.

Ruth E. Freeman, LCSW, Peace at Home Parenting Solutions founder and president, is a psychotherapist in private practice who has taught parenting education to thousands of parents over the past 30+ years. She is cofounder of the Connecticut Parenting Education Network and lead author of *Building Family Futures*, a University of Connecticut train-the-trainer parenting education curriculum. Ruth has also served as the family services director for the Cove Center for Grieving Children, family services manager for EASTCONN Head Start, and primary therapist at the Newington Children's Hospital Inpatient Psychiatric Services. Ruth's approach to parenting education incorporates her clinical experience with children and families in crisis as well as key concepts synthesized from a wide range of sources. Ruth freely and humorously shares the real-life blunders, challenges, and successes she has had applying positive parenting as a mom, stepmom, foster mom, and Nana.

Orinthia Harris, PhD, is a dynamic educator with more than 17 years of experience, both inside and outside the classroom. She is the founder and executive director of STEMearly, LLC, as well as a faculty member at the Center for Educational Improvement. As an education specialist and teacher trainer, she designs and delivers professional development and interactive keynotes around the world on the most effective ways to infuse 21st-century skills into any classroom. Dr. Harris has a passion for making learning engaging and has presented on how to effectively motivate and engage all students. Dr. Harris's research focuses on teachers' self-efficacy, its impact on the learning environment as a whole, and antiracism. She is committed to promoting access, equity, and compassion in education.

Kevin Hawkins has worked with adolescents and young people in various contexts for more than 40 years—as teacher, school leader, and social worker in the United Kingdom, Africa, and Europe. He lives in Valencia, Spain, and was previously in the Czech Republic, where for 10 years he was middle school principal at the International School of Prague. Prior to this, he was head of the Arusha Campus of the International School of Moshi in

Tanzania. Kevin trained in mindfulness in Europe and the United States, and he has taught mindfulness to students, teachers, and parents since 2008. In 2012, Kevin cofounded MindWell (mindwell-education.org), which supports educational communities in developing well-being through mindfulness and social-emotional learning. He is author of two books: *Mindful Teacher, Mindful School: Improving Wellbeing in Teaching and Learning* (2017) and *The Mindful Teacher's Toolkit: Awareness Based Wellbeing in Schools* (with Amy Burke, 2021).

Jeff Ikler has worked to serve the needs of students, teachers, and administrators for almost 50 years, first as a classroom teacher, then as an executive with a major school publishing house, as a coach to school leaders, as the cohost of the *Getting Unstuck: Educators Leading Change* podcast, and as the coauthor of *Shifting: How School Leaders Can Create a Culture of Change*. Visit his website at www.queticocoaching.com, and he can be reached by e-mail at jeff@queticocoaching1.com.

Melanie Johnson, MEd, an enrolled member of the Sac and Fox Nation of Oklahoma, focuses her life experiences on helping Native families build protective factors and resilience around their children to end the cycle of substance use. She is the program director for the National Indian Education Association (NIEA), whose mission is to promote educational sovereignty; advocate for culture-based education, including traditional knowledge and language; and improve educational achievement for American Indian, Alaska Native, and Native Hawaiian youth.

Jesse Kohler is executive director of the Campaign for Trauma-Informed Policy and Practice (CTIPP; https://www.ctipp.org/). Jesse is a passionate advocate and leader in the trauma-informed space who works on systems change to provide comprehensive support for individuals, families, and communities so that someday all people have the opportunity and support necessary to reach their full potential. Jesse can be reached by e-mail at jesse@traumacampaign.org.

Paul Liabenow is the executive director of the Michigan Elementary and Middle School Principals Association and the president of the Center for Educational Improvement.

Julia Murphy is the legislative aide to Massachusetts State Representative Smitty Pignatelli (Fourth Berkshire District) in the Massachusetts House of Representatives. Prior to joining Representative Pignatelli's staff, Julia worked as an intern for US Senator Edward J. Markey and as a political communications fellow for Senator Markey's reelection campaign. In 2020, she was a fellow at Biden for President and coordinated the Students for Biden chapter in Rhode Island. She is passionate about helping constituents by creating an open, inclusive dialogue and working to strengthen the link between people and the policies that affect their everyday lives.

In 2021, Julia graduated summa cum laude from Providence College with a bachelor of arts in political science, a minor in public and community service, and a certificate degree in public administration. She completed an honors thesis focusing on environmental justice and community organization in the greater Providence area.

Renee Owen, EdD, is a scholar-practitioner of adult learning and educational leadership. Dr. Owen is assistant professor and coordinator of education leadership at Southern Oregon University. She is also editor of the *Holistic Educational Review*, an open-access journal. Renee was a school leader for more than 20 years at unique public and private schools. As director at Rainbow Community School in Asheville, North Carolina, Renee was honored as an Ashoka change leader for her vision and work in making holistic education more accessible. Dr. Owen's lifelong work is for education to be a vehicle for helping people to thrive.

Michele Rivers Murphy, EdD, CEI's associate director of Heart Centered Learning, is a seasoned consultant, presenter, and educational leader. A change agent for more than two decades, she has helped transform some of the highest-needs neighborhoods and districts by improving student engagement, school culture, and academic success.

Michele has served as an educational leader at all grade levels. As an administrator, she created an innovative disciplinary approach as an alternative to in-school and out-of-school suspension that eliminated in-school suspension and decreased out-of-school suspension by 75%. In addition, she expanded high-needs programming to a mainstream setting, with a focus on real-life practice, service, and connection to community. She also created a 21st-century school community model, which she presented to the Massachusetts secretary of education.

Victoria E. Romero is an educator with more than 42 years of experience working as a classroom teacher, principal, and instructional and leadership coach. She is the lead author of two books: *Building Resilience in Students Impacted by Adverse Childhood Experiences: A Whole Staff Approach* (2018) and *Race Resilience: Achieving Equity through Self and Systems Transformation* (2021). Both books take a whole-school approach based on trauma-sensitive models that allow for the holistic social-emotional needs of staff and their students to be addressed as a community. Victoria's values about education are rooted in her belief that trauma-informed educators can create the trauma-sensitive cultures needed to mitigate the impact of social-emotional distress while simultaneously fostering resilience.

Martha Staeheli, PhD, is a faculty member at the Program for Recovery and Community Health in the Yale School of Medicine Department of Psychiatry and the director of the School Mental Health Initiative for the New England Mental Health Technology Transfer Center. Trained as a secondary English teacher and with a PhD in public health, she has extensive experience in population health and epidemiology; qualitative and mixed methods research design, analysis, and evaluation; and community and clinical intervention implementation. Her research interests are focused on recovery within substance use and mental health disorders; issues of health disparity and equity; and the health and wellness of underresourced community, clinical, and educational environments.

Meghan Wenzel, MS, is a senior researcher and writer with the Center for Educational Improvement. With a background in developmental cognitive neuroscience and education, Meghan is interested in early brain development and its implications for learning. She studied cognitive neuroscience at Brown University as well as neuroscience and education during her master's at Teachers College, where she worked in Professor Kimberly Noble's lab on neurocognition, early experience, and development, investigating how socioeconomic inequality affects brain development. Meghan has worked in a policy and advocacy nonprofit focused on improving the health, safety, education, and economic well-being of Rhode Island's children.

www.ingramcontent.com/pod-product-compliance
Lightning Source LLC
Chambersburg PA
CBHW020122240426
43673CB00038B/567